W9-CFJ-550

Also by Jean Giono

Joy of Man's Desiring
Blue Boy
The Horseman on the Roof
The Straw Man

The Song of the World

Jean Giono

The Song of the World

Jean Giono

Translated by Henri Fluchère
and Geoffrey Myers

COUNTERPOINT
A MEMBER OF THE PERSEUS BOOKS GROUP
NEW YORK, NEW YORK

Copyright © 1981 Aline Giono
Jean le Bleu copyright © 1932 Editions Bernard Grasset

First Counterpoint paperback edition 2000

All rights reserved under international and Pan-American
Copyright Conventions. No part of this book may be used or
reproduced in any manner whatsoever without written per-
mission from the Publisher, except in the case of brief quota-
tions embodied in critical articles and review.

A CIP catalog record for this book is available from the
Library of Congress
ISBN 1-58243-067-5

The paper used in this publication meets the requirements of
the American National Standard for Permanence of Paper for
Printed Library Materials Z39.48–1984.

Cover design by Amy Evans McClure

COUNTERPOINT
A MEMBER OF THE PERSEUS BOOKS GROUP
NEW YORK, NEW YORK

Counterpoint is a member of the Perseus Books Group

10   9   8   7   6   5   4   3   2

PART ONE

NIGHT. The river shouldered its way through the forest. Antonio walked out to the far end of the island. On one side, the deep water, sleek as a cat's fur; on the other side, the whinnying of the ford. Antonio felt the oak. He listened through his hand to the shiverings of the tree. It was an aged oak, more sinewy than a man of the mountains. It stood at the very tip of the isle of jays, right in the rush of the stream, and already half its roots emerged from the water.

"Is it all right?" asked Antonio.

The tree did not stop trembling.

"No," said Antonio, "it doesn't seem to be."

He patted the tree gently with his long hand.

Far away yonder in the dales of the hills, the birds could not sleep. They came and listened to the river. They flew over it silently, almost like fleeting snow. As soon as they had scented the strange smell of the moss on the other bank, they flashed back, flapping their wings desperately. They swooped down on the ash trees all together, like a net thrown into the water. That autumn, from the very outset, smelt of old moss.

From the other bank of the river, somebody called:

"Antonio!"

Antonio listened.

"Is that you, Sailor?"

"Yes, I want to see you."

"The ford has shifted," shouted Antonio.

"I'm coming on horseback," said Sailor. And he could be heard shoving a big tree-trunk into the water.

"He must arrive somewhere near the water-willows," thought Antonio. "With that new turn of the ford, the stream must run somewhere thereabouts."

"Hallo there," Sailor cried out.

He had already arrived.

"It's bearing up well," he said, "and keeping clear of the bottom. Go easy, it's been swelling like anything these last two days."

"Yes," said Antonio, "it's down below that it's brewing. Listen!"

He laid his hand on the man's arm. They both stood motionless.

From the bottom of the water there rose a rumble like the stampeding of a herd.

"The ford's on the move," said Antonio. "Come and warm yourself."

"Look here now," Sailor said, "there's no time to lose. Did you look at the water today?"

"Yes, and all day yesterday."

"Towards the main stream?"

"Yes."

"Did you see our trees go by?"

"No."

"You sure?"

"Yes, sure."

[4]

"You can be straight with me, Antonio. I'm old, but ready for anything. Don't say No if it's Yes."

"No, I tell you."

"Fir trunks. They're marked with a cross. I've always had them marked on four sides. Even if they roll, the mark's bound to be seen. D'you still say No?"

"Still No," said Antonio.

For a time neither spoke.

"Got any dry tobacco?" said Sailor.

"Yes," Antonio answered.

He fumbled in his pockets.

"Here's my hand," he said.

"Where?"

"Just in front of you."

Sailor took the tobacco.

"Now, what's it all about?" said Antonio.

"I've heard nothing of my red-haired twin," Sailor said.

"Since when?"

"Since he left."

"When did he go?"

"About the July moon."

"For how long?"

"Two months, at most."

"Two months for you," said Antonio.

"Two months for him, too," Sailor said. "I know him. I don't say it just because he's my son. I know how he works. He had fifty firs to fell."

"Where?"

"In the Rebeillard country, five days away on the far side of the gorges. He had to make the raft and float it down. That's why."

[5]

"Unless . . ." said Antonio, but he stopped himself and asked: "Filled your pipe? Hand me the tobacco."

"Here's my hand," Sailor said.

"Wait a bit, we'll have a light together."

"Is it still No?" said Sailor.

"It's more than No. I've rebuilt my dam," said Antonio, "and I've been watching the water for over twenty days. It's more than No. Had the trees gone by, I'd have seen 'em."

"They may have gone by at night."

"Not all of 'em," said Antonio. "At night, the stream bears towards the island. At least one would have stuck."

"What are you thinking about?"

"I'm thinking of Junie."

"It's her who sent me down to you," said Sailor. "If you're ready, I'll strike the light."

"Go ahead."

Sailor struck the flint and blew on the tinder. His mouth, in the thick of his white beard, was fleshy, with heavy lips, somewhat shiny and well filled out with blood.

He lit his pipe, then gave the tinder to Antonio. Antonio blew. He had a lean, wizened chin, and scarcely any lips.

"I'm thinking of Junie," said Antonio.

"It's her who started worrying," said Sailor. "I wasn't worrying. One morning she put her hand on my knee. 'What about the boy?' she says. 'The boy,' says I, 'what about him?' 'He ought to be back.' 'Give him time,' says I. 'The time's up,' she said, and she got up and opened the door. Daylight was breaking."

"What d'you think?" Antonio said.

[6]

"I don't try to think," Sailor said. "What I do know is he has cut the trees, made the raft, and must have set it afloat."

"Well, then?"

"Drowned maybe, I thought."

The ford went on galloping, and they could hear its big white paws paddling among the rocks.

"It's you I've come to fetch, Antonio," said Sailor. "Come with me to our camp. You must help me, and my wife's got to see you too. It's our twin, Antonio. If he's drowned, I've got to find him. We must carry him to his mother up there, and then bury him in dry ground in the forest."

"Let's go," said Antonio.

He groped in the dark to touch Sailor.

"I always wade across the ford," he said. "I don't know why, but it amuses me. . . . Hold on to my coat and follow me."

He went straight into the water.

"It's a bit lower down," Sailor said.

"It's here," said Antonio. "I've been watching the ford shifting down here for a good five hours. To my mind, it's going to stay here for some time. It's up against the end of the island. That's what's funny. Come along."

Antonio began to walk. As he got into the water, the cold gripped his knees at once. The water swirled around his legs and began to flap like a long weed.

"Hold tight," he said to Sailor.

He felt the life of the river.

It was always a big moment for Antonio. All day long he had been watching that river ruffling its scales in the sun, then those white horses galloping in the ford with large foamy splashes on their hoofs, and the back of the green water, up there, coming out of the gorges, angry at having been pent in by the gully of the rocks; then the water sees the broad forest spreading before it, and it lowers its lithe back and flows in among the trees. Now, it was all around him. It held him by a good bit of his body. It gripped him from his feet up to his knees.

"Hold tight," he said.

"I am," Sailor said. "I've been about rivers a bit in my time, too."

"That's life," Antonio said.

"The forest's better," said Sailor.

"Matter of taste," Antonio said.

They had almost reached the shallowest part of the ford. They heard the hiss of the surging foam. Suddenly Antonio felt earth, earth rubbing up against his belly. The earth of the bank with its hanging roots. He threw out his arm into the darkness. A tree. A birch. The bank. They had reached the bank.

"Climb up, quick."

"Already there," Sailor said.

"It's tricked me," said Antonio. "I thought I knew. One always does. But it doesn't reason like us, and that makes it difficult."

"I can see over here all right," said Sailor. "The clearing's on the left. Follow me; we'll go up through Jean Richaud's oak plantation."

He stepped into the undergrowth.

"One's always being too clever," said Antonio. "Don't walk so fast. Where are you?"

[8]

"On the left," Sailor answered. "Come in here."

On the other side of the brambles, the forest opened out in its stillness. The river could no longer be heard. The sound remained away over there in the foliage of the birches, like the soft rustle of rain.

"You know your way?" asked Antonio.

"I've lost it a bit," Sailor said. "But come on, the oaks are over there."

They trod upon thick mosses and a greasy humus which crackled slightly under their feet. The air smelt of wood and water. At times, a thick, sugary fragrance of sap was wafted, and Antonio smelt it on his right, then on his left, as if the smell had circled round his head slowly. Then, presently, as he went by he touched the trunk of a birch with its wounds. There was also a smell of green leaves, and there were puffs of a tingling perfume which flashed from some corner of the foliage. It seemed to be like the scent of a flower, and it twinkled, like a star which appears to be fading and then shoots out a long ray.

"What's that smell?" said Antonio.

"It's a willow that's made a mistake," said Sailor. "It has a smell of spring."

On reaching the oak plantation, Sailor stopped to feel with his foot for the dip of the path.

Antonio heard the sound of the forest. They had left the region of silence, and from where they stood, they could hear the night teeming with life in the forest. It came and touched the ear like a cold finger. It was a long, muffled breath, a throaty purr, a deep noise, a long, monotonous song from an open mouth. It filled all the tree-clad hills with its presence. It was in the sky and on the earth like rain; it came from all sides at once and it surged up slowly like a heavy wave, rumbling in the narrow corridors of the dales. In the depths of the noise, slight patterings of leaves scampered away like rats. Off they went and shot to one side, then slipped away down the stairs of the branches, and one heard the pit-pat of a light noise, clicking and soft like a raindrop dripping through a tree. Moanings rose from the earth and went heavily up through the sap of the trunks to the forking-off of the big branches.

Antonio leaned against a beech. He heard a slight whistling close to his ear. He felt with his finger. It was the sap dripping from a split in the bark. It had just opened. He felt under his fingers the lips of the green wood which were slowly widening.

"We've hit the right way," Sailor said. "Come on. We'll be at Christol's Pass in no time. I'm taking you along a new track."

"Can you really see here?" Antonio asked.

"No, but I can smell. This is my own forest. Don't worry. Can you smell the pines?" he said after a time.

Antonio sniffed.

"I think I smell oaks."

"And further on?" Sailor said.

"No!"

"I can smell the pines, anyway," said Sailor. "I know of only three in this forest, all of them at Christol's Pass."

Life in its fullness flowed gently over the hills and dales of the earth. Antonio felt it come up against him; it hit his legs, it passed between his legs, between his arms and his breast, against his cheeks, through his hair, as if he had dived into a hole teeming with fish. He began to think of the twin who was perhaps dead.

"Can you smell the pines?" Sailor said.

"Now I can," answered Antonio.

He could smell the pines now. They were close at hand; the smell already rose from the soft ground covered with pine-needles. Away in front of them they heard the pines singing, and another smell came too, alive and sharp, then silky. It stuck in their noses, and they had to rub them with their fingers to get rid of it. It was the smell of the mountain mosses; they were in blossom, crushed under little golden stars.

"Oh, Sailor!"

"What?"

"Nothing."

Antonio was thinking of the twin. That mud-stopped nose, those mud-stopped ears. . . .

They had just emerged from the forest and were on a high knoll. It was still night, but the darkness was greyer, for they were above the trees. There were only two or three stars in the sky and heavy clouds were sailing along with a noise like that of sand. A red glow rose from the depths of the forest.

"What's that?" Antonio said, pointing to it.

"My camp," answered Sailor.

The solemn song of the forest rose and fell slowly and struck northwards against the hollow mountains a long way off. A horn sounded somewhere in the east.

"The shepherds of Chabannes," said Antonio.

The smell of the mosses rose from its nest and opened

its beautiful anise wings. A magpie crackled in its sleep like the crushing of a pine-cone underfoot. A cottony owl flew silently by; it perched on the pine tree; it lit up its eyes.

In the distance, the horn kept calling. A bell began to ring. The belfry must have been far up in the mountains. The sound seemed to come from the sky.

"It's answering from the Rebeillard country," Sailor said.

There was a hush, and the smell of the river was wafted up. It smelt of fish and mud. The owl closed its eyes. A slight gentle howling seemed to call.

"There's still a wolf in Gaude Vale."

"The whole litter," said Sailor; "I've seen the tracks."

Foxes yelped on Jean Richaud's farm. Quite near the two men, a galloping sound went through the bushes. Silently the owl flew away. All the magpies awoke and flew down towards the river, bursting through the foliage.

"I'm thinking of the twin," said Antonio. "Have you any hope?"

"None," Sailor said.

"A pity," said Antonio.

As they walked down Christol's Pass the red glow began to throb in the depths of the forest. After a time, the tree-trunks stood before them like the bars of a fence. Antonio looked at the shoulders of his companion walking in front of him. He walked by an effort from his loins, more with the middle of his body than with his legs. He was a man of the forest, right enough; all the men of the forest walk like that. It is the forest which breaks them to it. From time to time, in the light of the approaching fire, Antonio could see Sailor's white beard.

They heard the crackling of the fire.

Two sombre-looking dogs darted noiselessly out of the brushwood. Sailor sang out their names.

It was Sailor's camp: three log-houses in the clearing. He and Junie lived in the one-story cottage; opposite, in the low hut, lived Charlotte, the widow of the first of the twins, who had been killed the spring before by a land-slip in the clay pit. Forming the third side of the square was a long shed, used as a barn and a work-shop. The second twin used to sleep there before he went away. In the area between the houses, a great fire had been lit. The three doors were open.

"Mother!" called out Sailor. "I've fetched your man of the river for you. Here he is."

"Good evening to you, Antonio," said the voice of a young woman.

She was sitting on the other side of the fire. They could not see her on arriving, because their eyes were dazzled by the blaze.

"Good evening, Charlotte."

She was a dark, wiry-haired woman, colourless and quite grey, despite the blaze: her forehead, cheeks, and lips were grey, and her long, hard face had high cheek-bones. Her eyes, of an intense yellow, burned large, like the eyes of night-prowling beasts.

"Sit down, Antonio," Sailor said. "I'll fetch mother."

From here Antonio could be seen properly. He was a man in the prime of life. He had long arms with thin wrists and long hands. His shoulders were rather high. His body was elastic and strong, rigged all over with solid but supple muscles.

[13]

He folded his knees and squatted in the grass.

"Antonio," said the young woman.

He turned his hard face, hairless and lean, towards her.

She was looking at him. Her mouth was still open but she withheld what she wanted to say.

"Give me your little girl," said Antonio.

The young woman opened her arms. The baby, standing on firm legs, was sucking at her breast.

"Go and see Tonio," said the woman.

She drew back her breast. The baby's eyes were completely dazzled by the fire. She tried to smile with her shiny lips. A large drop of milk was still welling up from the woman's breast; she wiped it off with the palm of her hand.

"All over," said the woman.

The child toddled round the fire. Antonio held out his long arms to her. He fondled her, rubbing his cheek against the child's cheek. The baby carried with it the heavy smell of the mother.

"So you've come, man of the river?" asked Junie from inside the house.

"Yes, I've come," said Antonio without looking round.

"D'you know what's happened through your fault?"

"I know what's perhaps happened through nobody's fault. Come out a bit, woman, and let's see you," he said.

He heard old Junie inside, walking on the wooden floor.

"I can see you without coming out, as if I'd made you myself," said Junie.

"Sailor told me about it," said Antonio. "If you'll listen to me, this is what ought to be done. We'll leave tomorrow, your man and me, and we'll walk upstream, one on

[14]

either side. If he's stranded, we'll find him. If he passes down, we'll see him. We'll walk up to the Rebeillard hills and ask around there. A man can't melt away."

"It's not for nothing that we named you Golden-Mouth," said Junie's voice. "It's because you know how to speak."

"No," Antonio answered, "it's because I can shout louder than the waters."

The young woman was gazing at Antonio. She remembered that cry which all the forest people knew, that cry which sometimes crossed the trees like the scream of a big bird to tell the joy of Antonio on his river.

"You must be sorry now," said Junie.

"What for?" Antonio asked.

He turned his face towards the open door through which came the voice and the drum of that barefooted tread stamping as it went, back and forth, over the deal boards.

"You didn't rest till you'd drawn us to your river, Antonio," said the voice. "I thought you sort o' loved me like a mother. Both my twins. They brought me back one on oak branches. We buried that one. But the other one? Who'll bring back the other one?"

Antonio raised his hand.

"I tell you we'll go and fetch him tomorrow morning."

"He's dead," said the voice.

"We'll bring him back to you as he is," said Antonio.

"What will be the good of that to me?" said the voice.

Antonio was stroking the little girl's head; he went right round it with the palm of his hand. The flames of the fire died down as if the air had begun to weigh upon them. The smell of the river crept down into the dale. The young

[15]

woman was watching Antonio; she was following all his movements.

Sailor came and sat near the fire. He was a thick-set man, but not heavy. He was a little shrunken with old age, and now he was round as a tree-trunk, without hollow or hump. The breadth of his shoulders seemed to spread throughout his body down to his feet. His white beard covered his face.

"You can hardly say anything," he said.

Antonio stared straight in front of him. He squeezed the little girl's mouth gently between his thumb and his fingers.

"What are you doing now?" Antonio asked.

"Nothing, everything is ready for the winter."

"Have you time to spare?"

"Yes."

"You and me, we've got to start tomorrow. We'll work upstream, one on one side, and one on the other, as I said. That may take us a long way. . . ."

"I've time enough," Sailor said.

"So have I," said Antonio.

The yellow eyes of the young woman tried to catch Antonio's eyes. Old Junie's step could be heard inside the house.

"Take your gun and some brandy," said Antonio.

He got up. The little girl, left to herself, looked up at him, and tried to speak. The young woman looked at him. Sailor looked at him.

"Going home?" said Sailor.

"No," said Antonio, "I'm going to sleep in the forest."

"Go to bed in the work-shop."

"No. Lend me a blanket."

"Do stay," said the young woman.

[16]

"No," said Antonio.

He went off into the forest. He had been lying in the bracken for some time when he heard a noise. He opened his eyes. The fire was still burning over there and its light was broken by a shadow coming his way.

It was the young woman. She was calling softly:

"Antonio!"

Then she stepped forward, almost noiselessly, with scarcely a rustle of her skirt.

She was calling around her, lowering her head a little to let her warm voice pass underneath the bushes. A bird, disturbed in its sleep, began to complain.

Antonio rolled himself up tighter in his blanket and buried his face in the moss. The smell of the warm humus and that call of the woman entered into him, lighting him up like a sun.

AT the peep of day, Antonio, wending his way across the lower wood, had gone back to the island. Towards the east the light shot right into the trees swarming with birds.

Every morning Antonio stripped off his clothes. Usually he began the day by slowly crossing the large black branch of the river. He drifted along with the currents; he felt the swirls of each eddy; with the quick of his thighs he touched the long sinews of the river, and, as he started to swim, he felt with his belly whether the water buoyed him up, pressing in on him, or whether it tended to sparkle. From all that, he knew whether he had to take the net with the wide or the small mesh, the hand-net, the netting-needle, the rod, or whether he had better go and catch fish with his hands in the pebbled shallows of the ford. He knew whether the pike shot out of the banks, whether the trout swam upstream, whether the fry shoaled down from the upper river; and sometimes he let himself sink, slowly treading water in the depths, to try to touch that huge red-and-black fish which was impossible to catch and which, every evening, came and blew across the stillness of the waters a long jet of foam and a child's moan.

That morning the grass was somewhat hoary with frost. Autumn had pressed down a little more on the trees. Em-

[18]

bers were glowing in the foliage of the maples. A small twisted flame climbed up the spindle-shaped poplars. The frozen dew, like glistening tin, weighed down the blades of grass.

When naked, Antonio appeared a tall man with long sinews. The night before in the forest, he seemed slightly shrunken in the darkness, but here he stretched himself out to his full extent. He was indeed the man of whom the people spoke on both sides of the river, from the gorges to the distant country downstream, as "golden-mouthed" Antonio. His feet were well arched. His heels were as hard as stone, resin-coloured, and well shaped. The fine arch of the foot advanced up to the toes, which were well separated and each in its right place. He had fine, light legs with scarcely any calf: just a small ball of calf, held by a net of muscles thick as fingers. The curve of his legs was not broken by the knees, but the knees were inscribed in that curve, which rose steadily, holding all the flesh of the thigh within its bounds. The caress, the knowledge, and the anger of the water were in that broad-shouldered man. At his sides, each thigh was jointed by a rounded bone, like the stump of a bough. He had the belly of a man who eats soundly, supple and flat and shaded underneath with fair hair accustomed to wind and sun; thick and curly hair like the fur of an animal, strongly rooted like the coat of a sheep dog. These hairs filled the hollow between his thighs and his belly, and overflowed on either side. Beneath them was planted that part of his body from which darted strange orders, making him, on certain evenings, leave his nets, jump into the water, slip downstream, and anchor himself among the rushes near the villages. He would hide himself in the neighbourhood of the washing-sheds and begin to sing with the voice of an animal. The village lasses would open their doors and sometimes run towards the river on the sloping meadows, where their linen skirts flapped like wings.

His golden skin, and beneath it a slight layer of flesh, would start throbbing from his thigh joints up to the hard sickle-shaped curve of his lower ribs. Antonio's respiration, confined on either side of his body, grew from there, or was held in check and quivered slowly as he lay in wait with his spear for a big salmon. From there it gushed up as he speared the fish, and there it rolled over onto itself as he took a deep breath before diving, or as he got ready to call the women with that howl of his. Antonio loved to finger his sides. Only there did the hollow part begin; for his legs, his thighs, and his arms were all strong and solid. From his sides upwards it was tender and hollow and there lay the real Antonio. He touched his supple sides and then his broad chest: he felt that he was well, and he was glad.

Daylight, by now, was beating down on the ringing vales full of men and beasts. Here and there curls of smoke crept out of the forest. It had been settled with Sailor that Antonio would shout when the time came to leave. Then Sailor was to walk up on his side searching every creek, and looking carefully at every beach. Antonio had said that the slightest scratch on the sand might be a sign, the tiniest shining thing sticking out of the clay might be the tip of a nail. Since they were trying to find the twin, it was better to put all the odds on their side, and go up the track step by step, without leaving anything behind unsearched. Antonio was to shout the signal, but before shouting he was

[20]

to examine the air, the water, and everything, to be sure of a good start.

"It's the last man of the house you're taking with you," Junie had said that morning.

And Antonio had stared at that old woman, all belly and breasts, that maker of dead children, that lifeless flesh of a face.

The air stirred from the north. The cold made Antonio feel like stretching. He rose to his full height, making the bones in his shoulders and arms crack. He laughed silently.

He, for his part, was to work his way up the bank beyond the great waters. He was first going to feel about the place; as he walked barefoot, he already perceived that the earth was contracting under the grass. Autumn would soon sour. It was a long journey that he had to make with Sailor. They had to cross the gorges. Once in the Rebeillard hills, they could inquire in the villages and the farms. A large purple scar crossed Antonio's breast. As he pictured the villages of that unknown country, he thought of his scar, and, as he touched that groove of badly healed flesh, he thought of Sailor's daughter-in-law.

While she had been looking for him, he had not stirred from his bed of ferns. She had walked a little farther in the forest. She had called again: "Antonio!" Then she had stayed there, and every now and again she had called: "Antonio!"

He himself had not stirred.

He ran his thumb right along the hollow of that scar across his breast. What had become of that woman for whom he had fought? Was she still in the house near the washing-sheds? He needed this mellow autumn, which deceived both women and water-willows in their bloom, to think again of that village fight. He had needed, too, the voice in the forest of that woman Charlotte, who had remained too long without a husband and was on the quest.

Besides that long furrow-like scar, he had another one, which was quite round, on his left arm, and another long one on his right arm. They dated from the time when, on the lower river, he was called "the man who comes out of the rushes." Every night the villagers lay in ambush by the river. Antonio swam noiselessly and emerged noiselessly. He walked noiselessly on the grassy paths, and went noiselessly into the houses where the women had carefully oiled the locks.

He had his three scars: a stab, the bite of a man, and the cut of a bill-hook which had laid open his breast. On that occasion he had awakened on the bank with the water right up to his belly. The water was red with his blood, and little pike were already between his thighs, nibbling at his testicles.

That is why he enjoyed fingering his velvety sides. The hollow part began there, the hollow full of images, which alone had remained alive, despite his wound, as he lay on the sand, bleeding all over. It was inside that hollow that the long moaning of the wind coiled itself like seaweed. It was from the time his belly and his breast had been fraught with memories of the villages, of their women, and of the fields downstream, that he had been called Golden-Mouth.

The morning drew on. He would first see what was happening to the river with its big, black, silent stream, and then he would shout for Sailor to start off. He was at the far end of the island. He dived.

[22]

His shoulders had grown so accustomed to the water that they had become like those of a fish. They were fat and round, without protuberances or hollows. They rose towards his neck, they strengthened the neck. The impetus of his dive took him into the ooziness of the stream.

He said to himself: "The water's thick."

He struck out with his leg. He had kicked as if against iron. He did not come up. He had long twinings of fibrous water curling round his belly. He clenched his teeth. He struck out again. A watery strap tightened round his breast. He was carried off by a living mass. He thought: "Till we see red."

That was his utmost. When he had exhausted his breath he heard a rumbling in his ears, then the noise became red and filled his head with a bloodlike rumble tasting of sulphur.

He let himself drift along. With his head he felt for gentler waters.

He heard within himself: "Red . . . red . . ." And the roar of the river, not the same as on the surface but that rasping noise which the water made carrying along its bed of pebbles.

Blood filled his eyes.

Then he turned round a little, steadying himself on the slender strength of the stream; he folded back his right knee as if to lean towards the bottom; he poised his head firmly on his neck, and, just as he kicked with his right leg, he opened out his arms.

He emerged. He breathed. He could see green again. His arms glistened in the foam of the water.

They were two fine naked arms, long and solid, slightly

[23]

filled out above the elbow, but well surrounded under the skin by muscles. The fine shoulders cleft the water. Antonio lowered his face until it touched his shoulder. Then the water swayed his long hair like seaweed. He struck well out with his arm and his hand gripped the strength of the water. He forced it downwards beneath him, while cutting through the stream with his powerful thighs.

"The water's heavy," Antonio said to himself. There were icy patches in the river which seemed as hard as granite, then soft and warmer undulations which treacherously whirled round in the depths.

"It's raining in the mountains," thought Antonio. He glanced at the trees on the bank.

"I'll go over to the poplar."

He tried to cut across the stream. He was rolled from side to side like a tree-trunk. He dived. He swam by a green-and-red trout which let itself drop into the depths, with its fins folded flat, like a bird. The stream was hard and taut everywhere.

"Mountain rain," thought Antonio. "We must get past the gorges today."

At last he found a slight flaw in the current. He bounded into it, striking out hard with his thighs. The water carried away his legs. With his hardened face turned against the stream, he fought with shoulders and arms. He dug with his big hands; at last he felt the water glide under his belly in the right direction. He was moving forwards. At the end of his tether, he reached the still water under the lee of the bank. He let himself glide on. The movement of his feet made small air bubbles rise to the surface. He clutched a hanging root with both hands. He pulled it gently to test

[24]

its strength. Then he tugged himself out of the water by it, bending forwards, streaming and glistening in the sunlight. His long arms hung at his sides, lithe and happy. He had fine hands with long, tapering fingers.

"We must get past the gorges today. It's raining in the mountains and the water's hard. It'll soon be cold. The trout are asleep and the current's in midstream. The river won't change for two days. We must get past the gorges today."

He got up and drew in a deep breath to shout. The air was sugary. Yonder, on the windward side of the forest, the old birches must have cracked their barks, and they were weeping their honey blood. He tasted the air. He still had the taste of the water in his mouth. He chewed it all together two or three times. Antonio's cry scared off the greenfinches from both banks. Then from the depth of the forest came the reply of Sailor's call.

Sailor was equipped with gun, wallet, and cloak. "Goodbye, Mother," he said.

Junie was looking towards the north.

"When you are in the Rebeillard country," she said, "go to Villevieille. Ask for the almanac-vender. Go and see him. If the house is full of patients, don't bother to wait. Only say: I have been sent by Junie."

"How do you know all that?" said Sailor.

"I know it," said Junie. "Do as I tell you. Trees that are grafted high up carry two fruits, one sweet and one sour. I'm the sweet fruit and he's the sour fruit. That's all; now go."

She was looking towards the mountains. She was gazing

[25]

at the blue mist between the high mountains and the foot-hills overhanging the gorges. It was the smoke and the breath of the widespread Rebeillard country, full of villages, brooks, and moving carts.

Charlotte had heard Antonio's call. She looked out of the window. Her father-in-law was going away. He was making his way along the wooded paths with the heavy plod of a man starting off on a long journey. Junie, with her hands on her belly, was watching him go. Charlotte listened. Outside, there were the ordinary daytime noises of the forest. And then, just that heavy tread of a man with hob-nailed boots. She went back to the hearth and piled up the logs under the pot. As she watched the blue valleys of smoke twining themselves in the big flames, she thought of Rebeillard.

Antonio made a bundle of his corduroy trousers and his gun. He packed in his knapsack his cartridges, powder pouch, and long knife, his bag for buck-shot, his file, and a coil of rope. He untied the bundle to add smoking and chewing tobacco. He swam across the river lithely, without effort and without splashing foam, taking advantage of the water's movements. Then he had a look. Nothing was wet except the butt of the gun because it stuck out a little. He dressed himself. As he stood on a small crescent-shaped beach, he could see upstream as far as the opening of the gorges. From where Antonio stood till far away into the distance the river gleamed in the sunlight and the trees were fine trees. Further up, the river seemed to be flattened out under the shadows. Beyond lay the Rebeillard country.

The river, which now flowed out of the gorges, had

sprung from a mountain land-slip. It was a deep black valley with black trees, black grass, and rain-soaked mosses. It
was hollowed out in the form of a hand, the five fingers
draining all the water from five deep ravines into the large
palm full of clay and rocks, whence the river darted like a
horse, with its big foamy hoofs.

Lower down, the water plunged into dark fir-clad ter-
races towards the call of another watercourse. It flowed out
of a valley called "Mary's Joy." Then, more at ease, it
rolled its fat waters along fine grassy meanders. Already
the voice of the highlands had been left behind on the distant horizon, and sounded like nothing more than the
breathing of a man. Sensitive trees grew nearer its banks:
willows, poplars, apple trees, and yew trees, among which
galloped almost wild horses and colts. The bells of unseen
flocks moved about among the hills. The river made its
way into the Rebeillard country.

It was an open country, ploughed all over, and surging
like the sea; its horizons slept under a misty haze. It was
composed of wooded hills, covered with red earth and clusters of twisted pine trees, of tilled valleys and small plains
with one or two farmsteads, of villages stuck on the tops
of rocks like honey-combs. Dogs ran out of all those villages and farms and went hunting by themselves in the
woods and in the fields. Cats crept along the furrows, brushing the ground, ready to spring upon moles. A small brown
bitch, all ears and loins, ran after an owl. The bird, dazzled
by the morning light, flew from tree to tree towards the
wood. The bitch flapped its ears as it ran. Beautiful golden
clouds had begun to sail across the sky over the countryside. They floated southwards, trailing their shadows be-

hind them. Between high-headed, motionless oaks slept a silent lake of air; a small greenfinch darted through it, clucking. Along a path winding up towards a village, a man led a mule laden with packets of tobacco. The old men of Rebeillard were on their thresholds. They had heard the mule's bells and were listening. Time hung heavy on their hands without tobacco. The women laughed as they looked at them and said: "It's coming up the hill. It'll soon be here."

From the hollow of the woods, pheasant-hens looked out on fields where the corn was still green. The bitch had stopped under the tree with the owl; at the same time it looked askance at a big golden beetle ploughing through the dung of a wild boar. An eagle hovered beneath the clouds. Cocks crowed and then listened to the crowing of other cocks. The eagle was watching a small stack of corn surrounded by hens, and as it swayed gently, it came down a little lower every time. On the threshing-floors of a village high up above the river, fires had been lit, despite the soft air of the morning. On long spits, red hares were being roasted, along with strings of rotting thrushes and two big legs of venison. The melted fat was sputtering in dripping-pans.

In her house the bride sat on her chair. She dared not move. She was wearing the usual full silk skirt, the heavy bodice, her mother's jewels, and the garland of laurel leaves. She was quite alone. She was watching the smoke from the meat being wafted along the road. She had fine, motionless eyes, like those of an ox.

At that time of autumn, birds migrated over the country in large numbers. Two foxes were following, at a jog-

trot, a flight of green-collared ducks. In a village in the
mud flats along the river, a big, strong, red-faced man who
had been a cartwright had just died. He was the fifth man
to die since the new moon. And of the same disease. Black
moss which gripped all round the belly and seemed to have
iron roots. It gnawed at the skin, then worked its way inside and got at the bowels fiercely. Then the men died yelling. That made the fifth, and the disease was spreading
faster and faster; already the cobbler was complaining and
holding his belly. A red crane had been trapped and, while
still alive, cut in two down the middle by a sharp stroke of
an ax. Now they were treating the cobbler with bird poul-
tice. The foxes were now walking among the water-willows,
still watching the tired ducks; but the birds had scented the
beasts of the earth, and they alighted in the middle of
the water. The river carried them away. A flight of thrushes,
thick and purple as a storm-cloud, changed the aspect of
the hill. It swooped down in the pine wood with a rustle.
The foxes yelped towards the open water. Villages, lost in
the ocean of hills, tinkled their bells, then were hushed
under flights of swallows. A long line of hazel-grouse, tapering like a lance-head, flew at top speed towards the lower
country.

The owl, hunted by the brown bitch, came to rest in
the heart of the wood. In the stillness even the thawing
hoar-frost could be heard dripping onto the leaves. The owl
winked with its marble eyelids, then fell asleep. There was
a kind of bird which in the Rebeillard country people called
"houldres." They were plumed with iron-coloured jackets
and golden ties, and were the birds which carried spring
in their throats. They had seen the hazel-grouse fly past,

[29]

and knew that snow was coming behind them. So they called one another to gather and fly off to their winter quarters. It was a warm dale, strewn all over with alluvium left by the river as it shrank into its own bed. All around, the bellowing of bulls and heifers was re-echoed incessantly. Maudru, the ox-tamer, lived there. When he walked along the roads of Rebeillard, he was always followed by four young bullocks by which he was loved more faithfully than by dogs. It was said that he was strong, and that his huge strength was heaped up within him in such disorder that he no longer had the figure of a man. In his red mouth the least word rang like the wrath of the air.

The river flowed right across the Rebeillard country, spreading over the land with its tributaries, its brooks, and its twig-like watercourses, like a huge tree carrying the little mountains at the end of its boughs. Lower down, southwards, it entered the gorges. All that could be heard down there was the thundering and splashing of the water and the screams of the hazel-grouse resting on the rocks. The day was still in its prime, but the mist was already thickening.

Antonio had entered the gorges shortly after seeing Sailor on the other bank. He made a sign to him that he had found nothing, then penetrated the juniper thickets. He remembered being told by boatmen that somewhere towards the middle of the gorges there was a small round house called "the old pigeon-cote" on the brink of the river. He was going to make his way there.

"Sailor must know about it," he thought.

He felt sorry that he had not made an arrangement with him about that old pigeon-cote. He looked across at the other bank. Sailor was no longer in sight. Shouting was useless; the river made too much noise.

Since he had left the island, Antonio had been carefully looking at every creek, every beach, and every overhanging bank of the river. He could not make it out. A large raft cannot melt away like sugar. The stretches of sand were smooth, without the slightest scratch. Yet the current drifted that way and, picturing what a fir log, roughly squared off and marked with a cross on its four sides, could do, one could only conclude that it must drift and get stranded there, on that sand.

At every new cove Antonio stood still for a time, thinking it all out again. On setting out, he only reckoned on an odd chance of finding the man's body, but he was sure of finding some logs. And yet there was nothing at all. The river was clear and clean. It seemed to say: "The twin? What are you getting at me for with your twin? I have not even seen him."

Antonio suddenly got a new idea. He pictured Sailor's son. One of those men who keep everything to themselves, who listen, who watch, who do not say No, but who think No, and it is No. Off he goes to Rebeillard. He's alone; builds his raft; fixes his timber-slide; gets afloat; follows the river. He's strong and lithe. So far so good. Ever since the July moon, the river had not gone wild and the earth had been calm all around. The twin found himself on an easy river, a child's water. What then? Against what did the twin lose the game?

Antonio reached a creek of deep water; it gleamed between the ashen branches of a birch. He walked down to the brink.

It was quite a little gulf, hollowed out in bluish granite. Antonio bent down and threw a pebble into the water. He listened to the glugging sound. A wan thing seemed to be sleeping. A long snake uncoiled in the middle of the water, just above the opaque depths.

It was a large fish, like a conger in fresh water.

This fish always sleeps in clean waters. It was certain that neither corpse nor wreckage lay at the bottom. The conger dived off, waving like a weed.

Every bush had its fox. They scampered off, long before Antonio's step reached them, with their tails stiff, like iron plumes, and they yelped as they ran up the crumbling banks. Above the river, kites and hawks soared, screaming.

It smelt of moss and beast. It smelt of mud too; that acrid, eerie smell of flint worn away by water. From time to time, there was also a mountain smell blown down by a head wind. Antonio tucked up his shirt-sleeves and sniffed all along his arm. He needed that smell of a man's skin.

Early in the afternoon, the mist which came from the Rebeillard country began to flow into the gorges. It was a river above a river. The waves smoothed it off from underneath. Puffs of mist blew into the crackling trees. Then there seemed to be a stillness as the voice of the water was gradually muffled. Antonio called out. His voice shot out three paces ahead of him and was then on him again. He was in a thick fog. At his feet a fox crouching in the grass stared at him with wide, astonished eyes. It had not heard Antonio's shout.

"Coming, old man," said Antonio to him.

The fox pursed up its chaps and showed its teeth. It

had huddled its body into a ball on its thin, shivering, rush-like legs.

Just after passing the fox, Antonio walked into a sort of dim, stifling daylight, where everything appeared without warning. With outstretched arms he walked among the trees. He could no longer use his eyes or his ears. He touched the branches with his hands. He pushed them aside to get by. He took off his shoes. When barefoot he felt the quality of the ground better. He was afraid of falling over a steep bank. He no longer heard the river. The fog flowed along his cheeks with a scarcely audible sound, like that of slipping flour.

Suddenly he said to himself: "What about Sailor?" He spoke aloud so as to hear his own voice. "Well, old man, what are you doing over there, on your side? You are the last man of the house. Foot it slowly. I shan't hear you from here if you fall into the river and cry out. How can we look for your twin in this?"

He walked on a few steps.

"If you had some sense," he said, "you'd stop and wait for me. You must have guessed that I'm now going to try and get to you. Now I've got to look for the father as well as the son.

"And if I had any sense," he said to himself, "I'd cross over before dark."

At that moment he heard a series of long-drawn-out, small, crackling sounds. He listened. That was it! A distant cart creaking on its axles, and then a barking dog, a gust of wind high up in the sky, the buzzing of a village. He had passed through the gorges; the Rebeillard country lay before him, spread out beneath the mist.

The sinking sun appeared at the bottom of the sky. It was red and shapeless. It sent a weak ray between the river and the mist. Above the water, the vaulted opening of a salt cave could be seen. Long, living crystal candles went down, slowly drawn by their own weight. A fairly wide stretch of the river was distinguishable.

"I'll cross over," said Antonio.

He stripped off his heavy trousers and his kit. He gathered some dry sticks. He built a small fire between two stones and lighted it. He left behind his knapsack, his gun, and his clothes, then jumped into the water to reconnoitre.

The water was warm. He drifted awhile, then began his great, eagle-like arm-strokes. The sunbeam followed him.

"It's possible," he thought.

He was thinking of all the kit he had to carry. As he turned round towards the fire that he had lit to show him the way, he plunged his head under the surface and saw the big conger following him. It was more than two yards long and as thick as a bottle. It swam near the man as fast as it could, then waited for him, gently swinging in the bosom of the river. When it was tinged by the sun it glowed like an ember, with small green flames flickering along the whole length of its quivering skin. It drew towards the man and opened its silent, gaping jaws, with saw-like teeth. Antonio touched the conger with both hands just when it swung its tail in front of him. The water-snake dived down, whirling as it went. Large oily eddies opened up before the swimmer. He struck out and then dived down himself, head first towards the bottom. The fish shot back with all its strength, and straightened itself out like a tree-trunk. It glided past, over the darkness into which Antonio sank, and turned round on its back. The sun shone on its belly. The conger's head emerged. It blew out a spurt of water and wailed. Its red eye gazed at the bank of the river. Antonio emerged noiselessly and sank noiselessly into the water again. He reappeared downstream. Up there, the conger whisked the water with its tail and continued to wail, with its snout straining at the bank.

The sun was disappearing. The cover of mist was darkening from one moment to the other. Then it closed in over the river. Antonio heard the fish dive. He got out of the water and started running towards the fire. Higher up he crossed the river, carrying all his kit with him. On the other bank, he had just time enough to see through a thinner veil of fog the trembling bars of a birch wood. Then night fell. He advanced towards the trees. He touched them. They had small, quivering stems. Under Antonio's feet the earth was soft like the flesh of a dead beast. He trod on alluvium. He imagined a narrow strip of mud along the river, between the river and the last rocks of the gorges. He advanced, hands first, towards those rocks. He walked slowly; he felt with his feet for safe places; his hands touched the trees. Beyond the trees, they reached out further and further into the night. Every now and then he expected to touch the cold rock, but his hand continued to sink into the darkness, and he walked on, step by step. He crossed a small brook. He heard the rustle of an oak. He breathed in the smell of rank grass. He realized that there were no longer any rocks to shut in the river and that now the Rebeillard country extended on either bank. He tried to peer ahead and around him. Nothing touched his eyes but the night, cold and flat as a stone. Once, as he bent his head

[35]

slowly forward to get nearer to some noise ahead of him, soft as the rustle of a silk scarf hanging from a drying line, his cheek was caressed by something slight and cold. It was a willow twig, with two tiny leaves.

Suddenly he noticed that the open country was lighting up before him.

The moon had risen above the fog. A hill raised its back with its fleece of pines. A ploughed field was steaming. Bare brambles with dewdrops glittering on all their claws gleamed in the hedges. Hills and woods, dark clumps of trees and bright fields, slowly unfurled and spread out until they filled the whole horizon.

Antonio stopped. He called out: "Hallo! Sailor! Hallo! Sailor!" Then suddenly he saw somebody ahead leap up in front of a red flame and he heard Sailor's voice.

CHAPTER III

He found him squatting near the embers, with his head in his hands.

"Seen nothing," said Antonio.

"Nor I either."

"Been there long?"

Sailor put his finger to his lips.

"Sh, sh," he said. "Listen."

They were in the shelter of a pine wood.

"The trees are making a noise," said Antonio.

Sailor looked at him with his eyes wide open.

"I've been here since nightfall," he said.

"What then?" said Antonio.

"Doesn't come from the trees."

The fire crackled. The blaze dropped with two small leaps, then hid under the embers, and started running along the ground among the little blue caves of burning charcoal.

"Has it been going on for long?"

"Yes."

"When did it begin?"

"When I lit the fire."

Antonio squatted noiselessly. He glanced at his gun. He drew it near him.

"No need of a gun for that," said Sailor. "It's in pain already; listen."

The moaning became more distinct.

"Evil country," said Sailor.

They could see the strange Rebeillard country through the haze, with its forests, white with hoar-frost and black with shadows.

"It's a cleft tree," Antonio said in a low voice.

"It isn't," said Sailor. "It's a voice."

Antonio stood up.

"Let's go and see."

"No," said Sailor.

"We must," said Antonio. "We're looking for your twin. I don't say it's him, but he may have cried out like that at night, up there in the open country."

They entered the pine wood. The moaning flowed along the surface of the grass without a stop.

"Who's there?" Antonio called out.

They had reached the top of the hillock, on the other side of the clump of trees. Before them they saw broad patches of moonlight on the backs of the hills, and shadow-streams in the dales.

"It's in there."

Beneath them was a valley, black with trees and night, from which emerged the frost-sparkling points of a fir wood. The moaning came from below.

"Not a man."

"No," said Antonio.

The moaning stopped.

"Come along," said Antonio.

"We can no longer see the fire," said Sailor.

"Let's go down."

The ground was strewn with pine-needles. The glimmer

[3 8]

of the fog shed a thin light on the undergrowth.

"Might be a bitch," said Sailor.

"What are you looking for?" said Antonio.

"I just want to make sure," said Sailor. "The country's evil."

They were now at the bottom of the coomb, and the dim light of the moon and fog had remained up above in the trees. They trod on great mosses. They heard something close to them like the panting from heavy labour, a scratching of feet, a naked hand slapping on a stone, then a heart-rending howl.

It was there, inside the bush.

"Light up," said Antonio.

Sailor struck a light.

It was a woman lying on her back. Her skirts were all turned up on her belly, and she was kneading this heap of clothes and her belly with her hands. Then she opened out her arms crosswise and shouted. She bent her loins backwards. She was touching the ground only with her head and her feet. She made a long effort. She opened out her thighs. She pushed with all her might, silently, without breathing, then she took another breath with a cry and fell back on the moss. Her head tossed about in the grass to the right and to the left.

"Woman," cried Antonio.

She did not hear.

"Go and fetch . . . go and fetch . . ." said Sailor.

Antonio tried to pull down the skirts. He felt that under there the woman's belly heaved with surging life, like the sea. He drew back as if he had touched fire.

"Go and fetch . . . go and fetch . . ." said Sailor, and

[39]

he pointed to the village. He tried to hold down that frenzied head which was beating about and hitting the stones.

"Run, Antonio."

"What?"

He tried to hold down the woman's legs. They slipped out of his hands. He dared not tighten his grasp.

"Run."

"Give her some brandy."

"Run."

"Hold her head."

"Run, I tell you."

The woman seemed to calm down.

"The child's coming," said Sailor. "Run quickly."

Antonio climbed up the knoll again. From all sides came the night, and that wan glimmer from the bottom of the water. Down below, their fire was dying down, like a blue coin. Antonio started running towards a ploughed field which he had seen glimmering. He shouted:

"Hey there!"

A flight of hazel-grouse passed over him. He ran across fallow land, then a meadow; it smelt of animals.

"What do you want?" cried a voice in the dark.

"Where are you?"

"Say first who you are and what you want. And stand still," said the voice.

It was the full voice of a man of the mountains.

"I am Antonio from the isle of jays. We've found a woman ill in the woods."

"You are one of those fellows who were warming themselves over there?"

"Yes."

"Come forward."

"Where are you?"

"Here."

The man was just by his side, but in his big cloak he looked like a tree-trunk, and he had spoken with his hand over his mouth to make believe that he was standing further to the left.

"I think there's a house over yonder in the small vale."

"Where?" asked Antonio.

"Go straight ahead, you'll see the light. Wait," said the man. And he laid his hand on Antonio's arm. "Maudru doesn't want fires to be lighted on his pasture. You're not from these parts, are you?"

"No," said Antonio.

"Go along then," said the man. "I'll see you tomorrow."

The meadow sloped down to a gentle coomb, with no trees, filled with moonlight. The house stood there with light shining through the joints of the shutters.

Antonio knocked with his fist.

"Woman."

"Who's knocking?"

"A man. It's for help."

The woman stopped moving.

"For you?"

"No. We've found a woman. She's going to have a child."

"Who's *we?*"

"Me and Sailor. Me, that's Antonio of the isle of jays."

"Did you meet the man who looks after the oxen?"

"Yes."

The woman unfastened the lock. He heard the leather

[41]

straps creaking as she undid the knots. She drew the bar.

"Come in."

She looked at him as he came in.

"You're a fine fellow," she said.

"Mother," said Antonio.

He wanted to tell her quickly about that woman yonder. He still heard the howling in his ears. He saw her thighs, naked like the thighs of a frog. He still felt under his hand that big, surging belly.

"She's shouting," he said. "Come quickly."

"Crying to start it and crying to finish it, that's the usual thing. Your wife, is it?"

"No. We found her in the wood."

"Pity. She would at least have started it with pleasure."

"Stop joking," said Antonio. "Come quickly."

She was a strong, dark woman, with signs of a moustache and big eyebrows. She was made like a man—tough hands, a man's nose, a hipless body, and only a bit soft at the breast.

"You'll be able to carry her," she said.

"I'll carry her," said Antonio. "Don't you worry."

He pictured her again: she was not big. He would carry her all right in his arms.

The woman shut the door behind them.

"Let's go through the pasture," said Antonio.

"No," said the woman, "let's go along the hedges. Whose fire is that up there?"

"Mine," said Antonio.

"Wait a bit," said the woman. "Don't tell me all the misfortunes at once. You've made a fire on Maudru's pasture, and you bring me a woman in child-birth. Walk ahead, and don't say another word—it's enough for tonight."

[42]

"It's over," said Sailor.

He had lighted another fire. He was kneeling near the woman. She seemed dead, white as hoar-frost, and without breath. Between her outstretched legs, she had a big bundle made with Sailor's jacket.

"Where is it?" said the woman.

"I've folded it in my jacket," said Sailor. "Only, cut the cord; that was beyond me."

"Is she dead?" asked Antonio.

"No."

"Give her some brandy," said the woman.

She opened the folds of the jacket.

"Why, there's the little chap," she said.

The child, all unclean, was gasping gently. Its small mouth was writhing silently. It was still attached to its mother.

"Give your knife here."

She cut the cord and made a knot.

"And who do you think you are?" (She was talking to the child.) "Because you've come in the forest, you're not howling like the others. Open that mouth of yours, come on." (She was shaking him.) "Yell now, youngster."

The babe began to cry.

"And, you there. Cover her up. You, who pretend you're so strong, carry her now. Pick up your knife, and come along. Now that it's begun to bawl, it's not likely to stop. Let's get off: frost's no good for all this."

Antonio picked up his knife. He looked at it. He had had this weapon for a long time. It had done many things before now but it had never before separated a child from its mother. It had done so now.

[43]

"What a business!" said Sailor. "Now what shall we do? Will you take the head or the feet?"

"I'll take her altogether," said Antonio. "You'll cover her up when she's on me."

She weighed next to nothing. Yet she was full-breasted and her flesh was hard. Antonio did not realize her weight: there was so much in that woman to make him forget that she was heavy. He felt only that warmth which she had now, and the round shape of that flesh, just fitting in the curve of his arms. As he lifted her to load her on his shoulders, he glanced at her face, without seeing whether it was beautiful or not. He was only watching for the pain on it, and he was glad to see that it was at last calm and freed from the moaning.

"Wrap up her legs," he said. "Give her my hood. Tuck it well under, between her and my shoulder."

"Coming?" cried the woman who was carrying away the child.

"Yes."

"I'll take the guns," said Sailor.

Antonio thought of the twin for whom they had been searching on the river the day before. It seemed more than ten years ago that they had found the woman. He was carrying her. She was folded on his shoulder like soft game.

"Open out my bed," said the woman to Sailor. "Be a little useful with your hands, old man with the guns. I didn't tell you to tear the blankets off. Now, now, a bit of common sense."

"D'you live alone?" asked Sailor. He carefully adjusted the blanket.

"Yes."

"Lucky," he said.

"Put her on the bed," said the woman. "Why lucky?" she asked Sailor.

"Lucky for the man who might have had to live with you. He is better off elsewhere. You can see for yourself if I haven't opened the bed properly."

"Heap the fire," she said, "and get some hot water."

"She hasn't spoken," said Antonio. He was looking at the delivered woman. She lay still. "I think . . ."

"You think, and you know nothing at all. Lend a hand. We must get her undressed and washed, and then warmed up, and you'll see. Put the baby's basket near the fire. And, you over there, old man with the gun, try not to roast the little one. Lift her up." She unhooked the clasps of the bodice. "Pull. She'll have plenty of milk. Look."

He was rather ashamed of looking at this defenceless flesh. Those breasts were overflowing with life. He had never seen any so beautiful.

"She'll be a good nursing mother. We must take her vest off. Looks as if you were afraid of her. Do handle her properly. What on earth are these two dough-fleshed men who have come out of the night? There. Pull off the vest. What we're going to see isn't as beautiful as all that. And, you over there, what's happening to my hot water?"

"It's all right," said Sailor.

"There, my girl. We're dying of heat in this place."

Antonio held the palm of his hand cupwise. He poured hot brandy into it and rubbed the woman's sides. He was afraid of his long, rugged hands. The skin he was rubbing was delicate and sandlike. He touched the lower part of the breasts. It was silky. He rubbed the globe gently, working

[45]

his way up towards the armpits. He felt in his hand all the valleys, all the folds, all the gentle hills of that body. They stole into him, they stamped themselves in his own flesh as he touched them, with their depths and their roundnesses. It hurt just a little, and then it burst within him, as a sheaf of corn, too tightly packed, splits open its bond and spreads itself out.

The delivered woman heaved a sigh. A long sigh, a fine sigh, at ease in the flesh and uncomplaining.

Antonio withdrew his hand.

"Help her up," said the woman. "I'll slip her vest on. Take her in your arms. Hold her up."

He pressed her against himself. He held her quite naked in his arms.

"Get off now," said the woman. "A sou to do and two sous to undo, that's what you need. Leave her alone; for the present she's no mind to begin again." She covered her up. "There," she said. "She's got a hot brick at her feet. Put your cloak on her into the bargain. That'll be all right. Now you can give us a draught of brandy."

The delivered woman was breathing. As the warmth stole into her through all the doors of her body, she began to smile. She had not yet opened her eyes. She was asleep.

"That's brandy from afar," said the woman as she drank. She looked at the two men. "You've not faces of these parts," she said. "Where are you from?"

"From the river," said Antonio.

"I'm from the forest," said Sailor.

"From the other end?" said the woman, pointing to the south.

"Yes."

[46]

"That reminds me," said the woman, "that you lit two fires on Maudru's pasture."

Sailor was snoring, stretched out in front of the hearth. The woman had lain down in the dark, on the opposite side of the fireplace. Antonio could not sleep. He was afraid of moving and making a noise, because of the delivered woman who was sleeping in peace and smiling. He opened the door silently and stepped out. Outside, the night was almost at an end. The stars were no bigger than peas. There was no longer any fog or moon, the sky was wide open from one edge to the other. The high wind was singing by itself. The house smelt of dry hay and fire. The expanse of sky and earth was filled with a peace and a gentleness foreshadowing day. The noises were pure and light. Antonio heard a step in the soft grass: it was the herdsman. He stopped at the angle of the house.

"You told me you were Antonio of the isle of jays?" he asked.

"Yes."

"The one they call Golden-Mouth?

"Yes."

"Don't disturb yourself," said the man. "Go on looking peacefully at your night. It's fine. As for me, I see every night. Do you know the names of those stars?"

"Which?" said Antonio.

He felt himself becoming Golden-Mouth again, singing among the rushes, floating in the river near the wash-houses, with his mouth out of the water, and his body immersed in the world.

"Those four there," said the herdsman.

[47]

"Those there?" said Antonio. "I've a mind to call them 'the woman's wound.' I'll call them that because they make a sort of hole in the night. They gleam on the verge. Inside, it's dark night, and one never knows what's going to turn up."

"And those, away there in the north?"

"Those? I'll call them 'the woman's breasts,' because they are heaped up like hills."

"And those, over there in the east?"

"I'll call them 'the eyes.' Because it seems to me that they are like the look of a sleeping woman who has not yet opened her eyelids."

The herdsman did not answer.

"Take my cloak," he said after a while. "It's cold before dawn for the like of you who stay still gazing at the night. I'm all right, as I'll have to go after my beasts. Don't worry."

Antonio took the cloak. The coarse cloth was warm with the man's warmth.

The herdsman went off in the dark. The night was slowly tearing itself away all along the outline of the mountains.

At dawn the herd drove out; Antonio saw the lyre-horned bulls emerge out of the western shadows. They came out of the pasture at the lip of the vale, and presently the rising sun struck their foreheads. At the tips of their horns they carried hawks and kites flapping their wings. Antonio walked to meet them.

"Man," he said to the herdsman, "thanks for your cloak. I have put mine on the bed of a sick woman who is sleeping in this house."

"Now, I can see you," said the herdsman. "I like seeing men. I've come this way with my beasts to see you. Usually I drive them down that way straight to the river. So you're Golden-Mouth?"

"I am," said Antonio. "You know me?"

"No, but I know the song of the three labourers. People say it's you who made it up."

"Who told you so?"

"The man who sells almanacs at Villevieille."

"Yes," said Antonio, "I made it up. Now I'm trying to find some way of catching congers."

"What's a conger?"

"It's a fish like a snake."

"Big?"

"Bigger than my arm. It's got eyes like blood, and a belly the colour of a daffodil. It sinks into the water like a root. It weeps like a child. It can eat iron with its teeth."

"One could listen to you all day long," said the herdsman.

Antonio looked at him.

He was a man built with a bit of brick-coloured flesh and plenty of big dry sinews, round as well-ropes. On the right side of his leather coat the letter M was painted in ochre, like a bull-mark.

"I meant to tell you," said Antonio. "Don't go close to the house, you'd wake her up. She needs sleep."

"Don't you worry," said the oxherd. "I'll go down by the birches since it's like that. You'll be here tonight?"

"Yes," said Antonio. He was thinking of the woman who would not yet be able to get up.

"See you tonight, then. Listen. I'm saying all this so that you won't be uneasy. I've hidden the fires under the grass.

[49]

Besides, Maudru doesn't come often. Have no fear. I call the woman of the house 'the mother of the road.' Don't trust her too much. She lives by her fingers." And he made a grabbing gesture. Then he called his beasts in a deep voice, and the bulls, carrying the birds on their horns, began to go down to the river.

"Is she asleep?" asked Antonio on entering.

"Yes," said the woman.

"The light's falling on the bed. You ought to cover up the window."

"Leave me alone," said the woman. "Now you're swaggering about and pretend to know everything. When a woman has been delivered, the next day is the finest of her life. Let her wake up in the sun. I've made coffee," she added. "D'you want some?"

"Give me some."

"Look at your mate; not even the light will rouse him. Neither the light nor the fire."

"He's tired."

"Why have you got such old mates?"

"I have no mates," said Antonio. "I live by myself. That's a man of the forest who's lost his son, and I'm helping him look for him in the river."

"What's he called?"

"Sailor."

The woman looked at Sailor sleeping. The blue day poured in at the window, and soon a wooden stool, the table made of tree-trunks, and the foot of the bed were bathed in light. The head of the bed was still in the shade. The sugar-coloured face of the mother was lost in the pale pillow and the sheet.

"The son was red-haired," said the woman.

"Really?" said Antonio in a surprised tone.

"And the tip of the little finger of his left hand was missing."

"Did you see him?"

"I see all those who pass by," said the woman. "I'm on the road. I saw that man right enough. He's an extraordinary sort."

"Come a bit nearer," said Antonio.

The woman leaned towards him. He drew her a little nearer.

"He must be dead," he said.

"Your mouth smells of sap," said the woman.

"I've been chewing a fig-tree shoot."

"Well," she said, "you're not a man like the others. No, I don't think he's dead yet."

"What makes you say so?"

"Listen," she said. Her hand stopped Antonio's shoulder, which was drawing back. "Keep near me. It's not common to find a man smelling good early in the morning. What I can tell you is that you're not the only two looking for him."

"Who else?"

"Maudru's men."

"What for?"

"Who can tell! What's sure is that the fellow outside has turned up with his oxen, and he's asked me for news of the red-haired chap. I'm the mother of the road. I'm

[51]

often asked about people, but seldom twice. First it was the oxherd, and he came down from the north with his bulls to ask me that, and ever since he's been watching like a sentry hereabouts, surveying the whole valley with his beasts. He's got orders. It's obvious. Maudru's men are everywhere. And all of them with their bulls. Sometimes the one here blows his horn, and they answer him. As I was saying, it was first that fellow, and then you two, who've come up from the south, and are also talking about the red-haired chap. What's the fellow done, that people are moving heaven and earth for his sake?"

"As far as I'm concerned," said Antonio, "the only thing he's done is to be the last son of that man asleep there."

The babe began to wail in its basket.

"Rock it," said Sailor in his morning sleep.

He woke up. He had slept like a stunned beast. His beard was all wet with slobber. He wiped it with the back of his hand.

"Well, then?" he said.

"Nothing," said Antonio. "All's the same as it was."

The babe wailed and tossed about. He struck his fist on the side of the basket.

"What's wrong with that little frog?" said the woman. "Here he is, wide awake on his first day. Nobody's seen the likes of that before."

"Is he nice?" said Sailor.

"Come and see him, old man."

They looked at him. He had tossed himself out of the swaddling-bands, and there he was, quite naked in the basket, flourishing his arms and his legs. He was not red like ordinary new-born babies; his skin was already turning

[52]

white, and, as he was covered all over with folds of fat, his skin laughed with a silky laugh.

Antonio looked at the mother. She was breathing deeply and regularly. The child took after her; he had nothing foreign in him. It was exactly the same mouth, the same nose, the same eyelids—both of them still had their eyes closed—the same forehead, the same cheeks with prominent cheek-bones. In the child the expression was only hinted at under a skin which seemed too loose, full of folds and grimaces. But one could see that he bore the grain seed of the woman's face, and that all would bloom and blossom out in the very shape of that woman's face there on the pillow. She seemed to have made him by herself.

The baby's mouth was writhing, and he slobbered a fine bubble of saliva. He started to cry.

"He wants to suck," said Antonio.

"He wants his sugar-water," said the woman. "As for sucking, that'll come afterwards. If only she'd wake up. I'd like him to take the breast, were it only to pull. It would bring her milk up."

She approached the bed.

"Now, my girl," she said, and she touched the hand of the confined woman.

A shiver ran along the pale woman's arm. She heaved a sigh. She opened her eyes. They were like two mint leaves.

"My baby."

"It's there, don't move."

"Is it living?"

"More than you, my fine girl."

"A boy?"

[53]

"A boy."

"Where am I?"

"In my bed."

She smiled very slightly.

"I can feel that," she said; "but where?"

"What a business!" said the woman. "We'll tell you bit by bit. For the time being, I woke you up for you to take that boy of yours a bit. Now you'll see him. Say, old man, bring me the baby."

"You're not alone then?" said the mother.

"You can see for yourself," said the woman.

The mother's eyes had not moved. She looked at the wall opposite her, and Antonio turned his head to see what she was looking at so intently.

"So you don't know?" she said. She put her hand on her bosom, which she felt was bare. "I am blind."

Her eyelids were like violets and her eyes were like a smudge of colour in fine, smooth plaster.

"Can't you see?" said the woman.

"No."

Antonio held his breath.

"Not at all?"

"No, not at all."

"Since long?"

"Ever since I was born. Give me the baby."

Sailor brought the child.

"Put him there, between my knees," she said.

"It doesn't seem true," said Sailor, looking at the mint-leaf eyes.

They were large and deep, and they gave that face a great light, a kind of glow which did not issue merely from the surface of the skin, but came from inside. When somebody spoke, she looked towards the speaker, but with a slight delay. Her eyes looked roughly in the direction of the spoken words and then stopped. Sometimes they missed the man or the woman. They looked aside.

She started touching the child. All three of them watched those long, pale fingers, those hands which were not merely supple, but which, by a miracle, seemed to have the enfolding power of water.

The baby stopped crying. He sniffed at the hand. He searched with his mouth along the trail of the fingers which glided over him, learning the lines of his face. He tried to suck. The hand always escaped. He began to cry again. She touched the child's eyes.

"He can see, can't he?" she said.

"We'll not know that till tomorrow," said the woman.

"It would be unfair," said the mother.

"He will see right enough," said Sailor. "Just now he seemed to follow the motion of my hands."

"He looks like me," she said. "It's my nose, my mouth, and everything, and I've felt that they're also my eyes. That's what I'm afraid of."

"Confined women are always afraid," said the woman. "As for myself, all the time I was with child I was afraid he would come out harelipped; and then he turned out like every other child."

"I know that I'd have liked to keep him in my belly for ever," said the delivered woman. "In there I knew him. Now, what am I going to do? It'll take me such a long time to know him properly. Nothing but his feet, his tiny legs, his tiny body . . ."

[55]

She began to weep silently but her expression remained unchanged.

"Don't cry," said the woman, "don't you worry. Don't get all upset. All that's bad for the milk. Your misfortune isn't a reason why he shouldn't have as good milk as the others. Give him the breast, just to see."

"There are three of you here," she said.

"Yes," said the woman.

"I've felt one of you there, at the foot of the bed. He's not said anything and he has been holding his breath. He smells of fish. I'd like him to speak, a word or two, and I'd also like him to go out while I feed my baby."

"Is it me you mean?" asked Antonio.

He had made a great effort to speak.

"Yes," she said.

"I'll go out shooting to bring you some meat to eat."

"Don't be cross," she said. "I felt you there, and you didn't speak. Your smell was not bad. You smell of water. All these days I've been walking towards the river which smells like you, and it was not for a good thing, 'cause I was afraid my child would be blind like me, and I preferred us to finish together."

Antonio felt himself trembling violently and he could not stop. He was trembling like the oak tree beaten by the waters at the tip of his island.

"You mustn't go to the river," he said, "you've no right to, either for yourself or for him; and your boy will be like everybody else. And even for yourself, you must think it over. You'll be happy to touch him and to hear him. There's good and evil in the world. You've still a great deal of good to experience."

[56]

"I don't know," she said, "but you did well to speak."

"I'll go and hunt for you," said Antonio.

"Yes, go away," said the woman. "Leave us both alone a bit. We've got to wash things which are none of your business."

"And my twin?" said Sailor, as they walked among the reeds.

"I've found more in this house than all along the river."

The osier-bed opened out before them, and beyond the osier doorway the flat river gleamed under the morning sun.

"Have you been told something?"

Sailor had stopped and he had moved his shoulders as if to turn back.

"Walk along," said Antonio. "It came about in a queer way. D'you trust me?"

"Yes."

"Leave me a free hand. What I tell you now is, there's no hurry at all, and tonight we'll know more. I believe your twin has launched his raft on a bigger river than ours."

"You think he's still alive?"

They had approached the river, and now they heard the water boil under the pebbles, and bullocks bellow in the distance. On the other side, a herd of oxen ran heavily through the juniper bushes, straggling all over the moor. In the middle of the herd leapt the black silhouette of a man with a flying cloak who was astride a russet bull. On the smooth brow of a hill, towards the depths of the horizon, other oxen moved on in the short grass. In the upland, the drover blew his horn. The cloaked man, singing the while,

[57]

stopped his beasts. They drove in a circle around him, then came to a standstill, panting.

Antonio and Sailor had just gone past the thick of the osier clumps. In the shallow pebbled stretches of the river another herd was bathing. The oxen were dancing in a watery spray, iridescent as the feathers of a pheasant. Their herdsman walked up to the open gravel. He blew his horn twice. The man with the cloak blew twice. The drover on the hill blew twice. Then the drover on the gravel began telling them a story on his horn, and one felt that he was saying all he wanted to say, deliberately and clearly. The others, at a given time, answered:

"Say it again, please."

He repeated his long sentence, with subtler modulations, and this time the two distant horns said:

"All right. All right. All right."

And the processions of bulls began to flow again along the moor and over the hills; the man's cloak flapped away over the beasts with their long, pale horns, then the herd rushed into a vale.

"He's living," said Antonio. "There are too many of them after him. People don't flock like that after a dead man."

The weather was treacherous and sly, like the end of spring, bright as a fine month of May. It was a rustling day, full of sound, as if summer were coming in. The milky strength of the air quivered in the distance and, up to the middle of the sky, ascended a tremulous veil of mist, full of light and yet concealing the high steps of the mountain which were covered with red trees and snow.

"Fine weather," said Sailor.

[58]

"Approaching winter," said Antonio.

"Don't care a damn for winter, if he's living," said Sailor.

Antonio checked him with his hand. The fresh tracks of a young wild boar were stamped in the mud. They stood still and heard the beast wallowing in the reeds. They advanced a few steps. They could see it now. It was digging like a pig. It ploughed up the mud with its snout, then lay in the cool slime and wallowed with all its bristles, showing up its belly in the air.

Sailor shot it in the belly. His buck-shot tore open large wounds. The beast did not stop snorting its happy snorts. It was still full of its joy in the sun, when its blood and entrails steamed on the black sand. It stretched out its neck and started laughing silently with its long fangs.

A lean youth ran along the gravel. He held a long ox-goad like a spear. He shouted: "Leave the animal alone." He reached them quite breathless.

Antonio had opened his big clasp-knife.

"Is it yours?" he said.

"It's Maudru's," said the lad.

"If you want to make us laugh," said Antonio, "smear moustaches on your face with mud, and then dance a bit in the sun. Perhaps that'll make us laugh, though we're not in very much of a mood for it, either my mate or myself. . . . But the best thing you can do is to mind your own business."

And he squatted near the warm beast to flay it.

"I said Maudru," said the lad.

"We heard," said Sailor.

Antonio cut round the foot of the beast and began to scrape the thigh. He looked up at the youth.

"You're in the light," he said. "Shift out of the way for me to see what I'm doing."

The lad stepped back.

"It'll be in the reckoning," he said.

"And paid cash," said Antonio, "don't worry."

The lad threw his goad away.

"If you're a man," he said, "drop your knife and come along. We settle accounts on the spot at Maudru's."

Antonio stood up.

The young herdsman bit his lip. He was lean as a rod. Antonio strode over the beast and stepped forward. He only pretended to stoop. He ran three steps. With one stroke of his arm he clasped the herdsman's waist. He squeezed.

"Son of a bitch," said the lad. He hammered at Antonio's shoulders and nape.

Antonio's arms were locked fast with all their strength. He pushed his hard head against the joints of the ribs and he heard them begin to crack inside the lad.

The lad was gasping. His face and his neck were swollen with blood to the point of bursting. He could no longer breathe. He held up his arms. Antonio loosened his grip. He pushed him off. The herdsman took three steps backward to recover his balance. He fell on the gravel.

"Maybe I'm the son of a bitch," said Antonio while the other struggled for breath. "But you, your father, mother, sister, brothers, aunts, and uncles, you're all a pack of bastards."

Sailor had loaded the beast on his shoulders.

"We'll flay it yonder. Come along."

Antonio picked up the goad.

"It'll make me a stick," he said.

It was a pike of fine holly, strong and wiry. The point had been whetted with a stone and seemed incorporated with the muscles of the wood. When the goad was brandished, it felt as light as a wing. In the middle of the handle the word "Maudru" was branded in big letters.

Towards the close of the afternoon, Antonio drew Sailor aside.

"Go and see what the herdsmen are doing," he said.

"What's the matter?" said Sailor.

"Go without saying anything as far as the clump of trees, and there lie down and watch. At nightfall they're bound to do something. Watch."

"Shall I take my gun?"

"No, take care. On this side, there must be two of them: the one of last night and the shady-looking customer of this morning. Have a look at them. Two on the other side: one with the cloak, the other from the hill."

He himself went and sat on the doorstep. The door was open to the autumn evening.

"Missis," said Antonio, "give me a few pots; I'll pickle some boar's meat for you."

"For once in my life," said the woman, "I know a man who's busy. Here's the meat jar, my lad."

She brought in the large jar which smelt of salt and blood. Antonio had made himself a brush with thyme-wisps and he scoured the inside of the jar. The mother was sitting up on the bed, holding her baby in her arms. She was singing him a lullaby:

[61]

> "Of all the stars of heaven
> It's you that I like best . . ."

Antonio put a layer of salt in the bottom of the jar, then he brought in a big slab of stone on which he sharpened his knife. After that he began to carve slices of meat out of the black ham of the young boar.

The blind woman stopped singing. "What are stars?" she asked.

"Lights in the sky," said the woman.

"What's that?"

"Lights like when you come near a town by night, with all the windows lighted up."

"I don't know," said the blind woman. "What do you mean with your day that you speak about so much, your night, your towns, your lamps, and your lighted windows?"

"Night's what you see yourself," said Antonio.

"And day?"

"Day," said Antonio, "why, it's the day, but it's a bit hard to explain."

"I think you really mean that the day's got a smell," said the blind woman.

"It's hard to understand," said Antonio.

He was carving the meat on the stone slab. He put the pieces into the jar. He sprinkled them with salt.

"What's your name?" asked Antonio.

"Clara," she replied.

"Why are you alone?"

She gave no answer. Her wide plaster-and-mint eyes were motionless in the shade. She realized that he was looking at her, for she no longer heard the carving-knife grind on the stone, and she turned her head away. Then Antonio imitated with his knife the sound of a man carving meat. Gradually the face turned again towards him, and the blind eyes gazed at him silently as he continued to imitate a man carving.

The woman lit the fire. She searched in the dark corner of the chimney. She handled the goad that Antonio had taken from the herdsman. She examined it. She came near Antonio.

"What's that?" she said.

"Nothing," he said.

" 'Maudru' is written on it."

"You're always talking of Maudru, you and the rest," said Antonio. "What are you afraid of?"

"Where did you get it from?"

"I took it from that lean herdsman."

"Is that your thanks to me?" said the woman in a low voice. "This house is all I've got, and my only peace is in being the mother of the road, and in eking out a living from one day to the next. You'll be happy when everything is burned up here. What arms do you think you've got, to go all the time against Maudru ever since you've been here? D'you know him?"

"No," said Antonio.

"I wondered you had so much pluck. Now, as to her," she said, pointing to the blind woman, "she needs rest. Oh, what have you done, lad?" In her hand she weighed the goad, as light as a wing. "It's evening already," she said; "I'm going to fetch water."

"You've got some," said Antonio.

"I want more."

[63]

"I'll go and fetch you some myself."

"No," she said, "I'm going."

Antonio watched her on the quiet from beneath his eyebrows. She went down to the river.

Sailor came back with muffled steps. He trotted noiselessly, making himself small in the shade.

"They're coming," he said.

Antonio jumped to his feet. He saw the woman over there running towards the wood.

"Take up your gun."

"They've penned up the bulls," said Sailor. "The two from the other side have crossed over, riding on two beasts. The two from here were waiting for them. They came this way at once. They're coming."

A bull bellowed in the water-willows.

"Load as if for big game," said Antonio in a low voice.

"What's the matter?" said the blind woman from her bed.

"Nothing," said Antonio.

He gripped his gun with both hands. He thought of his cartridges. He had four in readiness. He knelt in the grass and laid them out before him. He beckoned to Sailor to come near him.

"Shut the house door," he said in a low voice. "Lie down," he said aloud to the blind woman, "and don't worry."

Sailor shut the door, fastening it securely.

"Go near the laurel bush," Antonio said, "and if things go wrong, run towards the wood. The woman's gone there already. Don't trouble about me. Don't fire before I do."

Evening was drawing on more quickly. At the top of the

trees there were still some small flakes of light. Antonio still heard ringing in his ear old Junie's voice: "It's the last man of the house who's going with you."

"Damn the last man," he said to himself, "and damn Junie, and damn the twin! Damn the lot of 'em!"

The four men came out of the path.

"Stop!" cried out Antonio.

The evening was calm and green. In the house the blind woman was lulling her child with her pleasant voice.

"It's bloody nonsense," thought Antonio, shouldering his gun.

"We're bringing peace," said one of the men.

Antonio recognized the herdsman who had given him his cloak the night before.

"Have you come again for the names of the stars?" he asked.

"Yes," said the fellow, "for something like that."

All four of them had stopped at the edge of the osier-bed.

"We've come to stay a bit with you. You must know it's a hard job to tend oxen."

"What I know above all," said Antonio, "is that drovers are men. If they went four against one, the whole country-side down to the sea would know it, but if they tried to en-tangle me with their tongue, then I'd be at a loss. Come on, since you say it's peace."

CHAPTER IV

NIGHT came down with a big blast of wind. It did not steal in like water gradually dripping through trees, but could be seen leaping out of the eastern valleys. At one stroke it had first invaded everything down to the banks of the river, and then, while day still lingered among the nearer hills, it had got ready, crushing the osiers under its big black paws, dragging its belly through the mud. It had sprung down with the first blast of wind. Now it was already far off, ahead of them, with its cold breath; here, they were caressed by its warm body, full of stars and moon.

The laurel boughs were heard rustling, then Sailor appeared. He still held his gun levelled.

"So you want to make war on us?" said the man in the cloak.

"I want what's right," he said.

"Where d'you both come from?" said the lean fellow.

"Are you the chief of the country?" said Antonio.

"No."

"Then leave us alone."

"Let's all stay a bit without speaking," said the chief drover. "That'll make things clear for us. We'll have it .out afterwards."

This man seemed to be the leader. From time to time he

glanced into the night. At other times he motioned to them to keep quiet, and he listened to the crackling trees. The herdsman with the cloak sat down on the grass. Slowly. He tucked up his cloak. He carefully picked up the cloak-skirts over his knees. He crossed and uncrossed his legs two or three times, until he found the right position. Then he remained still. The lean young fellow who had fought with Antonio dug into his hollow teeth with his tongue. He was eating wind all the time and sucking up his saliva. He remained standing. The last man, the drover from the hill, whom Antonio had seen only from a distance amidst his bulls, proved now to be a giant of a man and short of breath. He breathed three times on end, then fetched a deep whistling sigh and sniffed. Then he would breathe again three times and start afresh, after which he would rub the nape of his neck with his big stubby hand. He lay down beside the others.

"We're not going to let you eat our stew," said the lean chap.

"I told you not to speak. And sit down; you're making a draught with your gestures," added the cloaked man.

Antonio was anxious about Sailor. He knew that when things came to fighting, the old wood-cutter was fond of vainglory and flourish. Antonio clenched his teeth. He himself had a mind now to let his gun off right in the middle of those seemingly peaceful fellows.

He said to himself: "If I shoot, I'll kill one of them. Sailor will shout: 'Wait a bit,' and he'll get in the way. He always wants to wait. He always thinks he has time. He'd be stabbed with a knife. I don't trust the man with the cloak. That's the one that I'd kill, though. Then the other one.

[67]

They must all have knives. If only I could trust Sailor."

He also thought of the blind woman inside the house. "Two on my hands," thought Antonio, "the last man of the family, and Clara." He called her Clara inwardly now, faced with the four herdsmen. "I shoot—I jump back. Sailor gets in the way. He's stabbed. Then they're three and I'm alone. I'd have no time to reload. I'd have to knock the young man down. Two and me. Run away. Yes, but the big one would then strangle Sailor. Nothing doing."

"You came from the south, didn't you?" said the first drover.

"We did," said Antonio. "Wait a bit." He called out: "Sailor! Come and sit near me."

"Let him pass," said the first drover.

"Near me," said Antonio. "Sit down."

In the dark he gently stroked the man's thigh.

"We come from the south," said Antonio. "I've told you who I am. This man here is my friend. For how long has the Rebeillard country been guarded?"

"It always has been," said the big herdsman. He panted as he tossed about heavily in the grass. He smelt of wild leeks.

"What does the schoolmaster say?" asked the first fellow.

"I say they come from the south," said the Cloak.

The lean fellow sucked his hollow tooth.

"We're not going to let you grab our stew."

"There's no question of stew," said the Cloak, "nor of your damned jaw, nor of punches on your ugly mug. Orders is what matters." He uncrossed his legs and tried to find a better position. "That's why I say: 'They come from the south.' "

The night was now spread out from one edge of the sky to the other, and it quivered with hollow rumblings like a big sail swollen out by the wind.

"Where are you going?" said the first fellow.

"About the country."

"What for?"

"Well, that may be private."

Antonio pressed Sailor's leg. Sailor's hand tightened on Antonio's hand.

"Should I tell them?" asked Antonio in a loud voice.

"Tell them," said Sailor.

Antonio touched Sailor's palm twice with his finger to hint: "I won't tell them." "Right," answered Sailor by squeezing his finger.

"We're looking for a man."

"Who?"

"A red-haired chap."

The lean fellow stopped sucking his teeth. The big man moved in the grass.

"Friends or enemies?" said the Cloak.

"What?"

"Help or hindrance?"

"Speak like other people."

The herdsman pulled his hand out of his cloak and made a sign that he gave it up. His hand was caught in the white light of the moon.

"I know what I mean."

"Speech has been given you to make yourself understood by others," said Antonio.

"He wants to know," said the first drover, "if you are a friend or an enemy of the red-haired chap."

[69]

Antonio touched Sailor on the knee.

"Listen," he said. "You came with your cloak as I was looking at the night, and you asked me the names of the stars. Afterwards, you put your own cloak on my shoulders and let me use it as I thought fit, and you went back to your oxen. I want to speak to you. Your mate there whom you call the 'schoolmaster,' I don't know him. He's there in his cloak, and he can stay there."

"That's what I'm going to do."

"He doesn't speak my language. He may not understand what I'm going to say. But you I know; I've had your warmth on me. It was the warmth of a genuine man. In this business, I know quite well you've come along here to find out who we are, where we're going, and what we're after. Somebody's sent you on this job."

"Yes," said the lean fellow.

"I'm not speaking to you there, standing in front of the moon," answered Antonio, "and preventing me from seeing the beards of the others. I'm speaking to that man over there who received the orders. You've not got orders, you? No? Then shut your ugly trap and, for the last time, get out of my light."

"You've not yet answered," said the Cloak.

"Here's what I say: I've got accounts to square with a red-haired chap. But that's my own business."

"After all," said the Cloak, and he looked as if he were speaking to himself rather than to the others, "the order is: a man and a woman coming from the north. But these are two men. They've come from the south. Doesn't tally. The order is: they mustn't leave Rebeillard. These two have come here. Doesn't tally. You're listening?" he asked.

[70]

"We're listening."

"Then, what I say is: if these two are also against the red-haired chap . . ."

"Look!" shouted the lean fellow.

On one of the northern hills a fire was kindling. It looked first like a small bird shining under the moss, then it opened out two big red wings, tapering like the wings of buzzards.

"He's been caught!" cried the lean fellow.

Sailor's teeth began to chatter.

"He's living," said Antonio under his breath, "and we are men."

"That's near Jacques's barn," said the first drover.

"Near the mountain."

"On the mountain."

"High up in the mountain."

"Look, everywhere."

All over the Rebeillard country, beacons were lighting up. They could be seen on the near banks of the river not far away, among the poplars along the alluvium, up to the far-distant highlands, and again higher up in the mountain. Gusts drove up the smell of the beacons in the plain, where they were burning mulberry wood. In the spells of wild burning, when the flames blazed, they could be seen hollowing out caves in the thick reddish-brown smoke, spreading out in the wind, writhing and throbbing like the plaited hair of highland women.

"There are too many of them," said the Cloak.

Black shadows passed in front of the beacons along the river. High flames beat up behind the poplars. In the hills glowing lights flowed from every verge, and deep-black tree-shapes unfurled against the red background of the

[7 1]

beacons. Then, high up in the mountain, bonfires sparkled in the black grass like eggs filled with sun; higher up, they shone like sheeps' eyes when the lantern is lifted up in the fold; still higher, they were almost in the stars, disappearing every now and then.

"You see," said the first drover, "you're not wanted for the red-haired chap; if he's not caught, he soon will be."

The full night-wind blew. The long wings of the beacons trailed among the black trees over the fluffy hillsides. From the other side of the river the bulls bellowed for their drovers.

Antonio held back Sailor, who was getting up.
"Sit still."

"Good-bye, everybody," he said to the herdsmen.

"Good-bye. I'm glad to know you, Golden-Mouth. I'm fond of your songs. We must be off now. That's the signal," the Cloak said, pointing to the night.

"Sit still," Antonio repeated under his breath. Sailor wanted to get up. His teeth were chattering. He was quivering right to the tips of his big hands.

"Good-bye."

"Good luck to you."

In the reeds yonder they heard the schoolmaster giving orders for the departure in an indifferent voice.

"You're listening?"

"Listening."

"What I was saying to myself was, suppose he went that way, across the hills . . ."

"At all events," said Antonio in a loud voice as he got up and with a groan stretched out, first one arm, then both arms, his leg, both legs—"oh!"—pulling right and left, forward and backward, "at all events, I'm going to bed and to sleep. Keep quiet," he said to Sailor.

He counted the noises in front of him.

"One. The Cloak, two."

A big voice called out for the bulls which served as mounts to cross the river.

"Three."

The beasts went off at a gallop towards the voice in the pasture which made a hollow sound under their hoofs, and, in the scuffle of the gallop, Antonio heard a slight rustle in the osier-bed like that of a wild beast slithering through.

"Four," he said. "The lean one is off. We're alone."

"We must be off," said Sailor.

"A minute."

"I'm off."

"Wait a minute, I say."

"It's one thing for you and another for me. It's my twin. He's in me like a knife-wound." Sailor touched his side. "It grips me, it's my boy. Maudru can go to hell, and so can you."

"I say, wait a minute."

"I say at once."

"Now, Sailor"—Antonio seized the old wood-cutter's wrist—"even if I have to bash your face in, I say, wait a minute."

"You're too young to hold me."

He shook his arm.

"Hands off."

Antonio held fast.

"Old fool," he said. He flung his long, swimmer's arm around Sailor. He pressed the man against him.

"Throw down your gun. There. I say, wait a minute. I'll crush your ribs. There. Trying to help a bearded old fool like you!"

"Hands off, I say."

Antonio let go.

"I say, wait a minute," he repeated. "Your twin is living. That's the whole thing. Maudru can go to the devil for all I care. He's not going to frighten me with his bulls and his men. But so far things have been pretty smooth. There's no point in rushing into it like an ass. We've got to unravel it thread by thread. Red Hair is alive. You know what he's like and so do I. No good worrying about him beforehand. And we are both here. That's what I mean. I'm responsible in this business. So I'm taking the lead. I'll be ready enough to take a punch in the eye from you if you catch me shirking. For the time being I say, wait a minute. A minute's not long."

"Angry?" said Sailor.

"Don't be a fool!" he said. "Swallow your beard and get along with you."

The leaves of the fig tree moved.

"Where are my fine fellows?" said a woman's voice.

"Ah, it's you," said Antonio. "Come along, you funk; here we are safe and sound."

The woman of the house approached.

"It takes you a long time to fetch water," said Antonio. "But I've a mind to tell you something. When you say: 'I'm going to fetch water,' if you want people to believe you, take a bucket at least, and don't go empty-handed."

"Well," said the woman, "in my opinion you're just cackling in your ignorance. But I know very well who we've got to deal with."

"Who?"

"Maudru."

[75]

"What then?"

"Why, those four fellows," she said, pointing to the darkness of the osier thicket, "if it had suited them, they'd have burnt the house, the woman and the child, and nobody would have said a word."

"Quite so," said Antonio, "and meanwhile us two would have been reading the papers, I suppose?"

The night had grown thicker with the smoke from all the beacons. Stillness had settled over it now. It no longer had any stars, and only a lustreless moon which hardly lighted up more than a finger's breadth around it. The fires were silently panting. Along the ground, far off and on all sides, a hollow trampling surged among the hills and the plains of the country around.

"I'd like to know," said Antonio, speaking to the night, "whether, in spite of everything, the mother of the road is capable of a bit of quiet courage."

The woman came near him.

"Let me feel your arms and your shoulders," she said. "Your voice was enough for me to open my house to you. I'm not yet an old woman inside. Allow me, my boy."

She leaned on Antonio's broad arm, with her head against his shoulder.

"I said 'fine fellow' when you first came in. Allow me, my boy, that's all I'm asking."

Antonio's muscles relaxed.

"What d'you want of me?" she said.

"To tell you a few truths."

She rubbed her cheek against Antonio's arm.

"We've got that red-haired boy at heart," he said, "like

[76]

honey sticking to a hive. We used our tongues a lot with Maudru's chaps. We all wanted to get one another's lips unstuck. We got one another to speak. Now I suppose we're going to rub one another's ears a bit. Don't worry, it'll be a long way from your place. Those four are off with their oxen. Listen to them. . . . We're off also, my mate and me. That's sure."

"Go on talking, if you let me stay like this," said the woman.

"All right, stay against my arm. You've not been sparing in your kind offices in this business. But I may be wrong in believing your house is our house, in this Rebeillard country."

"It's your house," she said.

"My pal and me are one," said Antonio. "Look here, if I wanted to feel you, I could. You see, I'm not moving my arm. But I believe we can be great friends if you do me a service."

"The service will remind me of your smell," she said. "What is it?"

"That blind woman," said Antonio. "You'll keep her for me?"

"If you like."

"Yes, I'd be very glad," said Antonio.

He called in a low voice: "Sailor."

"I'm listening."

"My heart feels all in a flutter," Antonio said, "as if I had breathed for a long time that over-tender smell of the water-willow which was blooming out in the forest last night. . . ."

"I knew you'd get like that," said Sailor.

[7 7]

"I'm quite lost. I need my river and its water. It's come upon me several times already, but never so strong, and never when the snow drifts slowly down the mountain."

"I'm always like that inside me," the woman said, "and that's why you must let me fondle your arm. We're poor fledgelings."

"The meadows smell strong in these parts," said Antonio, "and the trees' blood is so thick that the air gets its smell merely by passing through the branches. This country of yours is a heavy country, Mother of the road."

"All countries are," she said. "We're wrapped in meadows and hills like hard loaves in a wet cloth."

Antonio silently drew a long breath.

"Is she your wife?" she added.

"No. I found her last night."

"I'll keep her," she said.

Antonio opened the door.

"Your wallet," said Sailor.

"Give it here."

"Your gun."

"Give it here. Are you ready, Sailor?"

"I am. It's my son, you understand. . . ."

"Wait a bit," said Antonio.

He went in. A small fire flickered lazily in the hearth, hissing among the moist logs. In the flickering glow of the embers he saw that the mint-and-lime-coloured eyes were open.

"Hello, young woman," he said.

"Speak softly."

He went up to her silently. The baby was lying with his mother. He squeaked in his sleep like a young rat.

[7 8]

"Your voice is like a stone," she said.

"Well, young woman," he said.

He watched her without speaking. Now he could see her in spite of the dark, and unconsciously he made the motion of his arm which he used to make at the bottom of the river to stay in front of a big, sleeping fish. She was quite young, pale and smooth-skinned like a pebble, with the hard and full roundness of porphyry worn by water.

"I'm going," he said.

"I thought it was over," she said.

"What do you mean, over?"

"I'm speaking to myself," she said.

And she turned towards him as if to look at him. He drew his hand near her face, and let it stay there, only caressing the air which touched her.

"Everything's just beginning," he said.

"I don't mind," she said.

"What do you mean, over?"

"All those hard times. All that trickery of the earth. I don't mind. It's too easy, isn't it?"

"I still hear your words long afterwards," he said gently. "You don't speak like us. Tell me why."

"You don't speak like them, either; you almost speak like me. That's what made me say it was over for me, being deceived and running down sloping ways. . . ."

"You don't bear a grudge against yourself for being still alive?"

"No, not since I've been listening to you."

"May I touch your hand?"

"Here it is."

"It's cold."

"I've lost blood."

"Make it up again," said Antonio.

He held the small, cold hand in his. He dared not say: I'll come back.

"I'll come back," he said.

"It's too easy to deceive me," she said. "I don't mind. It brings its own punishment because it's too easy."

CHAPTER VI

"SHE has never seen the night," mused Antonio.

"Where's the road?" Sailor said.

"We'll follow the river.

"She has never seen . . ." mused Antonio.

The night was much more vast than the day.

On the earth everything was blotted out, hills, groves, undulating fields. It was simply flat and dark, and over the blurred trees the whole world was unfolding itself. In the depths flowed the milk of the virgin; flaming chariots, flaming ships, shining horses, a wide belt of stars spread out like stubble all over the sky.

"She has never seen . . ."

Now it was no longer that wild and hectic life of the earth; those cramped oaks, those beasts with the quick panting of their blood, that sound of leaps, steps, racing, galloping, and flowing waters, those howls and those cries, that rumble of the river, that wailing coming every now and then from the wind in the mountain, those calls, those villages full of corn and walnut grindstones, the high roads strewn with flint crushed by iron cart-wheels, that long-drawn stream of beasts forcing their way through the brushwood, the hedges, the meadows, the thick groves in the dales and on the hills, and raising clouds of reddish dust from the ploughed land, all that frantic scuffle of greedy life, fought under the opaque blue sky, cemented with sunlight. No, it was the cold silence of night.

"She has never seen night, swollen out with cold blood, like the river with its fish. She has never seen it, and I told her that night is what she usually sees in her dark head!"

"Shall we go up to that grove, yonder?" Sailor asked.

"Yes."

"Why are we following the river?"

"Not to go astray," said Antonio; "and besides, the ground is soft down here. They'll go higher up in the woods with their oxen. We'll escape them. You get me, old man?

"I told her: Night is what you see, you who are blind, within your dark head. Then she'll tell me: If it's like that, as soon as night comes, you lie down in the grass and look upwards. Well, don't you see anything? If not, you'd do better to sleep. Why do you look? It's too easy to deceive me.

"And what should I say to her? She'll know when I'm lying down, because she'll touch me. She'll put her hand on my eyes. She'll say: Your eyes are open. I'll say: Yes. She'll say: Tell me what you see. And what should I say to her?

"She could feel my arm and get to know the curve of my cheeks and my chin with the tip of her finger, as she's done with the babe. She could get to know me with the palm of her hand, feeling me all over, and knowing where I end. But she can't go round everything with her hand. She can't touch a tree from the bottom to the tips of its leaves. She can't touch the fox that jumps across the rubble like a mass of burning peat. She wouldn't know where all that ends, and all the trees and animals beyond and around. She

[82]

can't touch the river. Yes, she could touch the river, but she'd have to be able to swim. I can teach her to swim."

"What do you think he can have done?" Sailor asked.

"Who?"

"My boy."

"Who can tell?" said Antonio.

"To have all those people against him? And where are we going?"

"We're on the move," said Antonio.

A layer of stars rested on the contours of the land, and the night thickened in the firmament. The shepherd's star was the size of a grain of wheat. The wind was dropping. Day was coming.

"I'm on a footpath," said Sailor.

"Follow it."

"It goes up the hillside."

"Climb up."

"You know where we're going?"

"I know," said Antonio. "Don't speak all the time.

"She could touch me all right from top to bottom, and know all about me. She could touch the river, not only with her hand but with her whole body. She would get into it. She would part it before her arms, kick it with her feet; she would feel it glide under her arms, on her belly, and weigh on the hollow of her back. She could touch a leaf and a branch. She could touch a fish with her hand when I catch fish. She will touch my whole catch when I turn the net upside down in the grass. She'll touch them still alive when they dart in the water near her and flap their fins against her skin. She'll touch the wildcat of the forest which dwells in the isle of jays, and lets itself be touched when it

[83]

has eaten fish tripe. I'll kill foxes for her to touch. She'll breathe in the smells of the water and of the forest; of the sap, when Sailor fells trees round his encampment. She'll hear the crash of falling trees and the noise of the ax and Sailor shouting to warn people that the tree is going to fall on the right, and then, immediately after, the smell of the green boughs and sap, and then the smell that gets less and less every day, as long as the trees are left lying on the ground before being barked, until it seems like the tiny aniseed smell of flowering mosses. But how should we manage for everything else?"

He looked at the stars.

"The stars are growing bigger. They're like grains of wheat now," he said to himself, "but what could I do? I could give her grains of wheat to touch and say: They're like that. She can't feel the movements of everything. She'll be able to touch the wildcat when it's basking in the sun with its soft belly full of fish tripe, and she'll feel the movement of its sides. She'll not be able to touch the wildcat when it walks up there in the oak branches, when it jumps in the clematis, when it swings among lianas, hanging by its claws to jump into the willow. She won't be able to touch the fox when it comes to the river to drink. Nor the fish, either, which rises from the depths when everything's quiet, and suddenly leaps out of the water like the moon. She'll say to me: What's that noise?"

"It's changing into a road," said Sailor.

"Yes," Antonio said, "there are ruts in the grass."

"We can no longer hear the oxen," said Sailor.

"Did you hear them?" Antonio asked.

"Yes," Sailor answered, "didn't you?"

"No."

"They've been going up across the pastures on either side of us. Can't hear anything now. We've got along faster."

"Yes, we're shifting."

"What are you thinking of?"

"Nothing."

"I'm wondering what he's been up to, and where he can be."

"He's up there, over yonder," said Antonio. "Carry on, day's upon us."

Suddenly it grew very cold. Antonio felt his lip freeze. He sniffed. The wind sounded in deeper tones; its voice fell and rose. Trees gave voice; up above the trees, the wind sped along with a hollow roar. There were spells of heavy silence, then the oaks spoke, then the willows, then the alders; the poplars hissed right and left like horses' tails; then, all at once, they were hushed. Soon the night wailed quietly in the depths of the silence. The cold was oppressive. All around the outline of the mountains, the sky was torn open. The dome of night ascended high up in the sky, with three twinkling stars, as large as cats' eyes.

In the east a hill emerged from the shadows. Its black crest, with its undulating load of trees, was set off against a straw-coloured glimmer. Away to the south a forest rumbled, then its shaggy back heaved slowly out of the night. A greyish, shivering light flowed on the tree-tops from the bottom of the vale up to the flanks of the high peak where the forest ended. It could be heard up there beating against the rock; the rock was now all aglow. There was no light in the sky, only, in the distant east, a purple wound, interspersed with clouds. The light came from the hill, which, being first freed from the night, black as a charcoal-oven, shot a soft glow into the flat sky; the light fell back on the earth with a slight plaintive sound, then flashed towards the rock which threw it back again over the round hills, which in their turn suddenly emerged out of the night with their tree-clad backs. The shadows flowed between groves and hillsides, along vales, along banks, behind the network of woodskirts. A jackdaw croaked. Mountains and hills emerged from the shadows like wide, deep-green islands, lustreless, blackened by the reflection of that ocean which gradually drained down, ebbing along their enormous earthy roots, unveiling forests, pastures, ploughed land, farm-houses, ebbing lower and lower down to their powerful base against which the river wound its way like a silvery blade of grass. Flights of sedge-warblers and greenfinches mingled together over the alders, with their screams alternating like the creaks of a cart jogging along a rutty way. The night was now turning blue. There was only a reddish star left. The wind fell. The birds swooped down on the trees. The oak woods emerged. Day flowed suddenly in a flash along the river, far into the distant waters. The mountains lit up. The hills, set abruptly glowing, started their dance around the fields, and the red sun leapt into the sky, neighing like a stallion.

"Day," said Sailor. He looked round. His beard, his eyelashes, and his moustache were white with hoar-frost.

Antonio opened out his arms crosswise. He let them drop along his body.

"Poor thing," he said. He was dazzled.

"A cold day in the mountain," said Sailor.

"She's away over there," Antonio was thinking, "lying in

the black bed with that warm little toad by her side."

"When the morning's red, cold's on the way and the mountain's hard," said Sailor. "I can see the ice. Who knows if my youngster can make a fire?"

"Your twin," said Antonio, "I'll find him for you. I'll kick his arse all the way back to you, all the way down, if I find him. That's what I'll do, you old fool. D'you think I can spend all my life running like a lean cat about this damned country? Don't you think I'm entitled to a bit of quiet at my age, and to have a wife, and live in peace? Tell me, you son of a bitch, am I entitled or not?"

"Say, Antonio," asked Sailor, plucking icicles off his beard, "where did you learn your manners?"

Dawn lighted Antonio's face.

"Get along," he said. "Follow the path. The road's yonder."

The road undulated before them, over hills and dales, with maples at long intervals, shining in the sun.

The path which the two men were following cut across the road, then, further on, pierced through a wood. A woman was sitting at the crossways. She was a young mountain girl wearing wooden shoes. Her sandals were hanging round her neck on a string.

"You're waiting?" Antonio asked her.

"I'm waiting for Alphonse's cart."

"Where does this road lead to?"

"That way it leads to Villevieille."

"Are you going there?"

"Yes," she said, "but I'm waiting for Alphonse. I can't carry him so far."

She half opened her apron, which was folded over her stomach. A child was lying in the cradle of her lap. Patches of pinkish crust covered his face. He was slobbering and writhing his mouth.

"What's the matter with him?"

"Well," she said, "it comes and goes in fits. He doesn't seem able to get over it. I'm going to have my milk seen to. It may have turned bad when I got so frightened at the wolf-hunt. It's his father's blood that troubles him."

"He's got scrofula," Sailor said.

"No," said the woman, "we're all perfectly healthy in my family. It's my milk that is bad."

A cart made with rough blue timber was coming from the grove, driven by a man standing on the boards.

"How far's Villevieille?"

"It takes two days."

"Supposing we went with you, would it be any trouble?"

The man drew up his cart near the woman.

"They want to know if it would be any trouble . . ." she said.

"No trouble."

He wore a heavy grey corduroy suit and had big hands, which seemed helpless when they had dropped the reins. He rubbed them.

"Put the kid on the sacks. We'll walk along, we four."

The woman took off her pattens and laced on her sandals. She stamped her heels. Her skirts were swollen out on her hips.

Some time before the night drew in, Alphonse said:

"We'll sleep at the maple farm-house."

"Will they mind us?" Antonio asked.

The man laughed.

"You ask for leave, do you?"

"Not much," Antonio answered. "But if they're friends of yours . . ."

"It's on the road," he said, "open to everybody."

Soon after, they got on a mound from which they could see the country far away.

"It's over there," said the woman. She pointed at a long sheep-fold in a maple grove.

When they reached it, there were already two carts in front of the door, and, tethered to the trees, three horses and two mules still with their pack-saddles. A man with his cheek close to the grass was blowing on a fire. A boy was carrying water to the beasts. A little girl was cutting off the bands of the bundles of hay, and spreading the dry fodder under the horses' muzzles. Two mules were eyeing each other, turning round, rubbing their pack-saddles, kicking at each other's legs and laughing, showing their long yellow teeth. The horses were pushing the little girl with their muzzles and pawing the ground with their hoofs.

"Drink," said the boy.

The horse drove the bucket down with his head.

"Father," cried the girl, "the brown's trying to bite the mare."

"Leave them alone," said the man who was blowing the fire.

A little old man in a long coat with bulging pockets was looking at the border of the meadow. He was bending down, searching in the grass.

"I can't see any of your blue flowers," he cried out to somebody inside the barn.

[89]

"It's too late," said a woman's voice; "and then you're as blind as a bat. Come back and cover me up."

"True," said Alphonse, "you've not yet tried the blue flowers."

"I've tried everything," said the peasant's wife.

"The place's crowded," said Sailor.

"It's the road," the man said. "Lend me a hand. My horse hasn't been gelded. Hold him fast by the muzzle. Take the kid," he said to the woman. "Take him in. . . . We have to help one another, mate. If you see my Adrian chafe, twist the curb a bit tighter."

The big sleek horse noisily sniffed towards the mare.

"Come in with me," said the peasant's wife to Antonio. "They're more respectful when there's a man, and I'd like to have a corner, for I don't want the baby to catch cold; and then I'll have to suckle him."

"I'll take in the blanket for you."

"Take it, and the black bag as well."

Alphonse was unbuckling the harness.

"Be careful," he said. "He'll jump as soon as he feels himself free."

The horse quivered and prepared to shy. Slight ripples ran over his skin from the rump to the neck. He had propped himself firmly on his hind hoofs and, straining towards the maple grove, he shook his head and tired Sailor's hand. The mare was looking at him. The mules, rump to rump, pushed each other beyond the trees.

"Are you holding him all right?"

"Steady, you devil!" Sailor cried, and he punched the horse between the eyes.

"You'll hold him," said the man near the fire.

[90]

"We'd hold the Pope," said Alphonse, and he left a safety strap on.

The mare was prancing in the soft grass. She was calling by stamping her hoofs. She did not neigh, only waved her back as if the horse were already upon her, and she clip-clopped with her four hoofs.

"Easy," said Alphonse, and he tipped up the shaft of the cart.

The loosened horse jumped up. Sailor drew himself rigid from head to foot like a rock and gave a twist at the curb. The beast was like a boat moored at the bows with its stern bumping the ground in a powerful current; it was turning with its rump round Sailor. Alphonse caught hold of the belly-strap and pulled at it. The horse uttered a bitter neigh, then stood still. He trembled, the way mud, under the mere weight of the sky, trembles when stirred by water from below.

"Steady!" said Alphonse. "You only think of love."

The horse was complaining in a strange dark voice beyond man's understanding. The strap bruised the tender flesh between his thighs. The mare started to whine. The motionless mules held out their muzzles towards the horse and began to neigh gently. Far away in the woods, an ass started to bray. Dogs barked. The beasts were complaining bitterly.

"I'll have to make up my mind," Alphonse said. "The best will be to have him gelded. He'll keep quiet then. Come along. We'll strap him to that fir."

"I kept him like that," said Alphonse while Sailor was driving in the stake five paces away from the fir, "first of all because it flattered me"—he winked, and a smile ran over one half of his face—"and then, I felt he was more eager at his work. I made hay in the Robertes pastures, up there in the mountains, before anybody else, even Maudru. As long as he's alone with us, his work calms him down, but as soon as we get into the realm of females . . . I'll have him gelded. He'll be quieter and so shall I."

The horse was tethered by the bridle to the tree, and his hind legs were strapped and held by the stake. He no longer complained. He was staring straight in front of him, without blinking, like a dead beast.

Sailor and Alphonse went into the barn. The place was already full of people making ready for the night. A slight glimmering twilight still hovered in the windows and, right in the middle of the open door, the fire which the man had at last managed to kindle was blazing and sent long, red reflections darting up, that licked the straw of the litters like large dogs' tongues.

"Was it you that made that row?" said a voice.

It was the woman who had spoken about blue flowers to the little old man. She had made a kind of small room to separate herself from the others with a long, black, hairy carriage trunk, along with two big leather suitcases.

"Good evening, Miss," said Alphonse. "Yes. It's us. My horse is a stallion, you know. . . . Then you've left your woods, as well?"

"So it's you, Alphonse?" she said.

"That's right, and you see I recognized you at once."

"That's more than I can say," she said. "With this illness upon me, I no longer know what I'm looking at."

"How are you getting on?"

"Oh, badly, badly, and I can't get rid of it, Alphonse. So

[92]

father said to me: Let's go to Villevieille. And what about you?"

"Well, we're going for the kid's sake. I think my wife's diseased. She saw me when they brought me back from that wolf-hunt, you know, and I was bleeding all over. There's no knowing how things are."

"Everybody's got to have some sort of trouble," she said. "I saw your wife come in. She is down at the far end, I believe."

"Who's that?" Sailor asked, a few steps farther.

"Rich people," Alphonse answered.

There was a young man stretched out on the straw as if dead. An old woman was squatting beside him. She was watching him. Her lips were moving silently, and she never stopped talking like that to herself. A man was moaning in the shade. Somebody's teeth chattered. Three men, resting on their way, were eating raw onions.

"Hail, Maudru," said Alphonse.

"Hail," they all said together.

"Where's Maudru?" said Sailor in a low voice.

"It's not him," Alphonse answered. "His men only. They belong to the mules outside there. They go before the herd."

"Here you are, woman," Alphonse said. "He's found a snug corner for you."

She was sitting in a corner at the far end, on straw which had not been trampled on too much. She had fully opened her bodice, unlaced her stays, and brought out her breasts. The sick babe was sucking and whining.

Antonio stood in front of them. He was looking straight ahead of him, without blinking, like a dead man.

[93]

"Come along," Sailor said, pulling him by the arm. "Come along, we must clear off."

"Yes," Antonio answered, "we'd better."

Night had fallen. They walked along the road. The thud of the two men's steps could be heard. Then the sound became confused and merged into one heavy step. Then Sailor's step quickened and seemed more eager to walk on. Far behind them the mare started neighing tremulously, then the wind in the trees effaced that female whine, and all that remained was the soft sound of fluttering leaves in the heart of the night.

"I've not come into this country," said Sailor, "to hold stallions."

The trees swung their thick heavy boughs; crackling sounds ran down the length of their trunks and vibrated through the grass into the ground. There were forests on either side of the road.

"I want my twin. And I want to be certain."

Antonio's stride overtook Sailor's quick steps.

"When they said he was perhaps alive," said Sailor, "—and yet, they didn't say it, they only hinted at it, and I really believe now he is living—I started trembling like an alder. Of course, you've got your own troubles to think about, but I've got mine."

Dogs were barking in the vale. The naked road glimmered in the night. A hard and cold wind was now blowing in their faces.

"I see you don't care a damn," said Sailor.

"You're wrong."

"You don't. What I'm going to say means nothing to

[94]

you. To understand, you've got to be very different from a savage. And yet savages do understand sometimes. Do you know why I'm called Sailor?"

"Of course I do."

"Do you know all about it: the sailing-ship, the coffee-house, and that I was over ten years at sea?"

"Every bit: the coffee-house, the ship, and your ten years."

"Who told you?"

"Junie, when we were talking together."

In the uphill climb Antonio's big stride caught up Sailor's step more quickly. A buzzard screamed, and was then heard flying in the trees.

"I could never get her to tell me why on earth you came to live in the forest," said Antonio.

"She doesn't know why. I alone know. It was because I was used to a ship. I don't like the plain, or the mountain, but I like that forest, far away from everything. It smells of wood, it moans and creaks. That's why."

On top of the slope they came onto a wide barren plateau, without trees and almost without grass. The wind was galloping above the ground. It was blowing along the treetops. There were few stars. The waning moon lit up the strewn corpses of pale clouds.

"The kid," Sailor went on. "That's what you can't understand. I dragged Junie into the woods for that. I was ill, I was. It was at the time when I had my fits of African fever. I said to myself: Cut and hew, hew and cut, with a vengeance, and stick to it through thick and thin. My hands bled, but I built the house. Go to bed, I said to myself, and

[95]

mind you get rid of the fever. The children'll come there. Well, they did come. Two together. Twins. I longed for them so much. You can laugh."

"I'm not laughing," said Antonio.

"You, you're doing a good turn, but I, it's as if I was looking for myself. If they kill my boy, I'll set the country on fire. The river and the raft into the bargain. If he's dead, it's death for me. I'm not a whining dog. When the other one got buried and crushed in the clay pit, I said: All right. I would have said all right for this one too. I know myself. But, they are hunting him, and here I am. I'm not even doing anybody a good turn."

Antonio did not answer. They walked on for a while without speaking.

"I don't say it meaning you," Sailor said gently.

Antonio did not answer. He passed his hand over his cheeks and his chin. He had not shaved since they had set out. His beard was prickly.

"If I find him," Sailor went on, "he'll perhaps say to me: Mind your own business. Who knows what he's been up to in this country? But that's a thing you can't understand. There's no longer any sun, no longer anything. No Junie, you see, no Junie—nothing at all left. I want to be near him. And then, the rest of them can come along with their oxen. He's always given me trouble. Perhaps that's why I stick to him. Who knows?"

"Ravens," said Antonio.

They had just entered a place where ravens had settled for the night. Hearing their tread, the birds took wing. They flew heavily around them, striking their shoulders with their wings.

[96]

"The proudest kid in the world," Sailor said. "I blew in his throat when he had the rattles. I carried him in my arms. He kicked pretty hard at my ribs; the skin is still rough there."

Behind them the swarming birds swooped down, screaming as they went. Then, once again the plateau was filled with black silence and wind.

"Where are you making for?" Antonio asked.

"For Villevieille, to see the almanac-vender. I want to find out what my boy has done to the oxen."

"Don't you think we could sleep now?"

"Yes, now I think we could," Sailor answered. "I'm worn out enough now to go to sleep easily."

Antonio stopped. He unrolled his cloak. He lay down on the ground. He had covered his head so as not to see or hear anything in that wide plateau, with its grey road darting northwards.

There, in his warmth, he evoked pictures and sounds. He waited till Sailor had gone to sleep. Then with his lips he gently made the sound of a kiss. He had never heard such kisses before that night, yonder, in the house of the mother of the road. Clara had kissed the baby's arm. He had heard the same kiss again when the peasant's wife, lying snug in her corner, had kissed the sick child.

He pictured Clara with her warm baby near her. He thought: "A child! The child of a man! How did all that happen?"

He was lying facing the south and, through the opening of his cloak, he pictured in the night the grey road gently wending its way towards Clara, the lower country, the isle of jays, the river, and the great space of time that he would need to make her touch foxes, cats, fish, and feel the dawn.

He would have liked to be the only man appointed by life to lead Clara through everything of shape and colour. He merely thought of the joy of telling her, of the joy of taking her into things, of the joy of saying: "That's what it is; now you touch it. Well, d'you understand what it's like?" She would say: "Thank you, Antonio."

He repeated quietly under his breath in the folds of his cloak: "Thank you, Antonio. Thank you, Antonio."

A distant forest was wailing and speaking with dream words.

CHAPTER VII

"GET up," Sailor shouted.

The day was advanced. Away in front of them a horse drawing a light cart jogged along, shaking its bells. A small group of people on foot was coming from the south. Carts were creaking on the uphill slope. Drovers' horns were sounding from the woods.

"What's the matter with you?" Sailor asked gently.

Antonio rolled up his cloak.

"What's the matter with you, man of the river?" said Sailor, laying his hand on Antonio's shoulder.

Under his thick grey brows, Sailor's little eyes, blood-shot like a ferret's, glowed with tender affection, and his big hand grasped the man's shoulder.

"It's as if I'd been bled of all that made my happiness," said Antonio. "I don't know whether it's because I'm far from my river, or if"—he stopped rolling his cloak—"or if I've got into some other kind of river. What do you say?"

"You and me," said Sailor, "we both need to get drunk. That's what we want. We're fed up with everything. That's what's the matter with us. If everything's all right at Villevieille, I'll get drunk, that's what I'll do."

"So will I," said Antonio.

The day was overcast. A greyish damp plaster walled up

the sky from one end to the other. A volley of rain pattered onto the dry grass.

"I suppose we'll carry on, even if it rains," said Sailor, without slackening his step.

"Yes," said Antonio, "and let's have a fight. All's too soft. All's too womanish. Let's knock each other about a bit."

They walked on with long strides, well in step. They gradually overtook the light cart whose horse was no longer trotting. It carried a big, fat man, jogging up and down, covered with a shepherd's cloak which made him look rather like a bear. They passed him. The man was dozing on his cart. He had a broad birthmark, red as wine, covering the whole of his cheek.

The rain came from the north. It first began to dance on thistles which were as big as drum-skins. It hurried to the right, then to the left. It shrank the waste land around the two men. Juniper thickets gradually melted away before it, then disappeared; at last it advanced, stiff and cold, and it beat straight forward, slanting on the wind.

Sailor bent his head and pushed onwards. He had put on his fur cap. Antonio went bareheaded. Little by little, his hair, which was slightly curly, flattened out and straightened in front of his eyes. He was watching Sailor's feet and keeping in step with him. He rummaged in his wallet and took out his four cartridges. He looked at them, as he sheltered them with his hand. They were still dry. He put them in the warm in his trouser pocket.

The autumn rain extended for miles without a gap. At the bottom of the plateau, on the opposite side, the road was cut by a torrent which began to swirl muddy waters.

They were covered with froth which did not sputter away, but remained on the surface like the white of an egg.

Without speaking they crossed over, at their usual pace. Now they were alone on the road. Flights of dead leaves were swept off by the rain. The woods were being stripped bare. Huge water-polished oaks emerged from the downpour with their gigantic black hands clenched in the rain. The muffled breath of the larch forests; the solemn chant of the fir-groves, whose dark corridors were stirred by the slightest wind; the hiccup of new springs gushing out amidst the pastures; the brooks licking the weeds with their greedy lapping tongues; the creaking of sick trees already bare and slowly cracking in two; the hollow rumbling of the big river swelling down below in the shadows of the valley—all spoke of wilderness and solitude. The rain was strong and heavy.

A hawk flew by. It swooped down as if to try to fly under the rain. It skimmed the grass and screamed as it soared.

The road began to wind round a hill. Then, on top, it lengthened out across the moors. The fog was flush with it on both sides, but on both these sides there appeared to be steep slopes. The river could be heard breathing below. Dogs barked. Farms were crackling gently with the noise of fowl and goats.

"All right?" Sailor asked without slackening his pace.

"All right," Antonio answered. And he took a long stride to come abreast of him.

They could see nothing beyond the road. They were now too high up in the rain. The water no longer lashed their faces, but had become a soaking mist. It made no noises. It tested its greyish muscles on ghost-like rocks and on shadowy trees. Slowly it enveloped a maple on the roadside. The tree did not move, and even the smallest of its twigs remained motionless, yet all its red leaves fell. Through an opening in the dense clouds a wall of rocks suddenly loomed on the left-hand side. The foot of the rock was lost down below among the barking of dogs, but the summit rose through the thick of the cloud. The rock was black and dripping all over. Then again everything was blotted out. Ahead, the driving rain lifted, laying bare a huge, bristling hillock, lying athwart the road like a wild boar. Holes of bleak light bored into the clouds, now and again in the east, like the spell of a false dawn, then in the west, as if dusk were already there. At times, in the surrounding darkness, a strange glimmer kindled northwards, and it became impossible to know the time of day. It was like a vision of Doomsday, with everything changed, dawns and sunsets alike, and with the dead rising from their graves.

The road turned round and sloped towards the valleys. At the bend a cart with a canvas awning was lying overturned in the ditch. At the noise of their steps, a man emerged from the shelter.

"Are you going far?" he asked.

"Yes."

"Would you mind doing something for me? You'll soon get to the Cowhouse; tell the cartwright I'm here. I'm Martel of Revest. Tell him to come and help me. It's for somebody who's ill."

"You can count on us," Sailor said.

"Good day to you." And the man crept back under the hood.

As they went down, they entered again into the thick of

[102]

the rain. From time to time a tree covered with dead leaves loomed up and rustled under the rain, then faded out again behind them like a wet ember.

At the foot of the slope, a wretched hamlet of four cottages resounded with anvil strokes and poured out liquid cow-dung in the mud.

"Cartwright," Sailor called out.

They went in. A great lapping tongue of fire from the smithy licked them in front. They suddenly felt themselves drenched to the bone. A great icy branch opened out its frozen twigs on their backs.

"A man called Martel of Revest," said Sailor, "asked us to tell you he was up there with his cart overturned. Says it's for somebody who's ill."

"Right you are," said the cartwright. "I'll go along."

He was an undersized, thick-set fellow with enormous hands, twisted and gnarled like tree roots. He laid his hammer on the anvil.

"Have a warm," he said.

Sailor held out his hands towards the blaze. Antonio touched him on the arm. "Come on!" And he nodded towards the door. Sailor followed him.

As they were going out, Antonio looked at him out of the corner of his eye.

"All right?" he asked gently.

"All right," Sailor answered.

The last cottage of the hamlet smelt of fried onions and haslet.

Antonio began to whistle a song that hastened their pace. They pushed into the solitude of the rain.

They were now carrying the cold with them. Except in

the folds of their flesh and in the working joints of their limbs, which were kept warm by walking, they felt wide patches of frost on their skin. From time to time, by moving their shoulders, they sent a warm flow down their loins. The rills through which their blood passed were blooming with frosty flowers, sharp and cutting, with long, fine, icy thorns. Shivers caught round their wrists, coiling quickly like adders. Acute pangs bit at their knees. They had buried their chins deep in the drenched collars of their coats. They still kept some warmth under their chins, against their throats, a little nest in which the Adam's apple throbbed slightly as they swallowed the hard, cold saliva slipping down their gullets like stones. The water ran down their backs and their breasts. The innermost folds of their flesh held a small runnel of water which became warm as they walked then slipped lower down and was as cold as steel. They no longer had either skin or flesh: they were frozen and glossed all over by cold water. The only warmth which they had inside their sopping linen and the cloth of their coats was the fiery heat of their livers and hearts.

Antonio stopped whistling. He licked his lips. He started whistling again. The skin of his lips froze. The thickest part split and began to bleed.

"All ri . . ."

He cleared his throat.

"All right?" Sailor said.

"All right," Antonio answered.

They could just see a stag through the rain crossing slowly in front of them. Its antlers slanted low. It blew two jets of steam. Without hurrying, it made for the woods, prodding the spongy grass with its hoofs as it crossed the meadows.

[104]

Rain. There was only a feeble glimmer of waning light. There were no more smells, except for the smell of water; and no shapes.

The stag seemed to lengthen and grow in size. It looked round and gazed at the two men. Its eyes seemed to penetrate through the rain. It had thick reddish eyebrows, covered with water.

Antonio had wrung out his hair. The stubble on his cheeks had gathered in small flattened tufts, and his skin underneath was golden and shining like warm honey. Sailor's beard had grown longer, and he now had a long, narrow face and strong, lean jaws, the bones of which could all be seen.

The road coiled like a snake trying to extricate itself from entangled weeds. It found no issue out of the rain.

"Listen."

A confused noise of dancing and cries burst through the drumming rain. It came from a larch-grove on the left. It was a barn exuding fire through all its holes. Sailor went straight to the shelter. He pushed the door open.

They could see only big, quivering flames, a glittering golden foliage sputtering and crushing a red-hot brazier. Whirls of thick smoke curled up, hissing. Men were shouting: "Heigh! Ho! Hit hard!" They could hear the trampling thud of bare feet and the soft cries of a woman. Mules sneezed noisily and tapped their hoofs.

"Hey!" shouted Sailor, making for the blaze. On the other side of the fire four men and a woman, completely naked, were flogging each other with cypress branches. Their clothes were drying on cart rails.

"Same for us!" Sailor shouted.

He stripped off his coat and sweater, which were dripping with water.

"Just a moment," said the woman, leaving the dance. "Put them here, my skirt is nearly dry."

She was young, golden all over, with fine shadowy flesh along her spine and hard breasts scarcely in bloom. A dark man jumped through a gleam of the fire and started striking her sides with his branch. She panted under the blows as if she had just jumped into cold water.

"Quick!" said Antonio. "Hurry up!"

He had thrown his coat and trousers near the fire.

"Come, and let me rub you."

"Take some brandy," said Sailor.

Antonio took the bottle, and hollowed his right hand.

"Turn round."

He began rubbing Sailor's back. The palm of his hand soon burned.

"That's a good fellow," said Sailor.

His shoulders were covered with hair and his back was sinewy like that of an animal. His hips rang hollow, hard as horn.

"In front!" He turned round.

"It'll never get through those hairs."

"Go on," Sailor said. "Rub till I'm red. It's getting in all right."

"How old are you?"

"Seventy-five."

"Not so bad," said Antonio.

"Turn round," Sailor said, slapping Antonio's buttocks with the flat of his hand, "and let me rub you till I flay you. You'll see if I've got a strong hand at it."

He began to rub him with all his might.

"It does us good, both of us," he said.

The heat stole into Antonio's body in long sunny waves which made him gasp.

"You're slippery," Sailor said, "and supple as a fish."

Enormous shaggy arms of smoke were stirring the shadows and the lights.

Antonio looked at the young woman. She had fine thighs. She fought the man back with strong back-strokes of a thuya branch. She bent her knees, then leapt up, and her feet sprang from the ground. She slashed at them.

"Your bitch of a mother!" Then she added at once: "Help! Help! Oh, you swine!"

Slashed by the hissing green branches swung by the men, she dropped hers, hid her face in her arms, and started laughing with a whinnying laughter which set the mules prancing. She clawed at her hair.

"What a bitch!" the men said, flogging her twisted loins and her buttocks.

"Who wants a drink?" Antonio shouted, and he held up the bottle of brandy.

The woman snatched at the bottle and drank a good draught with her head upturned.

"Is it for everybody?" said a man.

"Yes," Antonio said, "but take your turn."

He drank, then handed the bottle to Sailor. The men waited, standing with legs apart. One of them was a fine man in the prime of life, with a flat belly, long thighs, and slender wrists. He wiped his forehead with a scarlet-and-gold scarf. Another had the frame of an animal trainer, with regular curving muscles and a heavy trunk, like that of a

[107]

marble statue. He had a large blue star tattooed on top of his arm. The other two were obviously brothers; they whispered in gasps, speaking the jargon of foresters.

"Mummy," wailed a tiny voice from the straw litter.

"Here I am," said the woman.

She went and leaned over a little boy lying there. She had fine buttocks, full and hard as iron. The child went to sleep again with a gurgle through its nose and throat.

She came back and sat near the fire. Fair, curly hair rose from between her thighs. The man with the scarf had gone into the shade, towards somebody else's moanings. The tattooed man was listening.

The brother foresters called out: "Clarissa!"

"Can't go to sleep," said a woman's voice.

"Keep still, then."

And they pulled down some straw to sit on.

"Bread," said Sailor. He cut up a clammy hunk which stuck to his fingers.

Antonio shoved a big piece into his mouth. He started munching slowly. A delicious saliva with the taste of wheat oozed down his throat.

The young woman heaved a sigh.

"Ill?" said Antonio, nodding at the sleeping child.

"The fate of the world," she said.

The light of the fire wound round her sides.

"All along the road," Antonio said. "The maple farmhouse"—he pointed towards the south—"and ill people all along. What's happening?"

"Fate," said the woman. "They're all going to Villevieille."

[108]

"It's not the time to go," said Antonio, "when the rain sings loud."

"When you're ill," said the woman, "nothing sings louder than your longing to be cured."

"Villevieille," said the brother foresters. They seemed to understand.

"The longing must be there," said Antonio, chewing his bread, "but you need to have sense too."

"Ah, your sense!" said the tattooed man, looking at his star.

The man with the scarf came back.

"I keep her tied up," he said, "not because I'm hard. I'm not hard, friends, but if I let her loose, she'd smash her head against the wall."

The brother foresters glanced towards their Clarissa, and listened, holding their breath.

"Day after day," said the woman, "alone on the red earth near Bédolières, with a man who's always away, floating timber. Wind and night, and every day the same, and the little one lying across my knees, slobbering at the mouth. You want hope, don't you? Then, you must wait and wait, until finally you think of the man at Villevieille, and rain or no rain . . ."

"Whom do you mean, at Villevieille?"

"The healer."

The brothers stretched out their necks.

"Listen, Clarissa," said one of them, facing the shadows, "listen to what's being said of that man."

"Well," said the woman, "he's a"—with her white hands, above her thighs and her groin, against her hard, blossoming

[109]

breasts, she was moulding the image of a man in the smoke and flame—"he's a little hunchback."

"No," said the tattooed man.

"All twisted."

"Straight as an I," said the man with the scarf.

"He sits behind his table," said the woman. "He has his hands placed in front of him. He doesn't move."

"He walks all the time," said the tattooed man, "all the time, striding up and down the room, thump, thump, thump on the wooden floor."

"He says: Come forward; come here. You go. He looks at you with his big blue eyes."

"He's got small black eyes," said the tattooed man, "like a guinea-pig's, and red eyelids."

"Ah, Clarissa!" said the foresters.

"Seems to be here, standing afore me," whispered Clarissa in the shadows.

"You know him?" the woman asked.

"I've seen him a hundred times," said the tattooed man. "I'm one of Maudru's men. I've been to Villevieille lots of times. I saw him when I was gored, there." He held up his arm. His armpit was barred across with a wide scar. "A hundred times."

"He's a little hunchback," said the woman, "as big as that." She held him against her, made of shadows and flames, between her thighs, her breasts, and her rounded arms.

The mules lay down in their warm dung. A stump of juniper burst on the edge of the fire. Wild vapour steamed out of the drying clothes.

"He's tall," said the man with the scarf, "with a broad

[110]

chest, a bit of a beard, and young. He touches you and says: It's there. He touches you, and it goes. He looks at you, he says: You may go. And you go. There you are."

"You've seen him already?" the woman asked.

"No. I just think he's like that."

"Stand afore me!" cried Clarissa. "Heal me, heal me, kind Sir!"

The brother foresters leapt towards her in the straw.

"Is there any knowing, I ask you?" said the woman to Antonio, looking at him with a long, weary gaze. "Is there any knowing, when we suffer . . . ?"

She opened out her arms. The form of the healer seemed to grow, and fill the barn with flames and shadows.

CHAPTER VIII

Morning came, bitter but clear of rain. The clouds had lifted and were now sailing higher up in the sky. They left ample room beneath them for the galloping cold wind which stirred the fine, clean firs and the washed grass.

The man with the scarf had dressed. He could no longer be recognized except for his scarf. His corduroy suit made him round and heavy, like a lead pipe. He was harnessing his mules. The four patients, who were gradually emerging from the shadows, had to be put up in the cart.

Antonio had gone out to look at the weather.

"Lend a hand to carry the child," said the young woman. Under her flowery skirt her fine hips were still swelling out, but the kerchief held in her breasts.

"Wait a moment," said the man with the scarf. "We ought to stow my wife at the far end and fasten her tight. Let's do that first."

He leaned over his sick wife. She was a madwoman with wild, violet eyes. She had her wrists and ankles bound with handkerchiefs. She jumped like a fish in the straw.

"Come along, Mary."

She tried to bite. He took her up in his arms. He shook her a bit to daze her, then sat her down on a heap of sacks in the rear of the cart. All round her he tied and knotted a rope, fastening it to the sides, to shut her up as if in a cage.

"Bring me your Clarissa," he said to the brother foresters.

They lifted up a stout, slobbering, dropsical woman. They stretched her out in the cart, with her head at the far end, and her feet towards the mules.

"Now yours," he said to the tattooed man.

"Just a moment," said Sailor.

They had to heave up a stout man, stiff as a log. His belly was surrounded by a thick dressing patterned with blood.

"Take him under the arms, gently, please. He's Maudru's nephew."

"Gored?" asked Sailor, pointing to the wound.

"Shot," said the tattooed man.

"When?"

"Yesterday."

"Hunting?"

"Fighting. Sh, sh," he said with his finger on his lip, as the man started opening his eyes. Outside, gusts of wind resounded in the valleys.

"Life is a funny sort of wheel," thought Antonio. He had just remembered his lithe river and he felt himself shut in among these mountains. He saw Clara with his mind's eye. He said to himself: "How was she dressed before being naked and bleeding?"

He gazed at the peasant's wife who walked behind the cart with its load of sick people. She looked fine, hale and sound, with her long, swinging stride.

"Funny," he said to himself.

In spite of her dress, he saw the woman naked as she had been the night before around the fire. . . .

He pictured Clara on the isle of jays. He tried to picture her in a linen dress. . . .

They had gradually come down to less deserted places. Among clusters of trees, undersized dark men, horses, and glittering ploughs were cutting open the smoking fields. Enormous clouds of ravens sailed silently across the sky. The light of the sky throbbed on their fluttering wings, and they flew by with no other noise than a muffled whirring which gently flapped back echoes with its felt-like hand. The birds swooped down in the furrows left by the ploughs, levelling the mounds of the opened fields under their black surge; then, as soon as the ploughmen plodded back, they soared up again in huge jagged flights, and went off, whirling around and around in the eddies of the wind. The mad-woman stared at them with her wild eyes. Whenever she saw that enormous mass of dark birds swoop down, in her delight a thick slobber trickled between her lips.

Sailor called Antonio. "D'you know," he said with a slap on the tattooed man's shoulder, "here's a chap who knows stories like a book?"

"They're things that have really happened," said the tattooed man.

Sailor said with a wink: "That chap, up there in the cart, he's Maudru's nephew. Hey, you with the tattoo, tell us a bit about that row. It'll stir our blood."

"It's his sister's son," said the tattooed man.

"What sister?"

"What in the name of bear's dung is the matter with you?" said the tattooed man. "Where do you come from, knowing nothing at all? Why, Maudru's sister! Give us a quid of tobacco. . . . She was called Gina," he said. "She had taken the Maladrerie estate for her share, up there in the chestnut trees. He can't hear us, back there in the cart, but

[114]

let's keep a bit behind so that I can explain who his mother Gina was.

"The Maudrus, they're divided as if with an iron rule. Men all alike; women all alike. When a mother in the family bears a daughter, it seems as if the girl had scraped all her stock of beauty out of her womb. Right away. And, mind you, girls always come out first. Right away. Boys come after, and they're made out of the remains. Stop a bit though. I'm not talking about nerves or brains or strength. Not a bit of it. I mean the finishing touch, the smoothness, the rounding off. That's what I say. Nothing more. Well, about Gina. In the days of the great Maudru (her own father and the father of the present Maudru), when she entered the bulls' stables (I'm about her age, and I've known her on an equal footing, because, mark me, in that family the rule is: I, Maudru, I am the master and, sons, daughters, bulls, and servants, nothing doing, you're all alike under my command), well, then, when Gina at that time entered the bulls' stables, even if we were tackling the fiercest black one, we always took time to steal a glance at her. It was worth being gored.

"A softness of belly which could be seen in spite of her skirt, and all around. What a woman usually looks like: legs, arms, and the rest, you know, but there was that softness of belly. Like a sun. It set your blood tingling, and then again two big lights on her body, then her throat, and on top of it her face in which she always kept her thick mouth closed —ah, prudence!—and her eyes which sang all the time like two fine greenfinches. That's what she was.

"As for me, I was a stable-boy in those days, but the fact is, she behaved quite the same with stable-boys as with

[115]

drovers, and she'd as soon walk about in ox-dung as go and watch the horses' volts. You may take my word for it. Besides, you've got to know that we were all of us men, only men, and from the youngest to the oldest we had fiery blood in us and the smell of bulls around us, and we were far from any woman alive on earth. . . . Well, you get me, don't you?

"When the great Maudru died, Gina says: 'I'll get married.' Our present Maudru says: 'You won't.' She says: 'I will.' He says: 'When I say No, it's No.' And, mark me, he's got guts in him. I know him—and that's something. Then she says: 'Is my arse your business?'

"Well, you can imagine! . . .

"In short, night came on. I remember it all as if it were yesterday. The big hall at Puberclaire. The fireplace blazing away. Weather like today's. I was mending a saddle-welt. Suddenly we hear a confused trampling pit-a-pat in the mud. We stop talking. I say to myself: the bulls are mad (it sometimes happens). A man says: 'No, horses.' We stayed there listening. Not a word spoken, and outside, on the dry pebbles in the stable yard, a big horse bursts in with a clattering of hoofs. 'On horseback!' yells out Maudru. Out we go. There he was, on his big horse, prancing like a bear. In no time we were all ready. 'Stop,' says he, and I remember how there wasn't the slightest sound and how we remained erect on our stirrups, as if suddenly turned to stone. Maudru held up his hand. Then high up in the wood we heard the cavalcade riding up and saw it: the whole forest was lighted up with their torches. Maudru lowered his hand, and said again: 'Stop.' Then we saw we weren't all there, but a good half of our band had gone away, galloping beside her, up there with torches, away where she, Gina, was leading.

"He said: 'How many are here?' We count up. Thirty-four of us were left. She had taken away twenty-three men. It was night. There was no knowing who had gone and who had stayed.

" 'Follow me,' ordered Maudru. 'Slowly.' And behind him, prancing along, we went to count up the bulls in the stables.

"I carried the torch. He went in first, cast a glance, and said: 'Right number here,' then added: 'Who's in charge here?'

" 'I am, Jérôme of Entrayes.'

" 'Very well.'

"We enter the next stable.

" 'Right number. Who's in charge here?'

"No answer. The man had gone.

"Maudru calls out: 'Benoît of Mélan.'

"No answer. Gone.

" 'Carle of Rustrel.'

"No answer. Gone.

" 'Vernet of Roumoules.'

"No answer.

" 'Flaubert.'

"It was a stable-boy.

" 'Here.'

" 'You'll be head here.'

"We pass to the next.

" 'Right number. Who's head here?'

"Burle of Méolans, Simon of the Rivers, Cathan of Echelles, Robert of L'Infernet, Antoine of Coursies, Jean

[117]

of Plan-Richaud—at every stable without drovers he appoints stable-boys. 'You'll lead here.'

"She had not carried away a single beast. Only men. From time to time we looked towards the mountain at the flaring torches.

"We went back home slowly, without saying a word. He had put me at the head of a stable, too. I've been a drover ever since. Once back at Puberclaire, Maudru stayed outside, and behind us he pushed home the great bolt of the gate. It was perhaps necessary for those who had stayed, and who stroked their beards, looking down at their feet without saying anything. But as far as we were concerned, all of us stable-boys, all the Ginas in the world might come and whisper through the gate. Now we were drovers.

"And there's an end of Gina's story."

"What a silly bitch," said Antonio.

"Wait a moment," said the tattooed man. "We'll stop a bit at Puyloubier well."

The wounded nephew had been moaning for a drink for a long while. As they went down, they had gradually approached the river. In spite of the shadowy clouds which sailed through the sky, the day was bright in the gusty wind. Between the hills one could see the wide waters gleaming. When he saw the real river once more, Antonio felt all his blood on fire. He straightened his back. He stroked the stubble on his face.

"I'll do just what I like, same as she," he said to himself. He was thinking especially of the linen dress. "Hallo, Sailor!"

"Are you waking up?" Sailor asked.

[1 1 8]

"Look at that."

The river below was knotted round the hills. A train of willows with fiery bark bordered the waters. A heavy barge emerged round the bend in the river. She was laden with blocks of granite. The current carried her away like a leaf, and she dipped her prow deep into the waves.

"It's swelling," said Antonio.

The quarry-man was standing astern, blowing his horn amid the waves of the river.

"Toine!" called out the wounded man.

"Coming," said the tattooed man. He was fetching water from the spring.

Antonio watched the man. His gaze was fixed. In his face, beneath the fat, the muscles, and the trembling caused by pain, traces of his mother's beauty could still be seen.

"Drink," said the tattooed man.

He struggled to sit up. His weak hand let go the cart-rack.

"I'm full of shot," he said. "Look, here too!" He touched the hollow of his throat.

The brother foresters wiped the dropsical woman's forehead. The young woman had put her hand like a warm pillow under the boy's head. The madwoman was looking for flocks of ravens.

"Cheer up," said the man with the scarf. "There's Villevieille, yonder."

"Where?" asked the woman with dropsy.

"There." He pointed away in front to a hill covered with golden grass. "Let's go," he said. "Let's get done with the road."

[119]

"He got the shot right in his belly," said the tattooed man, "ten metres off, with buck-shot as big as that." He held up his thumb nail.

"And what about the bitch, did she get married?" asked Antonio.

"She didn't, but she had five sons. She turned the song of the race into a lie. They were not ugly. She settled with her men on that Maladrerie estate. She traded in timber. There was no fighting. She ruled over business and her bed with a leaden whip. Five sons. Four of them died. One day she came down. Stiff, hard. The wind hissed about her. When at Puberclaire, she said: 'Where's Maudru? Go and fetch him.'

"They stood two paces away from each other. She said: 'Well, then?' He said: 'Well, what?'

"Two days after, she came back for good and all to Puberclaire. She carried her last son in front of her saddle. She brought back seven of the men. They were a little older, and rode behind her on their horses without saying a word. She said: 'You will take those back.' He looked at them silently, with his large blood-shot eyes. She said: 'I'll pay you.'

"It's about that time that Maudru had his daughter. A bit later. A year, maybe. Because, you know, everything had smoothed down again. Maudru married the master-tanner's daughter. She got drunk at once with men, bulls, dung, and that unceasing horse scuffle about her. She never got sober again. She looked at everything with those scared eyes of hers. She just had time to produce a daughter and then died. It was better for her.

"One evening Gina said: 'That girl shall be called Gina.

When one happens to be a girl in this place, one has to be called Gina to have any freedom.'

"Maudru doesn't speak much.

"The girl's called Gina. Damn me, if the name doesn't fit her!"

"Why?" asked Sailor.

"Look at him, poor devil, with his belly torn open."

"Is it her?"

"Not her, but for her. He fired at him ten yards off, like that. We'd known for three days he was lurking in that wood. He was alone. It could only be to find the way out. He wouldn't have gone southwards without her. The nephew made us scan every tree in the wood. I think, for my part, he had his eye on Gina the Second, himself.

"It was in the Rivolard forest, which is as dark as a cellar. We know the chap well: he's a devil. We were hemming him in, closer and closer. Then he shouted to us: ' A hundred against one!'

"We ran towards the shout. Nobody.

" 'A hundred against one!' from another place altogether. Still nothing.

" 'A hundred against one! A hundred against one!' He was singing it like a bird around us. There was no catching him. He made us sweat, right enough.

"The nephew then shouted: 'Show yourself, galley-slave! Look!' he said.

"We saw a white patch among the trees. The nephew fired. It must have been an empty shirt. The man got out of the bush. We only saw his red hair. He fired straight at the nephew.

" 'Take that to your whore of a mother!' "

[1 2 1]

"He was wrong there," said Sailor; "one should never abuse people's mothers."

"Villevieille! Villevieille!" cried out the man with the scarf. He had drawn up his cart at a bend in the road.

In the distance, on the ridge of the hill, there lay a large town, very old and white, like a dead man's face. Laurel bushes rose out of heaps of plaster and rubbish; they lapped their boughs heavily on the dilapidated houses, beating against the walls with their iron wings. Down below, the river seethed along under a dark bridge, and the town dipped in the waters from a steep embankment, dripping all over with a kind of oozy, reddish-brown slime. On a wall overhanging the river, broad ox-hides, like stars, were spread out to dry.

Grey-tiled tanneries stood out against the light-coloured heaps of ground oak-bark. The hollow thud of the fullers shook the dark depths of the earth, like the throbbing of a big heart heavy with blood. The low-walled town, starred with hides, climbed up the hill amid the wool of its smoke.

The thick breath of a baker's oven, sprinkled with glowing embers, leapt with its soft bear's paws from terrace to terrace. Higher up emerged some very old and bony houses, with ornamented roofs and pigeon-cotes. Out of the broad windows, quartered by stone crosses, stuck the stern heads of strawberry trees which had grown through the floors. When the weight of the clouds muffled the noise of the fullers, one could hear the song of the upper town. It sounded like a forest, but its rumblings lasted longer. The wind writhed through deserted halls, corridors, flights of stairs, and deep cellars. The wind died down; its song was now nothing more than the pattering of a drum; then the long wooden runnels

[122]

along which the water was directed started piping like flut€
Later the cloud lifted again, and the beating of the fulle
began once more to dart noises through the hollow plac
of the town which sounded like the trembling of fallen bul.
A smell of cattle-skinning, of tanner's bark and old plaste
squirted out under the flat hand of the wind.

All over its body the town was furrowed by long, blacki
scars of rain. Behind it, huge purple mountains, swollen wi
water, slept under a darkened sky.

"Heal me! Heal me!" wailed the dropsical woman.

"Restore me to health," said the wounded man. And l
spat a clot of blood into the mud.

CHAPTER IX

BEFORE reaching the town gate the cart drew up in front of an inn.

"I'm no longer any use to you," said Antonio to the young woman.

"Thanks," she said. "It's been kind of you to walk behind me with your bright eyes. . . ." She smiled. "The porter will help me put the kid to bed. Good luck to you."

"Same to you."

The tattooed man advanced towards the stables. He shouted in the courtyard: "Maudru! Help wanted!"

Three men ran out. They stopped as they saw the cart.

"Help," cried the wounded man.

"The nephew," said the man with the tattoo.

Antonio pushed Sailor on.

"Let's go. Let's go."

The town gate opened a little further on.

"I wanted to find out," Sailor said.

"You've done so now."

"I wanted to know more." He was looking back at Maudru's people, who were laying the wounded man on big rick-cloths on the ground.

"Stop, you two. Come along this way."

It was a gendarme. He was sitting in front of his lodge,

astraddle on a chair, with his arms on the back, his beard on his hand, and pipe in his mouth.

"Where are you going to?"

"To the town."

Under his unfastened tunic, the gendarme wore a soldier's shirt, with a number printed in marking-ink.

"What for?"

"Visiting a friend."

"Who?"

"Man who sells almanacs."

The pipe was stopped up. The gendarme sucked in vain. They could see his cheeks sink in under his beard.

"Have you got papers?"

"Yes."

"Let's see."

He tried to relight his tobacco. He rammed down the fire with his thumb.

"Is that your name?"

"It is," said Sailor.

"Haven't you got any others?"

"No."

"Nibles forest, where you're living, is on the other side of the gorges, isn't it?"

"Yes."

"Wood-cutter?"

"Yes."

"Ever bought timber down this way?"

"Never."

"Sold any?"

"Never."

"Sent anybody?"

"Never. It's too far. Not convenient. Poor job. I cut on the spot and I'm alone."

"And you? Fisherman?"

"Fisherman," said Antonio.

"What does this partnership of yours mean?"

"No partnership," Antonio said; "we are neighbours. It's like that."

"Let me see your guns. Loaded?"

"No."

"Show me the barrels."

He shut one eye and looked into the barrels of both guns.

"All right," he said.

The wicker chair creaked under his fat thighs.

"And now you know," Antonio said as they entered the town.

Sailor was pale under his beard.

"What on earth's he done, my boy?"

"He's killed the nephew, by God."

"Course he has—but before that?"

The street was straight and dark. In the back rooms of shops, lamps had already been lighted. Tanneries stretched all along the right-hand side of the street. From place to place, covered alleys, like tunnels with steps, led down through the factories and ramparts to the river whose yellow scales were seen gleaming down below. Here the fullers' thudding was overpowering and confused. It came from the depths of the earth, shook the glass windows of the shops, and made the watches jump between the watchmaker's fingers. After a time you got accustomed to it. In front of vegetable stalls, Spanish grocers cried out names of plants. Nobody could understand them. They laughed,

[126]

and with their thick lips they slowly composed the name: "On-i-ons." And they flourished an onion.

"No, thanks." The small, thin customer, in her tight neckerchief, weighed potatoes in her hand like fruit. People floundered in black slime which smacked under their feet. On either side of the street the runnels flowed red, rolling along big islands of animal fat. The draper had opened his shop. He was dusting coarse material which smelt of the fields. The butcher hooked onto his front window carcasses of young goats ripped open like water-melons. A little bent old woman pulled him by his apron.

"Tripe?"

"Come in."

He opened his door. The old woman went in under his arm. He followed her, wiping his big hands on his apron. An automatic piano danced with its clumsy copper feet tinkling with bells. Tanners came back from the fleshing, pushing wheelbarrows laden with hides.

"Antonio, I want to sit down," Sailor said bitterly.

"Come on, old man, cheer up a bit."

But he felt Sailor clinging to his arm. He watched him. The old wood-cutter had no blood left under his skin, and his hand was pale as grass.

"Find a corner for me to sit down . . . I think I have death on me."

"Lean on me. There. Two steps to the left. Up on the sidewalk." Antonio pushed open the door of a bar. "Go in."

It was like a dark cave. All the tables were empty. They could hear the roar of a big cast-iron stove, piled up with wood.

"Good day," Antonio cried.

Sailor dropped like a sack on the bench.

"Good day," said a fat woman out of the dark.

"Get me some hot wine," Antonio said. "Slip your kit off, Sailor," he added. He helped him off with his gun, his wallet, and his rolled cloak.

"Open your coat. Now, old man . . . You're done for if you don't pull yourself together."

He slapped his cheeks.

"Hallo, old man."

He pulled his hair. He unfastened the collar of his shirt.

"There. Lie down a bit and breathe freely."

"I've put in a whole litre," said the woman. The wine was already singing on the fire.

"All right for a start," said Antonio. "Have you got any pepper?"

"Yes."

"Nutmeg and saffron. Give me your canisters and the grater."

"Here's the spoon," said the woman. "Stir it up. You're big enough to do it yourself, aren't you? I've got some kid-stew on the fire over there."

"Carry on. Don't worry."

"You're from the mountain?"

"Yes. Go to your stew."

Antonio poured a spoonful of pepper into the boiling wine, grated some nutmeg, added some saffron, and started stirring while the big fire roared under the saucepan.

"Take the pewter mugs," said the woman.

"Drink, old man."

He held out to him a full measure of strong wine. Everything was steaming: the mug, Antonio's fists, and the thick ring of pink froth slowly circling on the wine.

"Wash it down into your maw."

"Ha. I've got many things in my maw already," said Sailor, stiff in tongue and body. "Many . . . a great deal too many . . ."

"Take that as well. Open your mouth. Don't be silly."

At the first gulp, Sailor cleared his throat. "Drink some yourself," he said.

"What I want is something to eat," said Antonio, sniffing towards the kitchen. All the same, he drank a full mug of hot wine, then called for the woman.

"Feeling better?" she said.

"Yes, thanks. It begins to smell of your kid-stew, out there. Can't we get anything to eat?"

"Certainly. I can even give you two platefuls of it."

"Yes. What we want is to get something hot to eat."

Sailor was pulling himself together.

Night by now had fallen completely. The woman arrived with her two platefuls of stew.

"You can't see," she said. "Do you want me to light a candle?"

"We don't particularly need light," Sailor said. "We know where to find the two main places, the plate and our mouths. It's pretty smooth work."

Night still hesitated to leave the town and to spread over the country. Above the roofs the sky retained the wavy green of forests and water. In the channel of the street the darkness was as thick as the mud, in which they could hear but not see men running about in pattens, wheels creaking along, and mountain mules floundering with their overlapping shoes.

"I'm thinking of that son of mine," Sailor said. "Who would have thought . . . ?"

"I would," Antonio answered. "Remember that wolf business. How old was he then? It's not ages ago . . . three or four years . . . he was sixteen. Sailor, when I was fishing of a morning, I glanced at the banks. No noise—but I felt as if somebody were watching me. Nothing. Only osiers. Then through the osiers I could see his red hair. Well, do you want to know? Your twin, I've always looked on him as a beast from distant parts."

"He's dropped upon this country like a lion," Sailor said.

"Children aren't made out of curds, old man. And we don't make them as we want. We make them as we are, and what we are, no one knows. We've got so many things in our blood."

"Yes. But what about Junie? You'd never find anybody more peaceful."

"What do you know about it? It's in the loins, I tell you. Think of Junie's brother. What's become of him?"

"Don't know."

"Now, you see. Don't be taken in by eyes or words. Soup. I've made soup. Eat your soup. There's a lot of talk about soup, but they never mention those flashes which dart across us like wasps, and when we've got children we realize that they were made with that. Not with soup."

"Yes," said Sailor, "the brother . . . of course, if the twin has got some of his blood mixed up with mine, his blood must be a bit queer. A little while ago I felt my legs cut under me. Suddenly I saw the nephew brought down,

[130]

the gendarme at the other end of the town, this country itself furrowed all over with Maudru's people and bulls. I said to myself: All that because of your son. To tell you the truth, Antonio, I left our forest to fetch the little imp, the kid, the child—the child whose red hair I used to stroke. And here I am, the father of a kind of mad lion."

"The main thing," said Antonio, "now we've got here, is to see the man who sells almanacs. What did Junie say about it?"

"Not much."

"Do you know where he lives?'

"I don't."

"Hey, Missis."

The woman came up with her saucepan.

"Do you want any more?"

"No, thanks. We've eaten like snakes. That's what was the matter with the old man just now."

"Hunger's bad," said the woman.

Antonio turned round on his chair.

"I say . . . But go and put down your saucepan. And then come along. We've something to ask you. D'you know a man who sells almanacs?"

She began to rake the stove with a big iron poker. The coals blew out a thick blue flame which lit up the whole bar, from the glass jar of pickled plums on the counter to the Vespétro liqueur advertisement at the bottom, upon which a paper horse among some bottles laughed between his bit.

"Yes, I know him; it's Toussaint, Monsieur Toussaint," she said, coming back with her cord slippers.

"Where does he live?"

"In the upper town. The last house."

"How much is this?"

"Let's say five francs. Follow the road up to the church square," she said, "and take the steps behind the steeple, then once you've got on top you can't go wrong. It's the last house—besides, it's the only one left inhabited below the bishops' palace."

They went up the road. Sailor had recovered his dogged strength, and followed Antonio's step. The clock-tower struck six. The thump of the fullers ceased. There seemed to be a great silence, and then there was the sound of a nibbling noise, made in the houses all over the town by the thousands and thousands of steps of housewives preparing the evening meal, the steps of the girls running down the stairs to fetch water from the fountains or meet their lovers, and the gambolling of children in the corridors. The tanneries opened their doors. Tanners came out, carrying their lanterns in their hands. A wild smell of rotten meat and salt reeked around them.

The church square lay on a high ledge of the town, away from the shops and work-shops. In a corner there stood the notary's house with its large scutcheons hanging over the door. In the opposite corner an old bourgeois house whistled a sour violin tune through the golden joints of its shutters. Between the houses a stone parapet towered over the lower town with its streets full of moving tanners' lanterns.

"There are the steps."

Antonio's foot touched the first step, the slabs of which were loose.

"It's full of weeds."

The wind drove the clouds away, unveiling the moon. The gaunt flight of steps climbed up right in the shadow of the steeple, then turned round, and at the turning up there, in the metallic rustling of a clump of laurels, a broken-down, rickety old house shone like an ox skull. The wind hissed in the steps, crushed the laurel bushes, struck at the house, leapt silently into the sky, and swooped down far away in the country upon a great forest which awoke and growled like a dog.

"It's up there," said Antonio.

Up there, in the shadow of the laurels, stood a long house with bright windows. A small ripple of moonlight glided along the curls of its roof.

The steps climbed up between wild gardens, covered with rank grasses, nettles, and leafless fig trees. Weeds spread over the decaying walls. The last autumn toads were piping in the rubbish with their glassy voices. The last two big steps of the flight stood out against the lighted house like surging waves. They came to an end on the threshold, cut by a big round door, almost a cart gate.

"It's here," said Antonio.

"Yes, it's here." Sailor was panting. He peered all around. "Their bishops' palace!"

Above the house they could see in the darkness of the sky a ruin bitten all over by rain and wind, a terrace fringed with marble balusters, vaults, and wide windows with stone mullions.

"We're there."

The town down below was hushed with its darkened streets. The river rumbled along its embankments. It was a very soft noise, silky and strangely sonorous.

"Listen," said Antonio.

Inside the house they heard somebody singing. The tune

was low-pitched, deep and wild. It said the same thing over and over again:

> "O my horse!
>   O my horse!
>   Canst thou swim through blood?
>   Canst thou cleave blood like a boat?
>   Leap in blood like a tunny?
>   Trample on men as on faggots in the mud?"

> "Tie a golden kerchief round thy head,
>   And I'll cleave blood like a boat,
>   And I'll leap like a tunny,
>   And I'll trample on men like faggots,
>   Provided I recognize thee if thou fallest."

Antonio grasped Sailor's arm.

"Gently," said Sailor.

"Shall I knock?" said Antonio.

"Yes, knock."

He seized the iron knocker and struck a good, ringing blow.

Silence. Soft scurrying steps. A door was shut, down below in the depths of the house. A slightly grating bolt was pulled back gently. The heavy step of hob-nailed shoes drew near, and the echoing walls clacked in answer.

"What do you want?" inquired a voice through the door.

"Is this where the almanac-vender lives?"

"It is. What's the matter with you to want him at this time of day?"

[134]

Antonio noticed that the voice came from across a wired peep-hole, and he felt eyes peering at him.

"Are you ill?"

"No."

"Well, then, what do you want of him?"

"The fact is," Sailor said, "we're sent to him by Junie. We were told to make sure and tell him that Junie sent us. Tell him as much, if you don't mind."

"Wait, then."

The peep-hole was noiselessly shuttered. The heavy steps receded in the house, then silence fell. Outside, the wind. Dry grasses were rubbing against the wall.

"They've stopped singing," Antonio said in a low voice.

"Was it here, d'you think?" said Sailor.

"Yes, down below, right deep down."

The door was opened noiselessly. Antonio felt it yield gently against his shoulder as it opened.

"Come in, both of you," said a small voice.

It was not a child's voice. It had broken, it had remained clear and naïve; it was the voice of a full-grown man, but it came out of the dark from the height of a child.

Inside, the shadows were thick, with never a break. The least motion set the wide sensitive stretch of corridor ringing. "I'll close the door," said the voice. "Feel your way to the wall, and walk along by it. We mustn't strike a light here. Sorry."

Antonio and Sailor shuffled along the flagstones.

"Go straight ahead," said the voice. "It's all clear. Have you got the wall?"

"Yes."

"Follow it with your hand up to the door yonder, at the bottom. The dark does not matter. Less than water."

"That may be," said Antonio, "but if it was water I could do it easier."

"I know," said the voice. "Here, it's just the same—it's only a question of assurance."

He reached the door before them. He pushed it. It opened on a large room hemmed in by shadows with a small island of light in the middle, carrying a large round table laden with books, papers, stones, herbs, and a lamp. The hand which pushed the door was long, with slender pale fingers, snaky as thongs of a whip. It vanished.

"Come in, gentlemen."

The polite and child-like voice urged them towards the light.

"Sit down, Sailor, and the other gentleman too."

Hearing the name, they looked around. Sailor! Who knew that name, born yonder, on the far side of the gorges, right in the Nibles forest?

It was a little hunchback with a big head. He emerged from the shadows.

"Jérôme!" Sailor cried.

"Yes," said the hunchback. "It's I. Don't shout, the house has ears. I'm Monsieur Toussaint. Sit down."

He slowly turned round the men to go and sit at his table. He walked on the verge of the circle of light. Half of his small twisted body clung to the shade and seemed to fill the whole room with its palpitating black flesh.

"You've got the armchair behind you, and you too, Sir" —he swung his long, supple arms and his watery hands in small, ceremonious gestures—"I always say 'Sir,' always, to everybody. It's a way of mine. I cling to it. Sit down, Sir. You are the one my sister Junie calls Golden-Mouth. I know. It's obvious. You can swim—the water, the wind, the forest, and the river. I cannot swim. I never go out. Thank you. I say 'thank you' because you can swim. Thank you for knowing how to swim. Sit down. Junie has told me. Golden-Mouth . . ." He stopped a moment at the opposite end of the table. The shadow swallowed all his head. There remained only the swelling of his right shoulder and, resting on his shoulder, an enormous lean ear, clawed like a bat's wing. The thin hand pointed at the table. "A bit of medicine, gentlemen. That's what it is. Pain. That mountain of mine in the bottom of which I sit, with my wings folded." He crossed his long arms. "My weakness." He drew out his chair slowly to sit down. "I'm glad to see you, Sailor. How is Junie? I've not been in the forest for a long time. Allow me to talk, gentlemen, I like talking." His voice glided against the echoes of the house without rousing them. "Well, Sailor, all that is all right as it is. Pain. I've dug my cave into it. Philosophers . . . No, I know you're bored. I even think you kicked my arse in the old days because I talked philosophy. I'm wrong. I'm sure you've missed me, Sailor. One needs a strong hatred for somebody in one's life. But sit down, gentlemen. Come, I'll sit down myself; if not, you'll remain on your legs."

He glided against his armchair with a rustle like a cat's. He sat down. He could be seen altogether now and looked like an insect: his knuckle-bone-shaped chin, dry and hard, and his great, limp, heavy forehead, leaning to the right. He had enormous eyeballs, bulging out of their sockets as if someone had trampled on his belly. His look had the warm green glimmer of foliage in the sun.

"One word more, Sailor," he said. "Call me Toussaint. It's as easily said as Jérôme, and they're accustomed to it, up here. I'm set on it."

He stopped talking and licked his lips. The house began to crackle gently like an apple lying on straw.

Antonio and Sailor felt as if they were estranged from the world. They were moved by that learned child-voice, by that look full of sap. The long, thin hands moved softly between books and herbs. Great visions were beating against their faces, smothering them like water: the past, the arrival in the forest, Sailor, Junie, the hunchbacked brother-in-law (he was called "the notary's clerk"), Antonio's howl down below on the river; the crash of falling trees, right and left, Junie in her young days. . . .

Sailor wiped his eyes. He thought he saw that May cloud over there, in the depths of the shadows: his glorious, youthful Junie.

"I had a purpose . . ." Sailor said sorrowfully.

"I don't blame you for it," said the hunchback.

Antonio's gun fell to the ground.

"Now, then, what have you come for in upper Rebeillard?"

"To find my twin."

"The one with red hair?"

"I sent him to make a raft. He's not come back. For the last four days that we've been walking we've been hearing a great noise in the hills and the woods as if my twin were

[138]

dancing his anger on the country with his big wooden pattens. What has he done? Where is he? That's all."

The hunchback licked his lips. "He's here," he said. He called out: "Gina!"

It was indeed a living woman who stood over there in the depths of the shadows, like a May cloud. She had said nothing till then, when she approached.

"Here is Danis's father," said the hunchback.

She put her free arm around Sailor's neck. "Then I must call you father, too," she said. "I am your son's wife."

She leaned and kissed his beard.

"And she is Maudru's daughter," said the hunchback. "Now, can you understand what's the matter, gentlemen?"

"Yes," said Antonio, "now I can understand everything."

He still heard the fierce beat of the song. Gina's eyes were flat and long, with big, dark pupils, her milky flesh was bathed in a white glow, her wrists were no bigger than rings on a man's fingers.

"As for me, I can't," Sailor said. "Not yet. Must I call you Monsieur Toussaint, or be familiar with you? His wife—what does it all mean? Maudru's daughter, what's that? And then? You've put that word in my ear like a sheep-tick. Maudru, what of it? What of it? What of him, anyhow?"

"He's my father," Gina said, "and he's a man, for that matter."

Sailor looked at her. "The twin's my son," he said, "and he's a man too."

"Not so big," Gina said, "and a girl-stealer."

"Since when are girls stolen?" said Sailor. "They've got feet and they follow."

"As dogs follow thieves," Gina said. "They say: 'Come, come,' and they promise."

"Promise what?" Sailor asked.

"Everything," Gina said.

"That's a lot," Sailor said.

"And they scarcely pay anything," Gina said. She put her hand on her forehead as if to cool it. She closed her eyes. She spoke to herself.

"And I could forgive him," she said in weary tones, "for not giving me the highways, the house, that freedom of ours he spoke of, I, who am prisoner. . . . But I can't forgive him for being less than what he seems to be, less than what he says, less than what people say, less than what I thought he was. Almost nothing. No, that I can't. I've been too badly deceived."

"My girl," Sailor said gently, "wedding time is a time for lies. What do you want?"

She opened her eyes. "I want him to be what he fancied he was, and what he had me believe."

"What did he have you believe?" Sailor asked.

"That he was strong," she said.

"He is strong," Sailor said.

"That he was stronger than my father."

"He is stronger than your father."

"You make me laugh," she said, "at you and at myself. D'you imagine I'm going to believe that? I'm tired of believing. At saying: 'I, I, I,' he's stronger, he is. At doing, he's not."

"What do you want him to do?"

"I'm worth what I'm worth," she said, "and he's got all for nothing. I want him to make my freedom, and to

[140]

make my bed, and I don't want to be a cuckoo in the bed of other people."

Sailor scratched his beard. "He'll make it," he said; "just wait."

"I've waited," she said. "Nobody can say I haven't, and I'm still waiting, but without confidence, so you see . . . One evening my father said: 'Nothing without me.' Your son said to me: 'Come, don't worry. With me, you'll see. I'll do this and I'll do that.' Oh, he's said things. Oh, at saying things! I came. I'm with him. I see. What have I? Nothing. If I wanted to be taken away from this place I'd only have to put a foot abroad. It'd soon be done. Who would defend me? He? He's not even able to find me a way to his country. Why? He daren't even go out in the daytime. Maudru? He said three words. He said: 'Nothing without me.' And he's all around the place, outside, and I've got nothing. That's how things stand. Your son, do you want me to tell you where he is now? He's just gone out to have a try, because after telling him over and over again . . . but he's there, close at hand, in the laurels down there, unable to move a step. Crouching with his rounded back, his gun on his thighs. . . ."

"Speaking of guns," Sailor said, "listen . . ."

Toussaint raised his long hand. "Wait," he said. "You're all inflamed by this fiery girl. Golden-Mouth has just struck his fist on the arm of his chair. Wait till I speak, before you turn my house into a blazing baker's oven. . . . Fetch your stool, my girl."

Gina went into the dark and fetched a stool.

"Sit down here near me, my girl."

He stroked her hair. She kissed the wan hand of the

[141]

hunchback, then pressed it against her cheek, and, with her head drooping sideways, she started weeping silently.

"Well, my men, let me speak before you become torches . . . while you can still understand what is being said. . . .

"You sent your son to cut down trees. He cut them down. He made the raft. He moored it in Villevieille creek. That was at the beginning of the August moon. Since then the raft has lain there, ready to leave. So much for the work. The twin came to see me. His mother had said to him: 'Since you are so near him, go and see your uncle.' She —knows I'm here, and what I'm doing. I've always kept on writing to her. At times I say to myself: 'Junie,' and I think of my sister. I picture her, far away, buried in that forest, and I think she must need the thoughts with which we used to play before you came from the sea, Sailor, to fetch her from our father's house, in the book-room. You, Sailor, you were still on the sea, with your seeds of red-headed children, still on your great ship full of sails. Junie and I, we used to talk. If you had not skipped into the port, Sailor, my sister would be a lady in Marseilles. Her husband would trade in oil or soap. She would have her drawing-room with great portraits of old gentlemen and old ladies, she would wear creaking shoes, and have her pew marked at church and at the theatre. At her age now, she would brush her bulging silk-clad hips into armchairs. You've made something better of her. I thank you on her behalf.

"I'm saying all that to put things in their right perspective. I see her now, not dead as she would be, but as she really is, bathing in the thick shadows of the forests, in her robust old age. I thank you for her. That's what I'm obliged to you for. But, it's for the rest that I sometimes sit down at this table to write long letters to her, where she and I become once more the children of my father in the book-room. For a long time somebody I know has taken them to her twice or three times a year. I want you to know everything. Well, then, she sends your son to me. Her son too. He speaks to me. He tells me tales. I gaze at him. In a family, Sailor, twins are a godsend. Laughing? Well, you always used to laugh when I spoke, then time went by and proved everything true. You'll see. Sailor, I say more: If one of a couple of twins dies a violent death, then the strength they had both together, the evil they had both together, what they were in the world both together, all of that goes to the one who's left living; it becomes his alone."

"That's an old saw," Sailor said.

"As you like," went on the hunchback. "The least I have against you, Sailor, is your shortsightedness. I pondered over that while he was here, that son of yours, there, precisely where Gina is sitting now. I held his hands, I looked at him; I touched his arms from the wrists to the shoulders. I felt him all over with eyes and fingers, and I said to him: 'Well, my man, and how are you getting on?' Then: 'What a fine chap you are, son of God.' In a word, all that a mere abortion like myself can say to a fine-looking twin who carries the share of two. And all of a sudden he disclosed to me his innermost self, all aflame, and he gave me all his tender cares, for me to cradle and heal, here on my knees. He's ten times the like of you as regards breadth of shoulders and strength of heart.

"But in that sort of open country"—the hunchback touched the pit of his stomach—"which he carries here, his own forests, his own rivers, his own mountains, he's worth

[143]

my sister Junie hundreds and hundreds of times over. I allow myself to be carried away when speaking of your son, for nothing has ever touched me more in all my life than when he made that great effort to pull himself together, that great effort of a double twin, and said to me: 'Listen, Uncle, this is what's happening to me. . . .'"

"I understand," Antonio said.

The hunchback looked at him. He passed his tongue over his lips. He let his eyelids drop slowly over his eyes.

"Yes, you, Golden-Mouth, you must understand well enough. On the border of the meadow where he was making his raft he had seen a woman."

"On that day," Gina said, "I was looking for washing-places."

"He started stammering when talking to me," said the hunchback, "and I saw him trembling before me. He told me what she was like. He tried to tell me of her beauty, and it made his mouth shine all over."

"On that day," Gina said, "it was summer. . . . I had tied a small silk skirt round my chemise, merely clasped round my waist, nothing more. It was hot—I was more at ease that way."

"How did it happen?" said the hunchback. "Who knows?"

He remained a moment without speaking. Gina wiped her eyes.

"He was marking his trees," she said. "He had kindled a fire, and had started heating his thick branding-iron red hot. I was looking at him through the willows. He caught the iron with his big bare hand, and stamped it, red hot, into the living trunk. In the middle of the smoke, I saw him

[144]

press with all his might. The sap was crying. He straightened himself up. The tree was marked with his name. And I saw that the man's hair was red, like his big branding-iron."

Toussaint gently stroked Gina's shoulder.

"Yes," he said, "as he stood there trembling all over, he just looked as if he were again seeing the girl on the border of the willows. He had lost his breath. 'Lost for ever,' he said, 'I shall never breathe again as I used to, before.' "

"I," said Gina, "I was marked by that red-haired man as if by a tree-brand."

"He told me he had tried everything before making up his mind."

"So did I too," Gina said. "Everything, you can take my word for it. I had known for a long time that my father wanted to give me to his sister's son. I went to the place where the nephew was eating with the drovers, and I told him: 'If you want me, take me at once.' In front of all the men he pressed me against him, he kissed me, and he felt all over my body with his hand as if I was his wife already. I thought: 'If it could only wipe away . . .' Ah, well. God flies, and try and catch up with Him on foot if you can!"

"So that you said nothing," the hunchback said, "when he came to fetch you. . . ."

"I said: 'Ho,' and again: 'Thank you, thank you,' times on end while he was holding me, to thank him for being there, for being himself, for being mine. That's all, and what else do you expect? What can you understand, you men?"

"I understand," Antonio said, "that for us it's not the same, even if we love as much."

An impulse made him look southwards.

"Yes," said Sailor, "but what about my son in all that?"

"I had warned him," Gina said. "Don't think I had con-
cealed anything from him. I even told him more than what
was likely to happen. . . . 'Nothing,' he said, 'all that's
nothing . . .' And he levelled everything out with his flat
hand. And I grew prouder and prouder of him. He was so
broad-shouldered, everything looked small by his side. I,
Maudru's daughter, had so often dreamt of such a man,
without hoping he could really exist, that I was mad with
joy to have him in my arms, and to find him still finer,
still bigger than the man of my dreams. I said to myself:
'How is it possible?' I touched him and I thought: 'It is
possible, fate is like a cattle-dealer: the better to deceive
you, he makes you drunk.'

"Wait a bit," she said to Antonio and Sailor, who both
wanted to interrupt. A fire, sparkling like a smithy, kindled
under her white skin. "Wait a bit, I've not done. It's too
big a thing for me not to regret my love. It's in my blood
to be generous, and if he knows of a single thing which I've
given grudgingly, let him say so. I've given everything,
I've thought of everything, I've fettered my hands and feet
for him. I told him: 'Take me away with you,' since it suited
him to take me away. I've given everything. When all's
said, my man, it's always give and take. Night after night,
over and over again, I revolved his promises in my mind.
The open road, down to your forest, far away. Life—it's all
I ask—a peaceful life, wherever he wants and how he wants,
but with him. But life, you hear me, father of your twin,
life, a house, mine and his, and let him make me bear
many children. That's what I counted up every night on

[146]

my empty fingers. Do you understand? He knew my father would pit himself against him. He knew my father would hem us in closely and fight to tear me away from him; and I had said to him: 'Here I am, caught like a kid; pack me on your shoulders and carry me away.' He promised me the open road. Is he then only a feller of trees, that son of yours? He promised. And he's not even able to cut a way for us through men, poor me!"

Her voice had gradually risen to a cry, and the shadows of the house were moaning with her.

Sailor was breathing hard in his beard; the hunchback was playing with a dry herb, and gazing at his fingers.

"Here he is," she said. She got up.

The front door, below, rang on its hinges.

"Speaking of guns," Sailor said, "I can tell you now. . . . Yesterday he fought with your father's men and killed the nephew."

"Gina!" cried the twin. He was running along the echoing corridor. The butt-end of his gun was striking against the wall.

PART TWO

CHAPTER I

WINTER in the Rebeillard region was always a sparkling season. Every night the snow fell, thick and heavy. In the halo of the street-lamps, Antonio had sometimes seen it fall straight as a shower. The towns, villages, and farmsteads of Rebeillard slept, muffled in those thick, silent nights. Now and again all the beams in a village would creak, people would awake, and thick clouds would skim the ground with their flapping wings, rustling along the forests. But dawn always rose in a great stretch of cloudless sky, swept by a gusty north wind. The sun, scarcely emerging from the horizon and crushed under the weight of relentless azure, would stream all over the frozen snow; the most stunted shrub would blaze up like a flaming heart. In the solid, metallic forest, the wind could not stir a single bough; it merely sprinkled a glittering spray over the dazzling whiteness. Bright, sparkling dust spread over the country.

Sometimes, on the flat, open roads, it enveloped a man walking along on snow-shoes, or else, surprising sick foxes at the outskirts of a wood, it made them get up and run to other shelters. The animals would stop in the sun, with their fur bespattered with frozen snow, hard as granite dust. They licked the sensitive parts of their bodies to warm themselves a little, then hobbled away again towards a distant, undulating slope. Daylight no longer came from the sun only, out of a corner of the sky, with each thing carrying its own shadow; light bounded from all parts of the glistening snow and ice, in every direction, and the shadows were thin and sickly, bestrewn with golden dots. It seemed as if the earth had swallowed the sun and was now the sole light-maker. It was impossible to gaze at the light. It struck at your eyes: you closed them, and you stole a glance at it to seek your way. You could look at it scarcely long enough to find the right direction; the rim of your eyelids instantly smarted, and, if you rubbed your eyes, dead eyelashes were left between your fingers. The thing to do was to look for blue or black silk rags in your cupboards. Sometimes they could be found in those baskets where little girls store their dolls' dresses. You made a bandage with them to tie over your eyes and, thus blindfolded, you could set out and walk in a kind of strange twilight which no longer hurt you.

About noon—that was the time people chose for short trips, mere saunters from farm to farm, or when they just wanted to take the stiffness out of their legs after getting tired of roasting them before the fire—men, women, or branded horses travelled across the country. They all plodded along slowly, appearing slightly tired, just as if they were trudging along at dusk. Those who wore black masks moved about apparently more exhausted; those with blue ones were a little better, but when they met, they started talking slowly without much enthusiasm, wearily straightening their backs, as if at the end of a heavy day's work. Yet it was midday, with a sun heightened to the utmost by the hundred thousand lights of the snow, and they had just got up from their stools round the fire. But it was because of these silk masks which they had to wear against the dazzling light, and because they carried the shade of evening in their heads.

At length, evening itself came. All the wanderers went home to their farms or villages. Two or three sledges still glided along at full speed on the outskirts of the wood with a heavy din of galloping and tinkling bells. One could hear in the wind people shaking the snow off their snow-shoes on the thresholds of their houses; then doors were shut, and farms and villages began to exude steam and smoke, like horses after galloping at full speed in the cold. The surface of the forests and the thorns on the bushes be-came blue as steel. All the glitter of the earth was suddenly extinguished, two or three stars rent the evening, then, from the mountain tops, the thickly heaped-up clouds dis-integrated slowly and snow began to fall again. Once night had closed in, nothing more could be seen. All that re-mained was to listen to the big clouds beating their wings across the forests.

After winter had settled, Toussaint had sent off his mes-senger. He had said to him: "Go and see Junie, and tell her: 'Your son is living; so is your husband. They are at Villevieille, at Toussaint's. Carry on as usual, and don't worry. They'll come back as soon as they can.' "

For the time being, they could not leave.

To begin with, there were two things: one good in a way, the other bad. Maudru had gone to the gendarmes. The matter was known from the outset. Antonio could go out in the town, for he was little known. He walked down from the house on the hill, and went to scent the wind of the affair among the tanners, and even among Maudru's men. They met in a wine-shop of the lower town called "Diversion Inn." But, in spite of that, they refused to allow themselves to be "diverted," either by the name of the inn, or by drink. They all roared out their great ox-drovers' laugh, when they saw the letters of the sign painted the wrong way round on the panes.

"Who can divert us from our aim?" they cried, slapping their hands on the deal tables. "Who can divert the like of us?"

"Quite so," Antonio would say. "Let's drink some hot wine; never mind."

And surreptitiously he got to know about all the hidden things. He had come upon the tattooed man again, and said to him: "It's much better than on the road, down here. Let's have a drink."

It was soon done. The tattooed man had two ways of behaving. When in the company of his fellow-drovers, he would sit erect on his chair with his body thrown backwards, his legs wide apart, and one arm resting on the back of the chair. He would begin by saying: "It's like this," and would detail a long story, opening and shutting his fingers, and twirling his big, red moustache. You could say as often as you liked: "What the devil are you talking about?" He would go on until the big, silent drovers cut him short with great blows of their fists on the table. Then he would become sad and lost in dreams. He would gradually go towards Antonio's corner and become his own good-natured self.

He sat down with great peasant politeness. "Hallo. How's your mother?" he asked Antonio.

"I've told you ten times over, I've lost her."

He carefully wiped the table before him with his big rough hand. He kept looking down, sighing all the time, trying hard to find what kind and polite things he could say. Then: "Ah, what bad luck!" he sighed.

"Whose?" Antonio asked.

"Mine."

He looked right and left to see whether anybody was listening. He touched Antonio's arm. "It's like this," he said. "When I've seen something, I've got to talk about it. That's how it is. I can't keep it to myself. If I see a rat move, I have to cry out at once: 'Here's a rat moving,' or I go sick."

"What's bad in that?"

"It's not me, it's them. They're always doing things, and never talking. Secrets. I like talking. What's bad in that, when it's among friends, you and me, here, quiet as we are, what does it matter, eh?"

He winked. It was always a rather extraordinary operation. His head was soft and greasy. He had no hair on his skin. He had no need to scrape his face clean from time to time with a razor: his chin, lips, and cheeks had only a youngster's down, although he was of age. He winked slowly and very deliberately whenever he was pondering over something which he wanted to say in private. That was again his form of politeness, as if to make people understand at once all the roguery of what was coming. But in his soft face the wink made a deep hollow, formed wrinkles,

[155]

and pulled out his cheeks, so that he no longer had a man's face, but a face like a vine-stalk. "Ho," they would say to him, "never do that before a woman with child."

"It's like this," he said. "I've been to see the gendarmes today. Not alone; with Maudru. He said to them: 'Well, what are you doing?' 'Well, you see we're getting ready,' they said. 'What for?' 'We know the man who shot the nephew is in the town,' they said. He looked at them, wheezing. He set his teeth grating as if he was cracking nuts. Their rifles dropped from their hands on hearing him. 'Steady, Maudru,' said the sergeant. 'Steady, yourself,' Maudru answered. 'Where did you hear that somebody shot the nephew? Who told you so? It's always the same thing,' he said; 'the government feeds you like turkey-cocks. All you have to do is to eat and sleep, then your blood tells tales. The nephew got wounded all alone, that's how it happened.'

" 'In the belly,' said the chief gendarme; 'it's a bit difficult.' 'Of course, your own sister's less difficult,' Maudru answered, 'but I tell you, a thorn bush catching onto him, a loaded gun, and the belly of an ass in the way—all that could have made him fire on himself. And I maintain it.' 'All right,' said the gendarme, 'then we'll stand off if you want us to.' 'Exactly,' said Maudru, 'I'm big enough.' And as a matter of fact, his head touched their low ceiling."

"And the nephew," Antonio asked, "how is he getting on?"

"He's passing out," said the tattooed man, "but not without a bit of a yell. He can live ten days, twenty if you like, but he's done for. He's half in the coffin already."

"And Gina?"

[156]

"The old one?" said the tattooed man. "The devil has taken hold of her. Since then, she's been a bundle of wolf's nerves."

"After all," Sailor said, "that's luck. With the gendarmes, we'd have been done for. To begin with, he has cleared my twin at one stroke of responsibility for all that might happen afterwards if the other dies, since he has declared it an accident. Secondly, he means to square the account man to man, and there we can always come to an understanding, either . . ."

"Either what?" Antonio said. "There's no 'either' about it. All we can expect is to lose either side in a free fight."

"That's what I mean," Sailor said. "But either night, or luck, or chance . . . With the gendarmes, there was neither luck nor chance; and night does not set on the gendarme country. That settles it for me."

"Did you sleep last night?"

Toussaint's house was all hollowed out with small vaulted cells, hewn in the walls. Their narrow windows opened on a high gallery overlooking the town, the fields, and the frozen forests. Two cells were bedrooms for Sailor and Antonio.

"I slept."

"I didn't," said Antonio, "and I heard. They sleep down below. She's again torn him to bits. Who knows what reckoning is in store for him? A man who has a wife like her, with all the words she says, may some day or other have a rather extraordinary reckoning. . . ."

They stood for a moment listening to the stillness of winter outside.

[157]

"All the more so, as she is in the right," Antonio said.

And then there had been the twin's adventure.

The drover who kept watch over the outpost of Puber-claire went out every morning when the farm was still asleep. He put on his snow-shoes and walked slowly along the outskirts of the Golden Wood. The sun had scarcely emerged from the mountains, and rose with a trail of reddish mist. Beyond the wood, the path ran across the open fields. At that time of day the bullocks' enclosures were still deserted. The snow was two-thirds of the way up the fence. The drover had a bearskin cap, two big necker-chiefs tied one over the other, a leather coat, sheepskin mufflers, and otter leggings strapped along his legs from his ankles up to his hips. He was heavy. He walked slowly. He just moved as much as was necessary. He had not yet put on his black silken mask, for the snow at so early an hour did not dazzle. He went straight into the open fields, turned left, plodded up Biéchard Hill, and went down the other side. He could no longer see the farm-house. He be-gan to see the river rolling its tarry waters between its icy banks. At the place called "the pear-tree enclosure" he went along the high cliff called the Ark. That was the shelter of the "houldres" and of all the birds (one or two of each breed) that carried spring in their throats. As usual, the sun already struck full on the rock wall, too steep to hold the snow, and the holes in the stone were prattling with a tiny bird's song, sung with the tip of the beak. A hazel-grouse rolled about in the snow, then hopped along, shak-ing its feathers.

"Fine morning," thought the drover. "They are re-

[1 5 8]

hearsing spring in the Ark. It's still far off, friends," he said
to the birds. "Luckily. What a flood we're going to have
when the thaw comes. You don't care a fig, with your wings
. . . but I, with my feet . . ."

Just as he got to Journas Heights, he saw a man below
who was making his way from the town. He was going very
quickly. Under his feet he had no snow-shoes, but long
boards like skis, the kind of thing which, in the high
mountains known as Upper Rebeillard, they usually call
"plaques."

"That's funny," the drover said. It was not the custom
down here, where winter was a slow season.

Down below, the man sped on, faster than a horse. He
pushed himself along with two sticks. The snow-field
stretched out in long waves, with hollows, ascents, and
slopes. The man flew over it like a bird. He was lightly and
loosely clad. He opened out his long legs. He shut them
again. He swung his sticks. He bent his body to the left,
to the right, to the left, to the right, swaying to and fro as
he glided at full speed on his boards, down the steepest
slopes, up the banks, on the ridges, then he dived and
seemed to sink into the snow. He disappeared, then emerged
further on, with his arms uplifted, rushing along at full
breast. He leaned forward, crouched, leaped, and glided
along again. He skimmed along the ground like a swallow
beaten down by a storm. Now he faced a row of willows.
He rushed headlong toward it with his arms folded, and
went through it in a sprinkling of snow-dust which the sun,
now higher up, lit up like lightning.

"There's a determined chap," thought the drover. "By
Jove, yes." He began to plod down the hillside towards the

[159]

willows through which the man had dashed. He had got interested in that headlong course. "I'll go and see," he thought.

On the other side of the curtain of willows, the twin, dazzled by snow-dust, turned his boards, squatted down, and stopped. Ever since Villevieille he had been rushing along at this wild pace. Nobody. He was alone. He looked towards the river. He knew the place, the winding creek where he had marked his timber. His large raft was sleeping under the snow.

The twin was strong in loins and thighs. His little body was formidable and highly strung. All the strength of his peppery blood was there, on his hips, accumulated in two enormous sinews in the middle of his back, just as the strength of the bow is in the middle of the bow. There lay the spring of everything in him. The whole way down from Villevieille to that beach with the raft had been covered by the supple play of his thighs and his loins, from the time when, waking up, he had stridden over Gina's body as she was still sleeping, till now, when he was unlacing his boards. He pitched his sticks in the snow. He wore no gloves. His blood was hot enough. He felt the cold only a long time after others. He looked around. He was alone. He did not put on a silken mask. He was not dazzled by the sun. He sounded the snow. Half a man's length, and underneath he could hear the beams of the raft ringing. He cut the layer of ice with his ax and then began to dig. He could not yet set the raft free. He wanted to know whether the iron bands still held.

"Queer man," thought the drover. "What's his idea?"

He had now reached the willows. He had hidden himself under the boughs and was watching the work.

The twin was chopping in the ice with his big ax. He tried to move the tree-trunks down below.

"What's he after?" wondered the drover. "Maybe digging for gold? . . ."

He had spoken to himself, half laughingly. These boards and the mountain kit had made him think of those gold-diggers who get thin up there in Upper Rebeillard, but then, speaking of gold, the twin took off his cap to scratch his head. "Red Hair!"

The drover slunk away slowly. He was bewildered: more of shock than fright, but nevertheless rather at a loss to be so near Red Hair. The latter had an ax, and he had none; the other was nimble, and he was not.

The screen of willows stood between them. He did not go up to Journas, but sidled off towards the larches, following the skirt of the wood. There he was hidden five times out of ten. He took advantage of a nook in the trees to look down below; the other took no notice. He continued to dig into the ice with his ax. The drover thought: "If only we were half a dozen!"

But he had to go up to the farm, and hurry, for the team would soon be leaving for Villevieille, judging from the height of the sun.

He hurried as much as he could, and had reached Bié-chard when he saw in the distance, close to the farm, the men about to leave for the town.

He could not resist the temptation. He could not run. He said to himself: "I'll blow gently; the fellow will not hear it." He blew a soft call on his horn.

[161]

In the creek with the raft the twin stopped his ax. He had a sharp ear. He put on his boards. He glided as far as the willow screen. He looked about. A drover had come there on his snow-shoes. There he had lain; there he had gone back to the larches.

He took a sweeping glance all round. Journas Heights bulged up like a cow's back; between the bottom of the hill and the river he could still see the track of his own boards, but going that way now was out of the question, for it was hardly possible to set out before the drovers arrived. He was Red Hair for all that, whatever Gina might say. He returned cautiously to his hole. He went and looked at the river. It had shrunk, and was lying flat a good way below its banks. It was frozen over for some ten yards from the banks to the middle. From the colour of the ice, the twin understood that it would carry and that it was likely to do so all along the bank. It was smooth, clean, and went towards Villevieille, just like a road.

He unlaced his boards and disappeared into his hole. He cut a passage through the snow down to the river bank. He looked up. On Journas Heights the larch forest crackled as if a herd were walking across its frozen branches. The twin half opened his coat. Underneath it he carried two iron skates, hanging round his neck from a strap. He fixed them on his feet and waited. The whole place was deserted. The morning bell was pealing at Villevieille. The first drover emerged from Journas. He had snow-shoes, no gun, and was heavily dressed. All right. Two, three, four, then ten of them, black as wolves, issuing from the larches, then remaining there a minute or two on the ridge, looking at one another, watching all round. They all had snow-shoes, three of them carried guns, one on each flank, one in the middle. One of the drovers pointed with his stick to the round place down below between the willows and the river, with the hole in the centre where the twin was hiding. They started moving down slowly. The twin felt his skates. They held tight. All right. He came out of the hole. He pretended to be surprised and jumped back into the hole, as if to hide. He had shown his red hair.

At that moment the drovers' net was prepared as they wanted: they held all the ways. The gun on the left covered the river, so did the one on the right. The others covered the bare and flat snow-field in front of them where it would have been impossible to miss a black-headed pin. Now at last they held that fox-like man. They all shouted together. They tried to run with their fur-covered legs and their big snow-shoes. The twin crawled off along his snow passage. He went down to the river. The bank hid him from their view. He stamped on the ice: it was as solid as a rock. At one glide he darted to a recess in the bank, and crouched there. He heard the drover with the gun go past him above.

He let him go past. He darted straight ahead, while they fired far behind him into the empty hole. He turned round two great bends in the river, climbed on the bank, and put on his boards again. He pushed himself down the slope. At the ascent he slackened his speed by bending one of his knees. He looked round. Far off in the distance he could see black men, as small as ants. They were floundering heavily with their snow-shoes. They were probably shouting but he could not hear them. They were waving their arms about. One of them fired his gun. The twin saw the smoke. A short time after, he heard the report re-echoing in the resounding countryside, from the hill to the river, from the river to the fir wood, from the fir wood to the mountain, where it set the narrow gorges of the mountain ways ringing.

The hour struck at Villevieille.

The twin went a few steps towards the slope of the valley. He leaned forward. He glided slowly at first, then his weight, the slope, and the swing of his arms carried him away.

On the other side of the vale, the town came towards him, growing rapidly.

CHAPTER II

"Haven't you got anything to clean my pipe?"
Antonio asked.

"Yes," Toussaint answered. "Let me fetch you a cleaner."

He walked to the door at the far end. His thin legs
gently swayed his body, burdened with oversized shoulders.
His long arms paddled around him. ("He walks like a
ship," Sailor had said. "I've been thinking of ships a lot
for some time; what does it mean?")

"Bring the lamp," Toussaint said. It was the first time
he had opened the door at the far end.

"Will the man you've sent to Nibles soon be back?"
asked Antonio.

"Usually it takes him six days. Today is already the
tenth, but we're in the heart of winter." He trimmed the
wick of the lamp. "Foul weather," he said.

All around the house, the wind rattled like a cart-load
of planks. On the threshold, Toussaint looked at Antonio.
"Where's Sailor?" he asked.

"Sleeping."

"Has he spoken of the sea again?"

"Yes."

"Bad omen," he said.

Whenever a lamp was carried into a room of that enormous house, the light took fright. It suddenly opened out two great golden wings, then crouched in the lamp, ready to die out. Toussaint quieted it with his white hand circling round on top of the lamp-glass.

"Yes," he said, "the man of Nibles may stay ten days or two months—one never knows."

"I've given him an errand," said Antonio.

"Far from Nibles?"

"No, at a woman's, called the mother of the road."

"I didn't ask you that," Toussaint said.

"Yet, I'd like you to know," answered Antonio.

The hunchback glanced at him over his bad shoulder. "Speak," he said. He secured the foot of the lamp between two big mountain stones.

"It's hard to tell you," Antonio said.

Toussaint's eyes were brimless: a great, bright light, almost still.

"Oh, it's only a woman," said Antonio. "Don't worry."

"Till now you've lived by yourself?"

"Yes."

"I wonder whether I can speak to you as I sometimes speak to myself," said Toussaint; "but I think so. You're a man of the country to the core, aren't you?"

He opened and shut his fingers as if, from time to time, flowers were being born out of the palm of his hand.

"I'll speak to you as I do to myself, shall I?"

"Yes," said Antonio, "speak. But don't forget I've mainly been brought up with fishes. I'm quite ignorant."

"Yes. But you've felt a lot. You're one of those men who can be compared to axles. You go your own way smoothly,

[166]

but you feel the wheel circling around you. How old are you? What have you done about women up to now? Why do you say: 'Only a woman'? Why do you say: 'Don't worry'? It's not 'only' that you should say, for it always means anxiety when something changes. . . ."

Antonio smiled. "You say: 'I'm going to speak,'" he said, "then you ask: 'Why, why?' I can't explain anything to you. What have I done about women? When I wanted one, I went down to the lower country and I could always find one. I'm forty. Now, it's quite another thing. Very simple indeed. On my way here with Sailor, we found a woman in the woods. All that meant more to me than just a fine lass, spring, and the twin. That woman was being delivered of a child in the brushwood, just like a sow. I carried her on my shoulder, I found a bed for her, warmed her up, washed her. She's blind. Before going, I told her: 'Wait for me.' I couldn't say anything else to her."

"You want to keep her with you?"

"Yes."

"Blind?"

"Why not? I'll teach her all the banks of my island. The river spreads all around; she'll run no risk, she'll only have to listen to that voice before stepping forward."

"Here's the cleaner. Clean your pipe."

Antonio sniffed all round. "There's a smell here."

"It smells a little of ether," Toussaint said.

The room was very sensitive to wind. Long eddying draughts fluttered about the lamp, rubbed against its glass, and the frightened flame flapped its wings wildly. One could make out in the shadows a broad chest-of-drawers,

[167]

and two or three tables pushed against the walls, on which bursts of light illuminated glass bowls, small glazed cases, tubes, and a big glass jar.

"I've dead insects here," said Toussaint. "Come along."

They drew near the table. It also carried a load of stones and herbs like the table in the room into which Toussaint ushered his patients.

"Take this lens. Look at this stone here."

Antonio turned the stone over in his hand. "It's fine," he said. "A bit soapy."

"Look," said Toussaint. "It's like open country. You see these green spots with their black enclosure, and those russet plains there with the thin dark line parting the fields. Seas, rivers, oceans, with their colours and their shapes. And it's merely a stone you've got in your hand. Do you know what all those coloured specks are? It's a small lichen, old as the world, living ever since the world was the world, still living, and not yet in bloom. One of our trees makes its own flower and sheds it again within four seasons. Just reckon a bit. Since thousands of years. What confidence! It's not bigger than a fly's hair, and it says: 'I've plenty of time.' Maybe if we looked at the world from on high, it would be the same, and we'd also say: 'What confidence! That's my game.'"

He moved his soft finger on the small universe of lichens. "There was a time," he added, "when I also thought of women. It was my biggest dispute with Sailor. It gives you so much strength, that for once I held my ground. Yet, it was the first time he was in the right and I wrong. Wait a minute, I'll show you some insects. Are you cold?"

"I am," Antonio said, "but never mind." He lit his pipe.

Toussaint went and fetched a glass bowl off a table in the shadows.

"It was a girl from down below," he said. "The strength from inside has nothing to do with this." He opened his arms to show his small warped wooden body and his thread-like limbs. "It's chiefly a matter of eyes and ears, and still, when I say 'matter' I mean genuine quality, and not that outward beauty which can be seen. You follow me? Look at this beetle; I call it 'Lady of the Moon.' Look, it's got moons all over its back. I prefer to give my own names. It's a matter of eyes and ears, indeed. You may touch it, it's not a goad. It looks frightful, but it's nothing: it's only the dibble for its eggs. With that, it can bury its eggs deep into the ground. A weapon of love. Yes, once I also had it in my head to . . . Understand me . . . I was younger . . . And it didn't go very far, though my mind was made up. At such moments you stand on a level with the greatest things: with whole countries carrying three rivers and two seas. . . .

"You see that female with her dibble. She bores through dry clods, and, down into the snug warm darkness she lets her eggs drop."

He remained silent for a time.

"You know the lower country well, don't you?"

"Yes," answered Antonio.

"You know Grand-Combe?"

"Yes."

"The slope up towards Chauplane . . . then the road makes three S's, and after that there's a house."

"Yes," said Antonio, "and then Marguerite."

"You know her?" Toussaint asked.

[169]

"I do."

"Well?" he asked after a pause.

"No," answered Antonio, "by sight."

"But you know her name."

"A man called her from the road. She came out of the house. I saw her; I was going to Chauplane."

Toussaint looked at the dead beetle.

"Then I suppose you can't tell me anything about her?"

"I can," said Antonio.

He drew two or three puffs from his pipe. Toussaint had put the beetle in the palm of his hand, and weighed it there.

"Hard to forget," said Antonio.

Toussaint looked straight into Antonio's eyes.

"I mean hard to forget, once one has seen her," pursued Antonio. "I was going to Chauplane. I stopped at the inn and asked: 'Who is the woman up there?' No need to say more. 'Marguerite,' they answered. 'Married?' 'Yes.' 'Long?' 'Three children, and still young,' they said. 'Obvious,' I said."

Again there was a pause.

"Happy?" Toussaint asked, as if speaking to himself. "Do you know?"

"It looks like it," Antonio answered.

A big winter star, fluffy with cold, illuminated the window.

"You believed, didn't you, that the earth was a joy-ball?" said Toussaint. He had resumed his child-like voice, with a light bird's warble entangled in the syllables.

"I don't believe anything," Antonio said.

"He who knows how to swim," went on Toussaint, "who can walk, who has strength in arms and thighs, who breathes well, who does good work, has the world on his side. He doesn't believe anything, right you are. Let's go near the fire; it's cold in here."

They returned to the other room where the fire rested peacefully between the big oak logs.

"No," Toussaint said, "the world is not a joy-ball. Give me the poker: these embers want stirring."

"It's warm enough," Antonio said, holding out his hands towards the blaze.

"My blood is weaker," said Toussaint. "I need a lot more fire for myself."

He thrust the poker into the fire, lifted the logs, and the blaze sprang out of the hearth showing its white belly.

"A big fire," he said. "World of necessity, not of joy. What confidence, I said a little while ago. So much confidence that we can no longer believe in confidence only. It's submission and obedience, that's what it is. Do you understand?"

"I'm listening," said Antonio.

"I myself have also obeyed," said Toussaint. In the shadows he followed the life of invisible beings. "I went and waited for her on the road," he said. "She stopped. You're looking at me?"

"Yes," answered Antonio.

"You've seen her, and you see me? You are right, that's the great thing."

"We're not strong only in our arms," said Antonio.

"You want to be polite," answered Toussaint.

"Not at all," said Antonio. "It's what I really think. Look: when Gina sits near you and you stroke her hair!"

"Kindness," Toussaint said, looking vacantly into the

[171]

distance, "maybe . . . When all's said and done, it's pretty much the same thing: looking after people. But there it wasn't the same thing at all.

"When you desire, you are not kind.

"It happened, as it might perhaps have happened to you; at least I say so to myself. It comforts me a bit—though all that's lost and over. Perhaps she saw me. If so, what am I to think? Perhaps she did not see me. That would be better. You know you don't always see people standing in front of you, do you?"

"No," answered Antonio, "I didn't know that."

"Well, she probably saw the man who spoke. She could shake hands with him. I've always had great strength of will. And I was longing so much.

"She gave me her hand," he said with his bird-like voice. "Yes, yes, she is mine in spite of her house at Chauplane, and her children, and her happiness. She is mine."

He got up. He stood a moment pondering, with his head lowered, shivering all over. He raised his head. He had his goat's eyes.

"Look," he said gently, "you're as tall sitting as I standing. I'd never noticed that. Let's see."

"You're taller," said Antonio.

"If you shrink down, of course, but stay as usual. Look. Taller sitting than I standing. That man on the road," he added, laying his hand on Antonio's shoulder, "was perhaps her husband."

"Maybe," Antonio answered.

"How big was he?" asked Toussaint.

"About my size," said Antonio.

"There you are." He sighed. "I'm selfish," he said.

"You wrong yourself," said Antonio. "Selfish? It's the last thing I would think about you. You're wicked only towards yourself. You cure people. Supposing you thought about curing yourself?"

"Selfish by compulsion," said Toussaint. "Alone. Alone in time, alone on earth. I can die tomorrow without leaving anybody's heart feeling empty."

"What about your patients?" asked Antonio.

"What the devil do I care!" Toussaint said. "I have them for myself, not for their own sake. Who walks by my side in life? Who's weak enough to want to go to bed with me? Who loves me? You understand: animal love? Listen."

He laid his hand on Antonio's knee. He raised his wretched face with its heavy eyes towards him.

"There are truths you can sense," he said, "and there are truths which I know. And what I know is greater. In summer, I go and hunt the Lady of the Moons in sand-pits. The sand is motionless, but the air above is restless. Then the sand begins to move, and the females come out. Thus, while you saw nothing, the sand was all bored through inside under the push of the females ascending from the bottom of the earth to meet the males. You see, that brown earth whose surface is smooth and still, but which writhes in the dark like molten iron in the fire. So much for them. And it's the same for others, green like chestnut shoots; for others again, blue like knife-blades, with a black spot on their heads; for brown ones like bricks; for those which are red all over; for black ones with green dots; for green ones with black dots; for round golden ones like small, dry onions; for long ones like pipe-stems; for hard and soft ones; for the sightless ones which make love while sleeping

[173]

like sacks being filled; and for the ones that shiver all over, more restless than the wind, which can look all around with their large crystal eyes. So much for love."

He tapped his hand on Antonio's knee.

"Seeing all that stir, you're led to think it's got some meaning: an air of joy, a blessing of the earth and of the sun which makes you rejoice. It's a chain, Antonio, the first link. All the rest begins from there. And I haven't yet made you touch the bitter core of those joys.

"You look at them: they make love. The earth has already crammed their heads with smells, and now it strikes with big hammers of joy on the shell of their skulls. You look at them: they are on with a frenzied, solemn toil, not much unlike pain. You feel quite clearly that they're not aware of it all. Obedience is obedience.

"That's the beginning, and all the rest must follow. Bellies are in a ferment. A steam like the breath of vats reeks on the world, flush with bushes and trees. Well, now, I'm sorry, but I can hardly tell you everything, and you already feel that if the flails of your arms strike for things like that, it's because somebody else holds the handles. Fights, sting for sting, eggs laid on the breasts of paralytics, meat carried about, beetles' skulls whitening deep in some hole by the side of a surfeited grub, butterflies' bodies sucked up like fruit, and carried away by the wind along with chaff. That's all.

"You said: 'Only a woman.' Good. Your bones are not yet crammed with powder like the barrels of a gun. Go on still making the best of fire and night."

The big clock was striking at the end of the passage.

[174]

"When I begin," Toussaint said, "time goes wrong. I'm thirsty. I'm going down to the water tank. Good night."

At the bottom of the passage, Antonio struck his lighter and looked at the clock. It was midnight.

He took off his shoes to go up the stairs silently. Upstairs the round window of the landing was filled with moonlight. The night wind had driven the clouds away. The whole country was visible: the black river, the snow-covered sleeping town, the hills with their pitch-dark shadows and their glittering crests. Over by the high mountains the sky was still murky and, now that the wind had abated, the long blue tentacles of the clouds started to grope again for the moon through the stars.

There was still a light in the twin's bedroom. It could be seen right round the door.

Antonio listened.

"Speak, now," said Gina.

"Yes," said the twin.

Then there was a long pause.

"That's what you wanted, you, son of the forests," she said (she hit her body with her hands), "this, my breasts, my belly, and this, here—and no more. That's all that you stared at through my dress, with your desire. Your eye has never really been keen enough to get into me beyond my skin."

"It has," said the twin.

"I'd like that to be true," she said, "but I've only to look at your eyes to know it isn't. What can you see with those eyes of yours? Nothing. Warm flesh, on which you burn to put your hand. That's all. What goes into you when you touch me? The warmth of my soft skin, that's all. You think some day you will be able to hear the noise of my blood? Never in your life! Deaf, deaf, that's what you are."

She remained for a while without speaking.

"And selfish, into the bargain," she added.

The bed creaked under the twin as he turned round.

"Selfish, me?"

"Yes, you. You've got selfish ears, eyes, and hands. You see for yourself, hear for yourself, touch and take for yourself. You look. You look at me. What do you see? You see nothing. You see for yourself. You see all the pleasure you can draw from it. Nothing more.

"Ah, God in heaven! What sort of a deal have You made? You were mad, weren't You? What have You given this creature, apart from his loins and his arms? Nothing.

"If I have a little warmth in me, it comes from Toussaint. Aren't you ashamed? At least he's plenty of heart given him for his share!

" 'When you're walking,' he said to me, 'it seems as if you were churning woman's milk. What children you'll make us, my girl!' "

"Wait a bit," said the twin. "You'll bear us some."

"I don't want any," cried Gina. "No," she said in a lower voice, "I don't want to bear you children. I'm not a mole to litter down in the dark, far from the sun, hidden, shut in among passages, walls, doors, and locks. I don't want to bear children and then be obliged to run away, carrying them between my teeth like a cat. You hear me? Your children? In the beginning when I said that, I said it to myself alone, making a channel with my hand from my mouth to my ear, and the inside of my belly was all soft with the idea. Now, I say No."

Again there was a pause.

"Or else, make me free," she said. Then some time after: "Give me a kiss."

Antonio began to climb the stairs, towards the upper story where he slept near Sailor. Half-way up, he heard her speak again. He stopped.

"You promised to give me the farm in the forest," she said. "We lie in other people's beds like cuckoos, and when I touch you, during the night, I hear in my hand your heart which says: I'm asleep, I'm asleep, I'm asleep . . ."

On the upper floor, the landing window opened onto the sky. Neither the town nor the valley could be seen, but only ghost-like mountains. Antonio went past Sailor's door.

"Is that you?"

"It's me," he said; "aren't you asleep?"

"Come in."

He pushed the door open. It was not shut, but just slightly ajar.

"He must have been waiting for me," thought Antonio. "Waiting for me?" he asked.

"I slept first," Sailor answered, "then I got up, and I half opened the door, to see you go past. . . . What's the time?"

"Past midnight."

"Come in," said Sailor to Antonio, who stood in the door-way. "Come right in, shut the door, and stay awhile with me. Perhaps I'll sleep afterwards."

"Shall I strike a light?" said Antonio. He had closed the

[1 7 7]

door, and the room was quite dark, for the window looked northward, on the opposite side from the moon.

"No, leave it dark, feel for the chair . . . sit down."

"Well, old man?" said Antonio after a time.

Downstairs they could hear the hum of Gina's voice still speaking. Toussaint's light and small step made the frozen snow in the garden crackle. The cry of a man mimicking a screech-owl sounded in the steep lanes. Another echo, then again another.

A final effort of the wind washed the face of the moon on the other side of the house. A faint white reflection lighted up the room.

"There," said Sailor, pointing to the window. Far into the night, the high, ice-clad mountains had started to glimmer. "I'm still thinking of the sea. Listen."

"No, it's Gina talking downstairs."

"Look," said Sailor. "The great ship has been moored just in front of us for three nights."

The moon lighted up the mountain tops. On the dark ocean of the valleys overbrimming with night, the lofty heap of rocks, snow-fields, and glaciers rose in the sky like a great three-master with all her sails unfurled.

"What ship?" asked Antonio.

Sailor pointed to the window.

"That one, there, outside."

"It's the mountain with the moon on the snow."

"No," answered Sailor, "it's the ship."

Outside, the mountain was creaking gently in the frost like a sailing-ship asleep on her moorings.

"I don't want to go," Sailor said. "I'm still wanted on

[178]

earth. And I tell her: 'Clear off, lift your anchor and put to sea.'"

"What do you think then?"

"The sea never lets you go. If she comes back, it's because my time is over here below."

"A bad dream," Antonio said.

The glaciers were swelling their top-sails in the night. The forests were rumbling.

"I'm bound for the shores of death," said Sailor.

"You've stayed too long without doing anything," Antonio answered. "Winter first, and then because we must prepare our stroke carefully, if we want to carry the twin and his wife off from this place, in spite of all those treacherous owls watching us. Another thing: we said we would get drunk. We've not done so. That's the truth."

"We'll do it," Sailor answered.

"Well, now, shut your trap, don't think of anything, get to sleep."

"Good night," Sailor said.

Antonio entered his room. He lighted the dip. The pork-dripping smoked, exuding kitchen smells. Antonio saw a fireplace full of blazing vine-branches, the black spit, and the golden pork-joint slowly turning. It was weeping into the dripping pan. The fat and the small bunch of black sage. The violet handle of the big meaty cutlet . . .

He carefully wrapped the foot of his bed in his sheep-skin cloak. He put out the candle. The sheets were icy. Then the bed stopped creaking. Antonio, lying motionless, with his arms pressed against his body, and his hands between his thighs, waited for the warmth to come.

It still smelt of savoury cooking, roasted meat, the hearth, ashes, the blaze, dripping, and the house.

"Life is short," he said without knowing why.

The warmth started to bathe his armpits, and he had loosened his arms a little. He stroked his thighs with his hands. He heard the softened noises of the night in a regular monotonous rhythm. He shut his eyes. He felt his blood pulsating in the nape of his neck. He said to himself: "Clara!"

A faint memory of the room, smelling of ether, stole into him. Between his half-closed eyelids, he could still see beyond the window white wings, a black carapace, and feelers, but he could not guess whether it was the moon beetle which he had seen that evening, all armed with love, pitching love into the earth with her egg-dibble, or else the keel, the sails, the rigging of the motionless ship of death.

Then he saw Clara's face with the mint-green eyes coming towards him, and he fell asleep.

CHAPTER III

On Sunday morning the three men got up at the black of dawn. The twin went down to the garden.

"Shall I help you?" Antonio asked.

"No, thanks, I'm going alone."

"Go under the fig tree," Antonio said, "and bring up the three big logs."

The twin was at the end of the passage, just on the first step. He looked round.

"I'd like you to go to the water tank," he said, "instead of my father."

"All right," cut in Antonio in a loud voice, "all right. Go along. I'll go to the water tank myself."

"What does he say?" called out Sailor from his room.

"He says I'm to go to the water tank," Antonio answered, "and we should like to see you a bit as well. We want you to chop wood. Come along."

A wintry dawn, blurred and wan, came in through the windows, through the joints of the front door, and through the three-barred panes of the fan-light. The house was still full of sonorous darkness. The twin came back from the garden and shut the door. Sailor came downstairs, walking in his thick linen slippers. Antonio pulled up the pails of water. He began to fill a huge cauldron hanging from the pot-hook in the living-room. The twin came in with big oak logs. Sailor knelt down near the fireplace, swept the ashes, and laid a fire with dry wood. He had brought in handfuls of resinous wood. The cauldron was hanging high up. There was enough room underneath to build a thoroughly good fire. Presently an enormous blaze shot up, and a noise of crushing and slaughter was heard when it began to lash round all those sticks dripping with oil. Then, the hollow roaring of the steady flame rose up the chimney.

Sailor shut the door. He touched the wall with the palm of his hand.

"It's already warm," he said.

The thick flames sputtered out of the hearth on all sides. White daylight mounted in the window. The twin cleared the middle of the room. He pushed the heavy table against the wall. He heaped the stools on the table. He swept the flagstones with a sedge-broom.

Sailor began to undress. Naked, he seemed to be touched both by the sharp cold of the window and by a tongue of flame.

"All right," he said.

In the town below, a church bell began to toll the morning angelus.

"Already warm?" Antonio asked.

"Yes. Need it. It's good. Not too hot. I like it," Sailor answered, his teeth chattering slightly.

He rubbed the white fleece on his breast with vigorous strokes. He seemed to take new life in the red bursts of flame. His broad, bare feet spread out on the floor. With great flutters, eddies of hot air beat all the hairs of his body. He straightened up his loins. Under his old skin the muscles

[182]

of his thighs swelled and girded his belly like the roots of a tree.

The twin and Antonio stripped off their clothes too. All three drew near the fireplace.

"The water isn't getting warm," Sailor said. "I'm tired of waiting for it."

"The cauldron's too high," said the twin. "I'll bring it down a bit."

He stepped onto the hearth-stone, and placed himself astride the fire. He caught the black handle with both hands, his arms turned inside. He took it off the hook.

"You'll burn yourself."

He made no answer. He panted between his tightened lips. He had all the weight of the water and of the cauldron at the end of his wrists. He hung the great mass on the lowest pot-hook, slowly, as if he didn't care about the flames which licked his arms, or about the weight.

He stretched himself to rest from the strain. Beside Antonio, golden all over, thanks to his life as a swimmer, and Sailor with his hairy body, the twin was white as milk. He did not give an impression of noble strength like Antonio, whose least gesture seemed to rest on the thickness of the air; he was broad-shouldered and rather square. Nor had his body that extraordinary mettle and temerity of Sailor's body, which one felt to be dependent on his head, and even completely carried away by his head into deeds and fights, with every sinew, every muscle, every bone as if moulded by obstinate sufferings. No, his stalwart body was unconscious, as it were. His breath scarcely made the point of his belly tremble. His well-undulated shoulders widened out like the ridge of a mountain. His head was like a child's, round, very small, and inflamed with red hair and eyebrows. There was another tuft of red hair at the sensitive joint of his thighs. As for the rest, his arms and legs were embedded in the block of his body as if in a rock.

The water was now singing.

"Turn round," the twin said to his father. He had taken a handful of box branches. He dipped them into the steaming water. He began to rub the old man's back.

"Strong. Quick. Hoo. Lower. There. Rub on. Good. Higher. Shoulder. Loins . . ."

Sailor was stamping and his bare feet clapped on the floor.

"Don't croak like a magpie," the twin said. "Meanwhile, Antonio, rub me," he said, "and afterwards I'll rub you down. Put your heart into it."

And he stood motionless while Antonio made him steam with the boiling water.

"Same for me," cried Antonio. "I'm frozen."

Sailor freed himself at one leap. The twin let his arms drop. Sailor thrashed Antonio with dry twigs.

"Rub with water, you bloody fool."

"It's to open the pores of your skin."

"They're open already."

"The shoulder, the shoulder," cried out the twin. "My shoulder's as cold as ice. Rub till you flay me, you damned idiot."

The three men were steaming like pork sausages just out of the copper.

Toussaint came in. He was wearing his great coarse cloth cloak and his boots, and he was bespattered with hoar-frost. He took off his fur cap. His face looked tired, his beard made black outlines along the wrinkles round his mouth, and his eyes were blood-shot from their long struggle against the night.

"Who's afraid of the white horse?" he said.

"What white horse?" asked the twin. He was still steaming with boiling water and blows.

"The horse of the mountains," Toussaint answered.

"I've never been afraid of a horse."

"One can never tell," said Toussaint. "That one frightens other people. Besides, after all, he belongs to your family. Only, I'd like to see you dressed. What I have to tell is serious. What a mania you have for stripping yourselves all the time."

"You shouldn't have gone out alone," Sailor said.

"I don't risk anything," Toussaint answered; "wherever I go, I run no risk. I'm attended, warmed, dragged, carried. I don't even have to move my little finger. Hurry up. Put your clothes on. How can you be naked so early in the morning? What sport! So you like to be naked, do you? What do you do? D'you stare at one another? Finger one another? What sport! Hurry up."

"We're rousing one another's blood," said Antonio.

"I'm bringing something that will rouse it much more," said Toussaint, and he took off his cloak. Underneath he was wrapped in furs. Over his sheepskin he wore a long, leather coat which reached below his waist. It was so big that he had to turn up the sleeves and tighten the collar of cat's fur.

He looked at Antonio. "I think we'll need you," he said. "So much the worse. If things come to fighting, fight you must."

Antonio remained silent and merely waved his hand as if to say: Please yourself. The fire dropped. The water was simmering quietly.

"The nephew's dead," said Toussaint.

Day now lighted up the whole window.

"Médéric, son of Gina Maudru and, I believe, of Carle of Rustrel. He's dead. It happened last night. And they say already that the evil horse is galloping on Maladrerie Heights. Put some wood on the fire. . . . Yes, Médéric, Gina's son," he added.

"Where have you come from?" asked Sailor.

The three men had put their clothes on.

"From over there," said Toussaint. "From the bull farm. I don't think you saw him," he said sadly. "I've been there every night. Pain draws me. It may be that. And I saw him suffer, but he was a man. Maybe his hands were a bit quick with the younger Gina. Yours. But he was very much attracted by her. He spoke. On the last day, the last night. A few hours more, and then time to speak is gone for ever, that's why one speaks. He wanted more of her than going to bed with her. He found himself before your gun."

He looked at the twin. "Your head is very small indeed, my lad. It's no bigger than a man's fist on your shoulders. The order of things is sometimes very difficult to understand," he said, speaking to himself. "Well, all's over! He's dead!"

"It seems as if you were sorry about it," said Antonio.

"Yes," said Toussaint curtly, then he noticed that it was Antonio who had spoken. "Yes, I am sorry about it," he went on. "He had begun to love that girl long before the twin. He was twenty-five years older than she. I think he made of her"—he stopped speaking and looked at the twin and Sailor sitting on the hearth-stone, listening to him— "he made of her in his heart what I myself did in a similar case. He was twenty-five years older . . . and I with my hump. I saw all that through him. It hurt him more than your shot, Twin. Yet, it was your shot that killed him.

"Ah," he said, straightening up, "you can't understand!"

He was agitated by a dull anger which excited his arms and legs, and filled his voice with manly tones.

"Now I know what sort he was, I should have preferred him to have had that girl, instead of you. It was so much like myself."

The sleeves of his leather coat had unrolled while he was moving about.

"Antonio, help me take this off. It was cold," he said. "They gave it to me; it's his coat. His arms were longer than mine, he was bigger. No, it doesn't fit me. Throw it away."

"Give it to me," said the twin.

He touched the suppleness of the leather, sniffed at the smell of the man which had remained in the fur collar.

"You said he wanted Gina?" he asked.

"Yes," answered Toussaint. "He wanted to leave for Champsaur with her, to take her high up, yonder, in the mountains, to be alone with her. Below them, from east to west, there would have been three hundred kilometres of open country, with valleys, rivers, farmsteads, pastures, and villages. These are ideas that come into your head when you yearn for a woman and when you feel rather weakly,

[187]

either on account"—his soft hand went round his face—"on account of your looks or your age. I know it well. A desire to be a long way off.

"What do you mean by sticking your nose into that cat's fur?"

"It smells of the nephew," said the twin. "It has his smell all over it. It stinks." He touched the coat collar. "He's dead. Good." He dropped the coat at his feet.

"You were on the same track," Toussaint said.

"And he happened to stand before my gun," said the twin.

"If it were to happen over again . . ."

"If it were to happen over again," said the twin calmly, "I would do just what I did, I would take my aim at him with the same eye, and fire off my two barrels at one shot into his belly—just as I did."

"Yes, but I say that I myself," Toussaint went on (he was wringing his thin hands, and the whole of his small, black, cricket-like body was quivering, while his fine goat's eyes were looking into the distance), "I say that if I myself had to do all over again what I've done since you've been here, I would do it otherwise. What are you looking at me like that for, Sailor? Yes, that's what I say. Your son came and spoke to me of love. Ah, he spoke of love. What can I do when people speak to me of love, to me, what can I do?"

He calmed down. "I have my own reasons for always believing in great things. I believed. I'm not sorry to have believed. I always give a chance. Love! And such a fine man. I must have believed that I saw before me, in the body of your twin, a part of myself, something of my old

[188]

desire. And that it was going to be satisfied. And what has he done, I ask you? The other man has also spoken to me of love. It's the other man who was like me, it's the other man I ought to have helped. It's the other man who would have done it."

"What would he have done?" asked the twin.

"The desire to be a long way off," said Toussaint.

Sailor rose to his feet. "You're still the old Jérôme," he said. "You changed your name for nothing, I'm sure. You flutter from one place to another like a swallow."

"To be away," said Toussaint. "Life. Order. Love is always to carry somebody off on horseback."

"That's what we're here for," said Antonio. "Steady, please, steady."

He raised his hand. Gina was heard coming in the passage. She was singing:

> ". . . with the carters of the whole parish
> This way and that, for my happiness . . ."

Antonio opened the door.

"What are you singing?"

"What I've a mind to."

"Your song isn't beautiful."

"It is for me."

"Go and make some coffee."

He shut the door.

"Now, I've something to tell you," he said loudly.

Toussaint turned his wild eyes towards him. He pointed to the door. "She's listening," he whispered.

"Well," said Antonio. "Champsaur, three hundred kilometres of open country. Good. But you forget this: a woman

[189]

goes to bed. If she does so with the man she has chosen, and if they agree, her body is happy. What has she to complain about? It's something. Maybe more than all the rest. Even if she has only that. It's all very well for you to say now that you would choose the other if it were still possible. But the point is that she has chosen this man here. You've got nothing to choose. She's the one who did the choosing. It's this man you must help.

"You may go and make the coffee!" he cried. "Get along, Gina."

She was heard going along the passage. She opened the kitchen door. She shut it gently behind her.

"It's this man you've got to help," said Antonio softly. He leaned over Toussaint. He laid his hand on his shoulder. Toussaint touched Antonio's hand, and stroked it with his limp fingers.

"Uncle," said Antonio, "you're right and you're wrong. Gina is right and wrong, too. You must always tell her she's wrong. The conclusion of the story lies with that man." He pointed to the twin.

The twin had spread out the dead man's coat. He was examining it. He fingered the supple leather. "It ought to fit me," he said. He put his arms into the sleeves. He drew up the shoulders. It did fit. It was even a shade small. "I'll keep it," he said, "after all. . . ."

Day by now had completely risen. A cloud sailed in front of the window. It was a dull Sunday. The thud of the tanners' fulling-mills, the songs which at times issued out of the work-shops, the rumble of the heavy iron gates which were opened to throw the old tan-bark into the river, everything was now hushed. A sharp, bitter north wind whistled in the tiled eaves of the roof. A shutter banged against the window of an empty room. In the depths of the silence, one could hear the creaking of the frozen mountains.

"What did you mean about the horse?" Antonio asked.

The big, surfeited fire silently spread out its glowing embers.

"When a Maudru dies," Toussaint answered, "the saying is that a big horse gallops away up there on the mountain top."

"And what of it?"

"Each time he carries somebody off."

"Where to?"

"Who knows? Where do you imagine? The fact is, sometimes one finds them dead at the foot of the peaks. Or else, they vanish without a trace."

"Old wives' tales," said Antonio.

"Yes," Toussaint answered. "But, to make it short, here's the point: Old Gina intends to do something. Her son has been killed and she wants her share of ceremonies and battles."

"I'm ready for her," said the twin.

"Even alone," Toussaint went on, "I would probably put the odds on her side. Ceremonies? She knows all about them. The nephew will be buried at Maladrerie with all Gina's husbands. It's up there, in the mountain. Ceremonies? She'll revive every bit of the ancient drovers' customs. The show will be worth seeing, I can tell you. Ceremonies? She's already assigned watches to the drovers in and around the farm. Fires, and everybody awake. The nephew alone has a right to sleep there now. Pailfuls of wine.

She herself goes from one group to the other, telling tales. The whole camp is astir."

"What about me, then, since you said I'd . . . ?" Antonio asked.

"Wait a bit. The burial feast will take place at Maladrerie, up there. In this town Maudru gives work to tanners, rope-makers, and iron-mongers. He's got supporters. Up there, you can count them, and know who they are.

"It's the tattooed man who'll go there to dig the grave. Go with him, and stay with him. Listen, look, and try to find out what they're going to do. I don't know," he added, "but it seems to me as if I'm betraying everything. I've little confidence left in you, Twin, and the other fellow's dead. I've still got his cries in my ears. Lies. Lies, everywhere in life. Only pain admits no lies—and you'll never be able to suffer, not you."

At about ten o'clock in the morning, the sky seemed to be startled. A patch of blue rent the clouds, and the north wind shook the trees two or three times, raising a puff of hoar-frost. Afterwards there was a great hush. The river could not be seen. It lay under the mist. Then it began to move its big thighs under the ice. It could be heard crackling and stirring, and there was a noise like the rubbing of big scales against gravel banks. There was no doubt about it: in spite of winter, the river warmed itself with its great movements, and when the rising mist stopped up the whole sky, spreading a pale, grey light, uncertain and almost warm, in the place of the glittering frost, one could see that all the ice on the river was drifting slowly southwards.

"Hallo," cried Antonio. He beckoned to the tattooed

man who was walking in front of him. They both leaned over the embankment.

"One, two, three, four; one, two, three, four," said the tattooed man, counting on his fingers. "November moon, Christmas moon, January moon—no, not possible."

They were looking at the river below them. The ice was drifting down gently without cracking.

"It's a mild day," Antonio said. "Happens like that sometimes. Means nothing."

"No," said the tattooed man, "nothing at all. The river moves, but the mountain doesn't."

"So much the better, today."

"Let's cross over the bridge," said the tattooed man. "We must first climb up behind the Blackbird Tannery. That's the way, by your leave, I'll explain it to you. Have you got your pickax?"

"Yes, carry on."

"To begin with, we won't take Gina's route. We're on foot, and for that matter, taking her way on a mild day like this we might get in for an avalanche. This way, we've got forests, forests, and more forests, then a short open space above, and, immediately after, Maladrerie. The fact is," he said, looking at the river, "it's really going. January moon, it's hardly possible."

They entered the forest. Down below, the town called two or three times with the clapping of shutters and the long creaking of a cart crossing the bridge. Then it ceased to give voice. The river was brewing something underhand, but seen from on high, through the white boughs of the first firs, it was dead. The silence of the forest closed on the men at every step.

[193]

"You'll dig the grave for me?" asked the tattooed man. "It's agreed, isn't it?"

"Agreed," Antonio answered.

"I'm too upset," said the tattooed man.

"No," said Antonio, "but you're afraid of the horse."

"Yes," he answered.

The trees and the mountains were petrified under the white dust of the cold. Not a quivering of branches, not a breath from the alpine meadows: a mineral silence. Forces were asleep in the vast muddy sky. Time slowly drew them towards the awakening. Already they were warm. A lump of snow fell from a fir. The bough scarcely moved. In a moment it was motionless as before. Nothing was ready. No birds. The snow was untrodden. No tracks, except the imprints of the wind during the night gone by.

At Fangas clearing, Antonio stopped.

"Tired?"

"No."

The forest and the mountain opened out onto the plain in front of them. Down below they could see a reach of river in the snow.

"It's moving," said Antonio.

At last there was something astir in the world, at the bottom of that gulf which the tortuous river scooped out in the white fields: a stretch of open water, shining like tar, was becoming larger.

"Nobody abroad," said the man. "We'll be alone." He pointed to the mule track on the other side of the river, ascending in the distance up the southern flank of the mountain.

Their snow-shoes sank two fingers' breadth into the snow. It began to be hard to pull them out of it.

"Dust," said the tattooed man.

They followed a steep mountain path, with trees above and below.

"Forward."

The mountain rose steeply in front of them now. They had to cut footholds with the edge of their snow-shoes before climbing. They ascended slowly like this, first along by the trees and then above them. An awful emptiness opened up below them down to the bottom of the valley where smoke and mist trailed along the snow-fields. Their fur leggings and ox-hide coats were telling heavily on every joint of their legs and arms.

The tattooed man made sure of his footing, stepped, and looked round at Antonio below him. "We are in the haunts of the horse," he said. "It's agreed that it's you who are going to dig the nephew's grave, isn't it?"

"Agreed," Antonio answered.

He cut another foothold with the edge of his snow-shoe.

The grey fur of the trees was far below now, and appeared quite small.

"Dust," said the tattooed man.

Some snow-dust slipped away. The mountain panted like a man's breast, then stopped.

The tattooed man put his big muffler in front of his mouth. "Slowly," he whispered.

The whole snow slope had become alive.

"Left," he said. "There."

Antonio thrust his left snow-shoe in the place indicated.

"Your weight," said the tattooed man. And he leant forward. Antonio leant forward.

"Your hand."

Antonio put his hand on the snow. He was now leaning on the slope. He touched the mountain with his whole body. The white abyss of the valley gently uttered its faint dismal whistling. The sound was so sweet that it softened the nerves and muscles, and loosened the grasp of hands and feet. Antonio's head was heavier than the whole mountain. The snow-fields below were heaving like a world hurricane. At times they would rise at full speed with their load of river and trees, as high as Antonio himself; he had only to take a step out of the slope to be sheltered. Then they would crumble down at great speed; they were still a long way below, and there was no need to move at all.

"Right," said the tattooed man.

Antonio got a footing with his right snow-shoe.

"Left."

Antonio placed his left snow-shoe.

"Hand.

"Up.

"Wait.

"Right.

"It's safe.

"Hand."

They went higher and higher up that steep slope which was ready to crash down towards the river and was pregnant with eager life within.

"Listen," said the tattooed man, after the pause. "Don't look up. Come up slowly. Take this root. Heave yourself up on your arms."

Antonio looked at his chest. He lifted himself up without moving his head. In front of him, his eye picked out a big black root with a layer of snow on top. He clutched at it with an eager hand. He pulled with all his might. He emerged up to the waist amidst a sparse pine wood. The top! He flung himself forward. He fell on the snow. He closed his eyes. He heard the tattooed man fall near him.

"There," he said.

"Come and see the way we came up."

They crawled to the brink. They could see a gigantic mass of snow-dust galloping right along the snow-field, rearing over the abyss, wrapped in its flowing marble mane.

"The horse," Antonio said.

"Yes," said the tattooed man.

They rose to their feet. It was the summit of a first escarpment of the mountain. On the opposite side of the wood, through the tree-trunks, they could see the ground curve down into a deep coomb where the snow was so thick that in spite of the murky daylight it had reflections like still water. Beyond rose the steep, bare rocks, vanishing into the clouds.

"Maladrerie," said the tattooed man.

"Where?"

"Here. You're looking for the farm"—he took off his right muffler and blew his nose between his fingers—"but first," he said, "we were off so quick, I didn't have the time to ask you. How's your mother?"

He started to laugh, shaking the icicles off his moustache.

"The farm's there, in the hollow. You can't see it. It's got its back to us this way. It's a low house: snow and roof all mixed up. There. Look. That big blot. That's it. In summer, in this hollow here, there's grass growing taller than you, and the quality's so good that you can smell it from the other side of the mountains. Before Gina's time, shepherds from the plains came up here with their herds on the first of June like clockwork. We asked them: 'Who told you the grass was ripe?' 'We smelt the wind,' they said.

"She lived there," he added after a short pause. "You'll see the house tonight. Coming to the feast? Come on, come to the feast. I can't exactly invite you, but I tell you: Come to the feast. You'll see. The burial ground is on that side. Come along."

There was not much snow on that summit, a thin layer only, with wisps of grass sticking out, for the wind of the past days had swept across it.

"Here's the burial ground."

It was a grove of slender trees too spindle-shaped to retain any snow. They were shining with a rich green fullness, thick and densely foliaged, like pillars. Antonio knew them for Italian cypresses. All the way round, a wall of huge stones separated them from the living mountain.

"She's buried them here," said the tattooed man. "One after the other. Walk around. You'll see a small gate. Look for a place for the nephew."

He looked up at the heavy, warm sky, in which the mist had gradually curdled into big clouds.

"The wind almost always comes from there," he said, pointing northwards. "Find a shelter for him near the wall or among the trees."

He stepped forward as if to go, then looked round. "Among the trees, that's it. Do it as if you were looking after yourself. One never knows. For that matter, how can we say that nothing remains behind?"

He turned round and came back towards Antonio.

"Look here," he said, laying his hand on his shoulder, "I've something to tell you. If it had been for myself, I wouldn't have put this wall all round. It cuts off the view. Listen: I'd like the nephew to have a fine view. Will you give a hand afterwards?"

"Why not?" Antonio answered. "I understand."

"We'll come," said the tattooed man, pointing to the wall, "we'll open these stones. It'll take two of us. Then, high up as he'll be, he'll see all the valley and the changing weather on the earth. Snow, grass, snow, grass," he said, swinging his hand to imitate the ebb and flow of seasons. "Snow, grass"—he lifted a finger—"one never knows . . ."

He went off towards the farm. From time to time, as he walked, he continued to swing his hand from summer to winter.

Antonio looked all around him. It seemed to be about three o'clock in the afternoon.

He entered the cemetery. Whole rocks without name or mark had been laid at the heads of the dead. He looked for a place near the cypresses. From there, when the stones of the enclosing wall were cleared, the dead man would have a fine view. He undid the pick from his belt. He took off his mufflers. It was not too cold.

There hung about the place a deeper silence than in the surrounding wood. It came from the cypresses. Like big sponges they drank in all the scattered noises, and they let flow from their foliage only a monotonous rumble which was like the deep heart of silence.

Antonio started to remove the snow. The black earth appeared. He cleared a fairly wide rectangle, the size of a man, two paces lengthwise and a good stride for the breadth of the shoulders. He began to dig. It was schist, already rotted through by frost.

The day was slowly waning. Dusk already blurred the distance. A pool of night was growing down below on the snow-fields, as if all the black water of the river had been suddenly roused and were overwhelming the valley.

"How's the work going on?" asked a voice.

Antonio looked up. He could see nobody.

"Here," the voice said again. It was a tree-and-stone voice, like the rumble of the forest from echo to echo. The man was sitting on the edge of the wall.

"Pretty well," Antonio said.

The man jumped into the snow. He walked with legs thrown apart, as horsemen do. His right leg was slower than his left, and less supple. At every step, he drew forward by an effort from his hip.

"What length?" he asked.

"Two strides."

"Breadth?"

"One."

"Depth?"

Antonio was already knee-deep in the earth.

"Good. Did they tell you to dig there?"

"No," said Antonio. "It's my own fancy."

"It's rather near the trees." There was tenderness hidden in the voice.

"It'll make them grow," said Antonio.

"True," said the man.

His head was poised directly on his broad shoulders. His chin touched his breast. He could look around him only by turning his whole body. He must have shaved from time to time, for his beard was straight as millet.

"I think it's deep enough," he said.

"Just a bit more," Antonio answered.

The man waited until he had finished clearing the bottom of the grave, then he held out his hand to help him up.

"What part of the country are you from?" he asked.

"Too long a tale," answered Antonio, and with a sweeping gesture of his hand he showed the whole world beneath them.

"You didn't come by the road, did you?"

"No," Antonio answered, "by the cliff."

They both walked towards the brink of the cliff, because there was still some light left through the trees. The man dug a furrow in the snow with his dragging leg.

"There," Antonio said.

The snow-fields slipped down, smooth as a steel blade; the night frost made the snow shrink.

"It's steep," said the man. Then: "Are you in a hurry?"

"No, I'm waiting for the body."

"So am I," said the man. "Let's sit down. We've only to button up our coats. Do you smoke?"

"Yes."

"Let's have a smoke."

They filled their pipes.

"This is the birch district," the man said. "You can't imagine what spring means here. These trees which are

[201]

like new-born calves. The skin, the slobber, the smell! . . ."

One could feel that he spoke only to ward off some worry or other.

Antonio looked down to the valley. A long, gleaming caterpillar crept along the snow-fields.

"The procession has left?" he said.

"Yes," said the man, "I've seen it."

There was such a display of torches down below that they lighted up the faces of the fields and the nocturnal woods.

"The dead are luckier than we," said the man.

"Not sure," said Antonio.

On reaching the top of the steep slope, when rolling in the snow, he had thought of the blind woman. Before nightfall, he had surveyed the wide stretch of the country under him and wondered: Where is she? There, or over there, or there again, far away, behind that blue mountain? Now, she was beside him, between him and that big man whose voice was gruff and kind.

"I thought you were older," said the man.

Along the whole length of the procession, they could see in the night the shining foliage of beeches, the white shoulders of hillsides, the black mouth of a ravine, the eye of a farm-window, against which wavered the flickering flame of torches.

"How young you are!" he went on.

"Not if you reckon from the day of my birth," Antonio answered.

"What then?"

"All the rest," said Antonio.

"Meaning what?"

"Too long a tale . . ."

He was preoccupied by that mint-eyed, shadowy woman, relying on him in her weakness, blind as she was.

Down below, the procession had just reached the mountain slope. Now and again a horseman rode forward, gliding like a star on the snow, to light up the shiny muzzle of rocks and the network of forests. He came to a standstill, lighted up by his flickering torch; he blew his horn to direct the procession towards him.

The man struck his lighter. He blew on the tinder to make the fire bigger and light the bottom of his pipe. His mouth was big, with ill-shaped lips, his nose like a dog's, with wide nostrils, and his cheeks were strong, all bones and skin. Over the glow of the tinder, he glanced at Antonio. His look explained his voice.

"Those who lie here," he said, "have never been as happy as since they are here. Are you married?"

"Yes," said Antonio, after a pause.

"What drives us to it?" asked the man.

"Everything," Antonio said.

"The dead are luckier than we." The man lowered his voice. It was now all kindness, and the fierceness of his words which sometimes rumbled more loudly in his throat was but the fierceness of a suffering man. "I've been married too. Why me? Why did she say Yes, I wonder? Why did I try and marry? Because everything drove me to it. You've hit it. And yet what is that force? Have you hunted?"

"Yes, fished mainly, mainly fishing. I'm a man of the river."

"Right, but you've hunted too?"

[203]

"Yes."

"Big game?"

"Wild boars. That's what we've got in my country."

"In what season are your battues?"

"Latter part of spring, on the borders of the wheatfields. Autumn as well."

"Wild boars which take you against the wind and make themselves at home. They wash their bellies and thighs in the dust, swallow long, black worms with their snouts upturned. Or else you can see the dam and her litter running about."

"That's it."

"Then you know. Good. I can speak to animals. There's no wizard's trick in that. Only natural. I don't mean I've spoken to wild boars. No. Only bulls."

"What's your name?" Antonio asked.

"Maudru.

"I've been married," he said after a pause. "A tanner's daughter. How much your hides? So much. I've never changed my mind all my life, but custom is custom. We went in, we drank a pint. She went to the cupboard, wiped the glasses, and handed them round: here's yours, here's mine, bang on the table. She brought in the bottle. She poured out. She leant her head aslant as she poured. Just to look at the brim, and not to spill the liquor. One day, at the farm, my sister helped me to a drink. Lean a bit more, I say to her. No, not the same. All day long I had the other way of leaning before my eyes. Nothing like it. Neither that, nor the fingers, nor the motion. Only going to the cupboard, opening it, taking the glasses, turning round, coming towards the table where I sat, only that. You might have put a thousand women to it, not one would have done it like that. But she could do it, she could. I wonder . . . Finally, I proposed to her. She said Yes."

His words rose painfully to his mouth and he breathed noisily over it all, like a strong wind on sprouting weeds.

"I'm boring you, am I?" he said.

"No."

"It's like a command," he went on. "What are you doing in life? Bull-raising? Farming? Your own strength . . . Your strength and yourself . . . No, ten times no. I say to you: that girl, that girl only. The movement of her body. There she walks. She stoops, raises herself, opens her arms, shuts them, takes a breath. She goes to fetch water. She walks, she walks. Look. Only her way of walking. Listen. She walks, her arms, her legs, that's her. Only her. I tell you to look at her. Look. Look. Look! It's perhaps the only time I've been happy," he said, panting. "What did you say?"

"Nothing," Antonio answered. "It's only my loud breath, but I'm listening."

"Well," said Maudru gently, "it's like that song of loggers. The boss sticks his hook in the bark, then sings out: 'Now, men. One more pull. One more pull—and off it goes.' I was blinded at first sight by that woman. One year, then she died, and that was not yesterday, but she's still there, between my bulls and myself, there for ever. Wild boars, you understand? You've seen; I've told you, so you know. The trees, our work, our toil"—one could hear his heavy hands fumbling about—"the beasts, and then everything else, in short, all that we've got to do. And that woman, there in the middle of it all, useless, like smoke.

[205]

To think of that? To see it, to have it stopping up my eyes? What's to be done?"

"Take another one," said Antonio; "everything drives us to it."

The din of a distant cavalcade rang through the mountain.

"Maybe," said Maudru. Then, after a pause, he said again: "Maybe . . . maybe . . ." And he silently drew at his pipe.

The first horseman who, in a fiery leap, emerged from the trees, started to shout, for he had just seen before him in the light of his torch the cypress grove of Maladrerie. He veered his horse and sank back into the forest, boring a great tunnel of light as he galloped. A cloud of snow-dust followed him.

The bier carrying Médéric's body lumbered up the last slope. The three pairs of bulls pulled to the right, then to the left. On the one side, after straining, they stuck their horns into the mountain clay; on the other side, their muzzles overreached the edge of the road, and they received the wet breath of the abyss in their nostrils. Each time, they caught their legs in one another, kicked short, blew two jets of steam and tried to shake off the yoke. On the seat the right-hand drover held the torch, and the one on the left had the goad.

"Ho!" cried Right, lifting his torch.

On the flat evenness of the night, the six bulls' backs shone out, glistening like pebbles.

"Aurora!" cried Left, standing on his seat. He flung his

long goad like a spear. It slipped through the ring in his hand and stuck into the shoulder of the bull Aurora, sniffing at the abyss. The six beasts surged back towards the mountain parapet, like enormous waves of red-and-white mud. The thongs whistled. The yokes creaked. The bulls bumped their thighs against the shafts. The bier turned on its iron pivot, jolted upon three wheels, pitched and tossed on the long-drawn grating of its rear axle. Médéric's coffin jumped in its ropes and the dead man's head bumped against the coffin boards. Then the beasts again made towards the dark brink of the night. Right shouted. Left flung his goad in the light, and a new effort of the bulls and of the bier carried Médéric up a little higher into the mountain.

Behind followed light carts, with white linen awnings, glistening like bubbles, in which lanterns hung from wooden hoops. Each of them was drawn by a bull with such ponderous strength that at each strain of the hip, the iron-work, pegs, nails, leather straps, and springs of ash, all rattled like a forest full of birds. Gina was in the first cart, black and mute, allowing herself to be jostled by the road without uncrossing her arms. The other carts carried men and women from Villevieille related to the Maudrus, small tanners who made their living out of the hides of the farm, and half a dozen plump girls, well washed and powdered, with silk kerchiefs wrapped round their necks and sticking out of their furs. They were drovers' sweethearts who went up for the feast and to sleep in the barns with their men afterwards. They crouched in the bottom of the last cart. They did not move, did not speak, only glanced at one another from time to time, smiling. In all the carts except Gina's they played cards or dice, or a kind of "mora," in which the players had to call out numbers while lifting up their right-hand fingers.

In spite of the rattle of the carriages and the hollow rumbling of the abyss lining the road, Gina heard the players' cries. She kept on saying: "Wretches. Wretches."

She drew aside the hood to look at the carts. She felt her bull flinch and sniff at his hoofs.

"Well, Gamma," she cried, "have you done licking your feet? The others are already up there."

Indeed, in front and above, the noise of the bier with the three yokes could no longer be heard. It was rolling on the even tableland.

The horseman had pushed his horse into a cleft of the rock. He held his torch high. "We're almost there, Mistress."

"I know," she said. "Tell those bastards to shut up, behind there."

The bull Gamma raised his head and started to bellow, swinging his muzzle. From above, Aurora answered. The bellowing flowed down the black valley, and one could hear the dead trees down below waking up. Gamma pulled on. Gina let the hood down.

The horseman could not overtake the procession. He waited in the cleft for the carts, holding up his torch. He held the reins between his teeth; he had drawn from his fur boot his long, woven rush-switch and was holding it tightly in his hand. When the first carriage passed by him, full of cries and peals of laughter, he lashed the hood with his switch as if he were punishing a beast. They stopped yelling. A man lifted a corner of the awning. He saw the horseman standing upright on his stirrups, with his torch on high, the reins between his teeth and his switch ready.

"All right," he said. And the cart went past, hushed.

When the next went by, he hit it in the same way, chewing meanwhile at the leather reins. "Shut up, you blackguards!"

He struck again, this time at a woman who had been frightened and had screamed.

He hushed all the carts, and when the last had gone, he emerged out of the cleft. He rode down a little in the darkness of the road. After the turning, he saw that a few windings below, the drover cavalry were coming. Then he walked his horse and went up the road again, with his torch on his shoulders. Only his head emerged from the night.

On reaching the tableland, the bier with the three yokes rolled slowly on the snow. The night, in front, was made thicker by the trees. Right, the torch-bearer, jumped down and went to touch the muzzles of the first bulls.

"Gee up, my doves. Beware of the oak-stump. There, Bosselé, take care of the fir. Straight on, Aurora, straight ahead."

He guided them slowly across the open forest. The huge bier tore off the barks, and the snow-clad cedar branches burst against the sides of the beasts and the cart-racks.

"Aurora's bleeding," he said. "Aurora's got a hole as big as a fist in his shoulder."

"Damn it," said Left, the goad-bearer, "I was obliged to do it. He sniffed towards the abyss all the way along."

On the ridge Aurora stamped his hoof in the snow.

"Make way," cried Gina, "let me pass."

She had taken off the front awning, climbed over the

cart-rack, and was standing on the shaft. She prodded Gamma with the butt of the goad.

"Follow me," she said. "That's the way."

Thus, at the bottom of the grove, the bier with the three yokes went sideways into a small heap of rocks. It stuck there as if stranded in a layer of snow so deep that it rose to the bulls' bellies. By holding up the torches, they could see, high up in the night, the glistening spindles of the cypresses.

"There," said Gina. "You'll have to carry him."

"We can get a bit higher up," said Right, the torch-bearer.

"Stop here," said Gina. "They've all been carried from here."

The carts were heard arriving. The cypress grove was breathing.

"Where's my blackguard of a brother?"

"Up there," said Left, the goad-bearer. Maudru had just appeared on the verge of the night.

The carts drew up silently around the mound.

"Unyoke the beasts," Maudru said. "They've worked enough."

"Clear off, then," Gina said. "They've smelt you. They'll trample on my burial ground."

"Unyoke them," repeated Maudru.

Men and women got down from the carts. There was Romuald the ironmonger, who supplied Puberclaire with chains. He was there with his wife and his two daughters. There was Marbonon of "Diversion Inn" with his big bear-skin coat. There was that big woman Delphine Melitta, owner of the three south tanneries, with her bonnet, her boots, and a whip, and that stiff air she had for everything in life, even when she had to ask tender things from men. There were the Demarignottes, the eight of them: the father and mother, the two sisters and four sons, all dressed alike, all speaking and walking alike, waiting for one another at each gesture, whether it was a low snuffle or tightening a belt. There were the five tanners from the rue Bouchoir-Saint-André who were under some obligation to Maudru. They drew up towards the torches, so that Maudru might see them from up there.

The awnings had been drawn back. The bulls were being unyoked. Gina had sunk into the night.

"Hold my foot," said Héloïse Barbe-Baille. She was alighting from a carriage without a foot-rest.

Bertrand-le-Gaz made a step for her with his knee. "Be careful," he said, "it's slippery."

He wore otter breeches. Héloïse felt her foot slip. She clutched at Bertrand's neck. He would have given a thousand otter skins for that.

"Thanks," said Héloïse.

"Don't mention it," he said.

Héloïse smiled. So did Bertrand. She went up among the snowy rocks towards the burial ground. Her fine round hips, smoothly swathed in fox furs, were swaying.

"What shall I do?" Bertrand thought. "Shall I follow her? Suppose I told her tonight . . . ?"

He had leaned up against a small cedar.

"Clear off, man," said Thomas. "You're blocking the daylight."

They had stuck torches on top of some goads, but these lighted up only the high branches covered with snow.

[2 1 1]

"Come along," Thomas said. He had brought his little wife along with him, and with her thick load of furs she looked like a baby marmot, lithe, with short gestures, and sleek with fat.

The girls were standing apart and gazing at the drovers unyoking the bulls.

At that moment cries were heard at the outskirts of the wood. The drover cavalry were arriving. As soon as they reached the tableland they started to trot. At the top of long poles they carried paper lanterns and sheepskins in the shape of bulls' heads. The eye-holes, encircled with rings of soot, flashed forth flames, the light osier horns danced above the lanterns like butterflies' feelers, and the manes, made of dried sedge and corn-silk, hissed about the lanterns.

Aurora looked at the wound in his shoulder. He went away blowing towards the unyoked beasts. He spoke to them in low tones in his bull's language.

"What's the matter with you down there?" Maudru cried.

Aurora bellowed softly. He began to climb the mound. The other bulls followed him.

Left, the goad-bearer, had untied the ropes and let loose the nephew's box. Four drovers worked together to heave the coffin. They bent under the weight. Bertrand-le-Gaz slipped his shoulder under the middle of the coffin, and raised himself a little.

"What's the matter?" Maudru asked.

Aurora approached him.

"Who's the son of a bitch who did that to you?" he

shouted. He touched the bull's wound. It oozed and throbbed under his fingers like a rotten fruit.

Left, the goad-bearer, placed the corner of the coffin on the fleshy part of his shoulder. "Let's go that way," he said, "there's a path."

"Aurora," Maudru said, "now, my pretty, now, my pet . . ."

Aurora rubbed his fat muzzle against the ox-hide coat.

The eight Demarignottes entered the cypress grove. The father carried a torch, the mother had taken a torch, so had the four sons, and the daughter brought up the rear carrying a lantern.

"Where's the grave?" cried Left, the goad-bearer.

"Here," Gina answered. She had been standing for some while on the edge of the grave.

Ropes were slipped under the coffin. It was lowered into the hole. "Just right," said Bertrand-le-Gaz in a low voice.

The mane of the bull-lantern was hanging still, trembling slightly in the hot air of the flame. The sound could be heard of Aurora blowing and of Maudru's hand stroking the bull. The snow was crackling under their steps.

The four drovers shovelled the black earth into the hole.

Gina turned round and went away. The Demarignottes went after her with their torches. Delphine Melitta lashed at her fur top-boots. Maudru climbed down the mound. The bulls paced around him, leaving near the master wounded Aurora, who from time to time stopped and tried to lick his shoulder.

Maladrerie, lost in the snow, had just lighted up all its

windows. From the chimney, in a cloud of smoke, leapt the red gleams from the big fire in the hearth.

The tattooed man emerged from his shelter under the cedar. He entered the burial ground. Only the cypresses were talking in low tones.

He called: "Antonio!"

He now had to cut that opening through the wall, so that at the first call of dawn the nephew lying in his grave might see the entire face of the earth spreading far and wide in front of him.

CHAPTER IV

4

ANTONIO came back on Tuesday morning. Toussaint was tidying his reception-room. He had finished sweeping the floor. He had taken a cloth and was dusting the furniture.

"I was worrying about you," he said.

There still lingered in his eyes that gleam of painful madness, that weariness, that disquiet which they showed when he had come back from the nephew's bedside. He occasionally looked at the window and strained his ear towards the door.

"The weather's fine, isn't it?" he asked.

"Yes."

"I'll have patients."

The gestures with which he was dusting the furniture were already circling, and he moved his fingers as if he were reaching outside the commonplace world and touching, far in the depths of the air, the mysterious womb of hope.

Antonio talked of the meal at Maladrerie. "Where's the twin?" he asked.

"Upstairs," Toussaint said, "in bed. For three days," he added, "he and Gina have been like fishes teeming with spawn. They hover round each other, they follow in each other's wake, they smell each other. They are in bed. They emit light merely by walking about."

"Sailor?"

"Wait," Toussaint said, raising his hand, without Antonio's being able to tell whether he himself had to wait, or whether Sailor was waiting for something.

"Well, then . . ." he said.

He had been to the funeral feast. In a corner. Old Gina was at the head of the table. She ate standing. Looking at nothing, seeing nothing. Now and then she spoke as she chewed her meat. Antonio could not hear.

"What does she say?" he asked the tattooed man.

"Wait a minute," said the tattooed man. And he put his finger to his lips with a "sh, sh."

Antonio had tried to listen. He could well see that old Gina was the mistress there, and that her true estate was that area of snow and night, that immense farmstead with its giant's breast whose ins and outs were lost on each side in the quivering shadows of cob-webs, that fireplace which had been hastily stirred to new life for the burial meal, that furniture, dusty all over with white dust from the walls. The very drovers seemed to have lost their master, and Maudru kept silent and motionless, except when he carried huge pieces of bread to his mouth, moved his big, stiff leg under the table, or glanced from time to time towards the stable door through the joints of which Aurora moaned with the gentle voice of an enamoured beast.

The company was eating as was the custom. The eight Demarignottes ("You'll see them everywhere," Toussaint said, "they've no convictions"), sitting together all in a row, with their elbows on the table, seemed at last to be at their journey's end. Marbonon often filled his glass. Romuald had placed his daughters between himself and his wife, and tried to protect them from the wildness and the weird hissing of battle which flowed in the silence. Delphine Melitta ("I wanted to know that one," Toussaint said; "she's on their side, now. What on earth can she want from Maudru, what has she her eye on?"), Delphine Melitta was eating composedly. She had taken her gloves off her beautiful long hands, which were quite white. She never once took her eyes off her plate. She had unfastened her fur and had opened her collar a little. Her fine throat and the beginning of her shoulder could be seen. At times, as if unwittingly, she glanced at Maudru.

Toussaint went all over the list again on his fingers: "Demarignottes" (he laughed); "Romuald, it's to sell his chains; Delphine Melitta, we'll come back to her, I want to get it all clear. She owns three tanneries with a hundred and twelve tanners. Out of the hundred and twelve she holds a good round eighty. We'll come back to that. Héloïse Barbe-Baille, to be free for a night. Bertrand-le-Gaz, for Barbe-Baille. Thomas, he's dangerous. He's a man. On Maudru's side. Why? I don't know. Brave, trustworthy, strong. A knowing man. That is, you cannot make him believe that black's white. Well. You say that all told, counting them all without the drovers, there were thirty from the town? Thirty. Good. Of the lot, only Thomas can draw men on his side, and Delphine Melitta. Good. And Gina has spoken."

Yes, she had, all of a sudden, without any change in her

demeanour of a dark and straight woman, without warning; in the midst of the silence, as if it were a long-expected, well-matured thing.

"You know her well?" Antonio asked.

"I do," Toussaint answered.

"What she said," Antonio went on, "has touched me everywhere: shoulders and arms and legs, everywhere, as if with her hand, to know whether I was ready to fight, and, as she said . . ."

"Golden-Mouth," muttered Toussaint.

"As she said . . ."

She had spoken without hatred, indifferently, using the little words of a woman. Around her, all her house, which had sheltered her life. There she stood, with her old hopeless flesh. She lowered her arm across her breast while saying that she had rocked that child. Speaking of his father, she said: "That man, I loved him," and with a slight swaying of the hand she evoked the riders' cavalcade to the funeral. She opened out the palm of her hand to show how he had stroked her breasts when she was a young woman, how he had laid her on the beds of that enormous mountain house, how he had made the child with her, little by little, not straight away, but slowly, by dint of love, understanding, and union. She evoked her great, tragic life, clad in love and hayfields, and joys more dazzling than hawthorn hedges. And there she was, standing before the table, lean and erect, with nothing left but her cotton shawl.

"Yes," said Toussaint, "I know her well. I know all that she can say, and how she says it. Believe me, when she put on her black gown and her thin shawl, when she tightened her waist to make herself lean and flat, she knew what she

[218]

was doing, and what she was going to say. Golden shawls! She still has boxes full of them, and she would not wait till the middle of the spring to take them out, at the same time as light-coloured skirts. I've known her a long time, and I've seen her, lately, again and again, more than need be, always knowing what she'd do, and what she wants. What'll she do? Just as before, neither more nor less. Not that she's quite indifferent about Médéric's death. Women always have a corner out of which tears flow when you press it. But what she wants above all is fighting."

"She is like our Gina," Antonio said.

"Yes."

"I meant her face," Antonio added. "She must have been quite like her when young."

It was still very early in the morning, and Antonio must have walked a good part of the night. He went upstairs to go to bed. He looked out of the window.

Yes, there was something new, even strange, in the air. The sun was heavier, and, in the blue of the sky to the east, a wide strip of a still deeper blue had just opened.

"Our" Gina did not go downstairs until the stroke of midday. Antonio had already got up. He had gone to the kitchen and had found the fireplace cold and the shutters closed. He had opened the window, lighted the fire, rummaged in the bin, found eggs, scoured the frying-pan, and was about to fry them when "our" Gina came in. He could hear the patients on the other side of the wall speaking or shouting, and Toussaint.

Gina was tired and pale; and Toussaint was right: she carried a smell and a light about her. She was not dressed. She had put on only her big fur cloak, but merely by her

[219]

small white ankles and wrists one could see that she was naked under the furs. Her eyes were wide open under her meadow-saffron eyelids.

"I've come to fetch some bread and cheese," she said. "We won't come downstairs."

Antonio was breaking the eggs into the pan.

"Just to stay a bit by ourselves," she said apologetically.

Antonio made no answer. He looked round towards the fire to avoid looking at her. She went out.

Antonio was thinking of that way opened in the sky, by which something came and touched the earth. He heard within himself desires, the wind and noises of the river.

He ate there, by the fireside, with Sailor. He began again to tell the story of his two nights at Maladrerie. He did not speak of the conversation with Maudru. No more than he had done in the morning with Toussaint. That was for himself alone. Then Sailor fell asleep on his chair.

Out of doors the day was setting off for joy and movement.

All the patients in the morning had been easy enough cases. They had brought along with them the fragrance of the forest and the open air. They were healed at once simply by being at the healer's. They were talking from chair to chair, about the road and the fields, about the long glide they had made from the upper villages down to Villevieille on snow which was already soft and which carried them reluctantly.

"You must speak lower," Toussaint said to them; "I can't hear the disease."

He had stretched out on the table before him a little five-year-old child who was half naked, and he was fingering him gently with his slender hands. The mother was gazing at him, following all his gestures, even the slightest movement of his fingers. When Toussaint laid his finger on a small blue vein on the child's body, the mother held her breath, and remained in suspense, her eyes wild with hope.

"Here we are," Toussaint said. He stood there with his hand resting on the child's chest.

"Be quiet," said the mother towards the place where the folks were muttering.

"Where do you live?" Toussaint asked.

"Near Méolans," the mother answered.

"You'll look at the larch trunks. You'll find this lichen there, look. Take it fresh, with a piece of bark. About a handful of it. Boil it. Break an egg into it. Give it to him in the morning when he wakes."

"Will he be healed?" she said.

"He is healed," Toussaint said. "Look."

"Breathe," he said to the child.

The child started to breathe. His lean little breast, all strung round with big ribs, rose and fell regularly.

"Hurts?" Toussaint asked.

The child glanced at his mother with a smile.

"Put his clothes on. Don't forget what I said."

"Now it's your turn," Toussaint said, "you, my good woman, talking about hazel-grouse, come this way, please. It's time to speak now. What's the matter with you?"

"Can I . . . ?" said the mother. She looked questioningly at him. Her fist was clasping a big silver coin.

"Yes," Toussaint said, "there, on the table."

He had not yet found his balance and his peace of mind

[221]

in treating those insignificant pains. He could not yet forget the bright morning on the other side of the windows, nor the clear sky which had just cleft under the weight of the weather, like a piece of timber which opens the way to its sap; nor could he forget young Gina, glowing with love, naked, up there in her bed.

The light was turning to afternoon when two big lads came in carrying an old man. Toussaint was just feeling a woman's head.

"Stand back," he said to her, "and wait. That man needs examining first. Come along, you over there. Put him on my chair, there. Hold his shoulders, you. Take care of his head."

The old man's head, lacking support, was too heavy for him to bear, and was swaying on his lean, weak neck.

"Can't he open his eyes?"

"Yes," said one of the boys in a frightened voice.

The eyes opened. Their fierce light was clamouring for help.

"Does he eat?"

"No."

"Does he sleep?"

"No, he suffers."

He seemed to be upheaved by an extraordinarily powerful breath.

"Undo his waistcoat," Toussaint said. "Tuck up his shirt."

The skin showed all yellow, with bluish circles on the belly. The whole body was terribly thin. Every bone had already its skeleton's position under the skin.

Toussaint's hand alighted on the evil flower of the belly. He waited. He seemed to have emptied all his life and strength into his hand, everything: his eyes, ears, nerves, and a kind of strange material sensibility which grew under his hand like the root-hairs under a tuft of grass, and he felt it enter into the sick man's body.

The mystery was the giant's breath in that wretched body hardly as big as a pair of bellows, without fat or anything, and without any flesh to nourish. What did he nourish with these torrents of air? What made him do it? Who was in need of all that human air, inhaled and blown out like a whirlpool of water in the river?

The thin, sensitive roots of his hand stole down into the purple shadow of the old man. They touched the liver. There was the liver: right the way round. Rather clotty. Still supple, a bit juicy. They went up along the skin, towards the ribs. The heart! Like a toad lying in a foliage of blood. They felt round it. It was leaping. It was escaping. The point began to strike big blows in the tree of the veins. The lungs. The great light of the lungs. For whom, that great light? The sensitive root-hairs turned down towards the belly, swept away by the streaming torrent of air. The belly!

Suddenly Toussaint felt a muffled bump in his hand. Then, nothing more. His sensitive strength had just been cut off close to his skin. His hand was now only a dry, useless hand, no different from other hands. Death! He had just touched death in the old man's body.

There it was, in the pit of the belly, with its thick violet wreath, its bony forehead, its dry mouth, athirst for air. The command!

"Dress him," Toussaint said.

While they carried him away, the man once more opened

[223]

his eyes and looked at the living people's faces with that terrible look from which they all shrank.

Toussaint drew near the window. It was the long twilight of winter. The sun was crumbling in the west.

"Death," he said between his lips. At last he felt at peace within him and clear. Bounteous death, happily inevitable!

"You've forgotten me," said a woman's voice.

"Yes," said Toussaint.

"You told me to wait."

She advanced from the shadow to the wan spot which was left in front of the window. Her laced bodice held fine breasts with their hard buds.

"There's nothing the matter with you," he said.

"No," she said, "I've had nothing since the time when you cured me. Only to give me a more serious disease," she added after a pause.

"You must leave me," Toussaint said.

"I cannot speak easily," she said, "for all is hidden that used to give me joy and happiness. On the first occasion you cured me. Cure me again this time. For all my life."

"I can do nothing in the way of a cure for that," he said.

"You alone can do something," she said. "I wouldn't have come if somebody else could have cured me."

"You've never seen yourself?" he asked. He was gazing at the sinking sun and the flashing green clouds.

"I've seen myself," she said, "and that's what comforts me a bit."

He looked round towards her, with his head leaning on his hump. His forehead was glistening. A big vein was bulging on his temples. His thread-like arms were hanging limp under the weight of his long hands.

"And me, have you seen me?" he asked.

She closed her eyes.

"I see you," she said.

"Seen me as I am?" he said.

"I wouldn't have come back if somebody else could have cured me."

"You must go," he said, "and never come back."

There was a long hush, in which one could hear the murmuring song of the metallic sky. Night was rising. The woman walked towards the door. She waited.

"You're never alone, then?" she whispered.

"Never," Toussaint answered.

She went out.

Gradually silence filled the great room. The straw chairs had relaxed. The table had creaked. Now even the stones of the walls no longer spoke.

Toussaint passed his hand over his face. Now it was sensitive again. He touched his forehead, his eyes, his nose, his mouth, his sad mouth into which ran the frightful wrinkle of his right cheek. Under his skin and flesh he felt the bones.

The night had already ascended half-way up the window. No more noise. He was alone.

He was at last at peace with himself. He could feel his face with his hand, look at his hand in what remained of the daylight, and see without pain what wretched skin, what sorry flesh, what faulty frame of bone made up his body.

He had touched death in the depths of the old man. Death! Pure strength. Fortunately thou canst not be soiled by our cures, or our commands, or our prayers.

It was there by his side, familiar. It alone gave him hope. It alone gave him peace.

Two knocks were heard at the front door.

"So soon," Toussaint said. "It arranges things better than I thought."

He crossed the passage. He opened the peep-hole.

"What do you want?"

"Patients."

"It's too late," Toussaint said.

"We've come a long way."

There were three men. He saw them in the greyish dusk. One of them had his head bandaged in a stained dressing, the other his arm in a sling, and the other his face eaten by a black lupus.

"Come in."

He drew back the bolt, then shut the door again. Night in the house had grown thicker.

"Follow me," he said.

A little light remained in the patients' room.

"Don't sit down," Toussaint said, "and tell me straight away what the elder Gina ordered you to come here for."

The three men were standing in front of the table laden with stones and herbs.

"I know," Toussaint said. "It's clear enough. It looks as if it hasn't made much impression on her that I spent night after night drying her son's sweat.

"Come. What did she tell you to do?"

"She said nothing for you, Sir; it's about Red . . ."

"And to begin with," cut in Toussaint, "what's all that mockery of disease? Was it she who told you to make up that fine black ulcer on your face? Take it off at once. What did you make it with?"

"Clay," the man answered, "curds, and spurge." He tore off the plaster.

"Let me see," Toussaint said. He touched the man's cheek. "Just barely in time," he said, "and I'm not even certain of that. Does it hurt here?"

"No."

"There?"

"Yes, it hurts a bit there."

"On top of the skin," Toussaint said. "You're in a pretty mess."

"A light," said the man.

"What for? I know," said Toussaint. "I can tell you. You must never joke with wounds. I can see that woman cares as much about you as about an old petticoat. What does she care if glanders do eat your face?"

"A light," said the man.

"If you like," Toussaint answered; "but what will be the good of that? You've done too much already."

"A light!" cried the man.

"A light, a light!" said the other two.

"Silence," Toussaint said. "Above all, silence. Red is upstairs, and he has never masqueraded with imaginary diseases. Now, silence. Otherwise he'll come down, and in your pretty state! Gently! Have you got matches? All right. Wait. I'll take off the glass. There." He secured the glass on the lamp. He regulated the wick. "There. It'll soon be done. We'll see. Don't move."

They didn't move.

[2 2 7]

"You're in a pretty mess!" he said.

They were three of Maudru's drovers. The mark was on their coats. The tallest of them had taken off his bandage. His forehead was still stained with red colour. The arm of the other, which was supposed to be in a bad state, was out of the sling. The man with lupus tore from his beard small clods of clay, curdled milk, and the green pus of grass.

"If I wanted to look after bullocks," Toussaint said, "you'd say: 'Look at him, he's going to get himself gored, he is.' And now you're playing with my bulls. Well, then, reasoning as a man should, I say to myself: 'Here are three fellows who are going to have their ribs peppered.' What do I do about it? Nothing at all. I watch. It's not I who've put you before the horns of the disease. What then? What's my right? I'll watch. One has not so many opportunities for a good laugh in life. Get along, my fine lads. Do your job."

"It hurts here," said the man with lupus, pointing to his jaw.

"Come here," said Toussaint. He had sat down. "Come nearer, stoop down. There. Under the lamp."

The man with lupus knelt down between Toussaint's legs. They no longer spoke. Toussaint fingered the man's cheek.

"You must go home," said he, "wash your face with brandy, have a shave, boil this plant, and apply compresses. If it gets bad, you'll come back to me."

The man got up again.

"Never joke," Toussaint went on. "You must salute man's illnesses"—he made the gesture, touched his forehead and saluted—"politely"—he bowed. "And you say to it: 'Pass along. Don't touch me.' And if it passes along, you go on saluting for a long time, saying: 'Thank you, thank you.' That's what must be done."

He went to the door slowly. He drew the three men towards him with a nod of his head.

"Be off now, my friends."

He listened to them walking in the passage, heard them open then shut the gate. Then he also advanced into the shadows and drew the big bolt. He spied through the peephole: the three men were walking down the street. The man with lupus touched his cheek, then examined his hand in the moonlight.

Toussaint went into the kitchen. The fire was dying. The stools near the fireplace told of the long wait of Antonio and Sailor. Toussaint felt that he had not eaten all day long. He opened the cupboard. He found some cold boiled potatoes. He picked one up, peeled it, and ate it without bread or salt as he went to bed.

THE river was now heaving up from underneath. From time to time it was seen to move. You had to gaze at it for a while: it was still motionless under the cold, then you could hear something like a rush of breath coming down from the mountain. You looked at the trees, they stood still, but when you turned your eyes again on the river you noticed that it had burst its old skin, and that a patch of new skin, black and sensitive, was splashing between the ice-blocks. Then the water was tarnished with frost, for it was still very cold.

But now they were real heaves, and at times it threw into the fields big icicles which started shining and blazing, went out when a cloud passed overhead, then again began to throw cold flames against the sun. All along the banks, at places where the river had been able to rub itself against the hard trees, there was already a fine stretch of black water, quite free. It tasted the air, and no longer froze. It only made wry faces with its ripples, and with the moire of the great current which animated it from underneath. To see the river move, one no longer had to spy at it like a weasel pretending to be asleep. It was now at its ease. It even indulged too much in making noise, and at times it cracked as if from one end to the other just to heave its frozen back a little and let it fall again. Then, the freed water of the banks overbrimmed into the fields, and by dint of licking the snow, uncovered the ancient face of the earth, the face which had been forgotten, the face with a scraggy skin.

There was even a rainy day. It seemed very short, with its unusual noise. The tiles sang, the runnels clattered down the sloping lanes like new strips of steel. The whole sky, disturbed by the sighing of a somewhat heavy wind, made the dark vales of the mountain and the morose lyre of the bare woods sing in the swaying of the rain. On that day the river swelled up with savage joy. Full of hollow thunder, it suddenly surged forth, uprooting willows and pulling down poplars far from its usual lair. It shook Villevieille forest. It flung against Delphine Melitta's tannery a high wave, upright like a man, packed with gravel and ice, which crashed against the walls. The tanners ran about in the snow with their big leather boots. From the bottom of the lower country rose the moaning of the hills. One could hear the river pressing up to crush them. Birds flew up from a cliff at the bend of the river. They whirled over the town with their wings swollen with rain and so clean that one could see all the colours of their feathers. They soared high up till they blackened the clouds, and as they hovered round they looked at the whole countryside. From up there they could see all Rebeillard under the rain. They told one another what they saw. But one which must have been a male greenfinch soared right up towards the mountains and vanished in the clouds. It came back at top speed, and one could hear it screaming, without being able to see it through the mist. It flew across the ring of birds like a stone, and all followed it, winging their way rapidly towards the cliff of the Ark. The sky remained empty with its rain. Nevertheless, the rain stopped on the verge of the night. The next morning everything was silent and crushed under the frost.

But the sun did not come back. The sky remained muddy and alive. Above the motionless earth, above the river, which, labouring under the cold and nearly exhausted, could only moan gently against the sand of its gulfs, the sky, under the mighty strain of its gasping, raised and lowered its breast of clouds. Heavy mists sometimes trailed all day long on the surface of the grass. At other times the clouds were so high, so far, that through their transparent body one could see the sun like a heart doing its work of blood-pumping.

Black silk masks were no longer needed. The snow was no longer blinding. In the middle of the soft fields, men were now to be seen barefaced, with sunburnt chins, mouths, and cheeks, but with foreheads and eye-holes still pale. They looked at the weather with joyful uneasiness.

The mountains were no longer visible. They were hidden under a thick mist which descended to their feet.

"Your ship can no longer be seen," Antonio said. "No longer. She's gone."

Indeed, over by the mountains all that was left below the fog was a row of firs, like the border of a great forest extending over a plain.

Sailor came and looked through the window. Since the world had begun to warm up, he had joyful moods, fits of anger and desperate depression, as sudden as gusts of wind. He had said a hundred times over: "Open the door, and let's be off. Junie is waiting for me yonder in the forest.

Yes, she is. Let's go, and damn Maudru." Then Antonio had to say to him: "You want to lose everything. Now we've waited such a long time, don't you see they are out there? That's what they want. Stay where you are. What with spring, freed roads, freed water, spring, we'll see."

"Spring," did he say? Sailor looked round towards the mountains and lo, above the mist, on a clearer patch of sky, there rose like a royal foresail the square glacier of the Ferrand. "Well," he sighed, "fate is fate. We'll wait. There's only one thing worrying me: it's poor Junie by herself yonder. Yes, you're right. We'll wait. What pleases me, after all, is that we'll get them out of this place, my twin and his wife. Yes, we'll get them out of this prison, don't be afraid, my children. Let me at least be of some use once more." And he gazed at the mist as it rose gradually. It blurred out the top foresail. All that remained was the mist, but it was swollen out by the great motionless ship, which awaited her passenger.

"Nothing left," Antonio said. "Look."

It seemed as if the mountains had been levelled out. The fir forest extended over a new plain like the black surge of the sea.

"Yes," Sailor answered. "Once we rounded Cape Horn and were sailing up towards Goat Island. Weather like today. It cleared off. We all yearned for lemons. We'd been sopping in brine for months and months. . . ."

"Always talking about your sea," Antonio said.

"Can't help it," Sailor said.

"You never spoke about it before," Antonio said. "Yet we had plenty of time, there. Never a word."

"Well," Sailor answered with a slight, grey smile, "it's

[2 3 3]

always like that: when you're far from embarking, you're careful not to say a word about it, but as soon as you're signed on, then you speak of it. On that day, I tell you, the island lying there, and that yearning for lemons! We make for lemons. Slowly, by guess-work. Weather clogged up. I run up the jack. Then, just as I'm alone looking towards the stern, I see gliding ahead of us, like a bird, a great sailing-ship, all sails spread from jib to ensign.

"The *Grace Harwar* of Greenock, in the mist, with scarcely a splash. . . . She had missed us by a hair's breadth."

"Listen," said Antonio.

Outside there was a new sound. The whole country was listening to it in a hushed stillness.

"Open the window," Sailor said.

The air was warm. On the other side of the mist, a water-fall rang in the mountain.

Freed water!

"This time," said Antonio, "it's spring."

"Spring," Antonio said, coming down the stairs. "Spring?" It was bitter to say it. He had not realized his loneliness at first. Clara had not come. Of course, without news from the Nibles messenger, he couldn't know things for sure. But still, she might have . . . No. It's over. And then after all, what he had never thought of was . . . that she had been with child. There was the other man . . . Or somebody else. No, it's over. He saw her again. She was there, made up of so many habits, there, close enough to touch her, to see her, to hear her coming down the stairs with him. No. The flowering osiers, the pools of bright

[2 3 4]

morning on the river, the clouds of nightingales, the fish leaping out of the water. Spring! Spring!

He went up again to Sailor's room.

"We said we'd get drunk," he said, coming in.

"I was thinking about it," Sailor said.

They went out through the small back gate opening on ruins. They had crossed all the house barefooted. Toussaint was busy with his patients. Since spring had announced itself with the first convulsions of the river, Toussaint hungered after sick people. In the twin's bedroom Gina was singing in low tones. He himself was doubtless lying on the bed.

"Be careful," Antonio said, closing the gate with the stealth of a cat. "Let's stay here a bit."

They were hidden behind a huge laurel bush, still half laden with snow. It was mid-afternoon.

"I don't think we'll run great risks on this side," he said. "As they chiefly expect us to go out all four together, with our goods and chattels, it's the door of the lane they're watching. After all, they don't care a damn if we go to the town, do they? What does it matter?"

"Nobody seems to be about here," Sailor said.

"Come along," Antonio said.

He let himself slip down into a long empty cistern with no roof on it. On the farther side of the decayed wall there was a passage into the corner of a cellar.

"Don't strike a light," he said. "It only lasts a moment; feel along with your feet. Got the stairs? Follow me."

After three broad steps of a winding staircase, they found themselves in a little more light, then still more, and they reached the edge of a long corridor lighted by ten windows

[2 3 5]

facing the town. In the shadow of the stone balconies, in the passage, they recognized that they were in the bishops' palace.

"All the same, last time," Antonio said, "there was one of them here. I don't know whether he was there to watch, or only passing by. He was there, you see, after the third window, flattened against the wall, near that patch of ivy. I could hardly make him out. He didn't move more than we are now. He must have heard me. Today, it's empty. Come along."

At the end of the passage the stairs took them on a level with the lanes, but they went down still lower into a broken-down cellar.

"All these dead houses communicate," Antonio said.

The sound of the waterfall filled the sky now. Everything was still motionless, but everything was listening, and one could already hear in the depths of the silence confused noises of a heavy sleeper who began to toss about and sniff on the brink of sleep. Above them, in the lane, somebody ran by.

"A woman," Antonio said.

They heard skirts flapping.

They stopped in the middle of a series of half-crumbling cellars, going down the slope. At the end, the daylight looked like a moon.

Women were singing. People were heard running. Then a woman cried, and her cry was borne on the air like the song of a flying bird. Then she cried with a steady cry, and all the women started to sing.

A hollow thud shook the earth; a fuller started to beat

very quickly as if it had gone mad, then the great steel brake was heard creaking, and the fuller stopped.

"There's too much water," Sailor said. "They can't start it, they're trying."

As they went further down, under the lower town, they could hear life getting more and more intense above their heads.

The long tunnel of cellars came to an end in the yard of a house. They went out. A tanner was unfastening bundles of ox-hides. A woman was playing with her little daughter's ball. She hopped first on one foot, then on the other, spin, double spin, one hand, then the other. Her coil of hair was hanging loose down her back. Thick shreds of fog, driven on by the wind, trailed along the streets, and from time to time girls scampered away, with boys at their heels. They escaped up the corridors of the houses. They screamed when the boys overtook them, but they were soon silenced, for the boys took advantage of the dark to kiss them. Thus the boy and the girl suddenly saw, in the shadows of the corridor, their two faces, sunburnt in the lower part, with pale foreheads, and their eyes, restless with spring, come nearer and touch each other like two seeds below the ground. Meanwhile the other girls who had stayed at the base started to sing. They well knew that yonder the couples were busy kissing. That is why they sang: that was the game.

"We won't go to 'Diversion Inn,'" Antonio said. "The place will be packed today."

"A quiet place," Sailor said.

"Not easy to find," Antonio said, "just for that reason."

He pointed towards the river. A continuous rumble blew through the houses of the waterside, the steep lanes ascending in steps, and the vaulted passages. The river was galloping with all its hoofs.

"That, on the contrary," said Sailor, "is rather peaceful and soothing. Just like this, you know." He showed the trailing mist which rushed headlong against the poplar in the egg-market, divided against a tree, went and hit big soft blows against the prows of the roofs, and splashed off in useless spray. "The movement of things does me a lot of good."

"Strange," Antonio said. "I get upset by it."

"We're no longer after the same thing," Sailor said.

They went into a small wine-shop, lengthening out like a fox's lair, and lighted at the rear by a wide window, opening on the tumult of sky and river. There was nobody there except a lean young girl, with buttocks shaped like cloves of garlic. The big stove was burning up well. The girl was lightly dressed in a short skirt and an old bodice which was too big for her and which hung loosely around her small mottled breast.

"Brandy," Antonio ordered.

"Bring us the bottle," Sailor added.

They sat down close to the window. From there they could see the river down below, flowing from below the bridge. The embankments were deserted. A violent wind, which swept along with the rushing water, bent the riverside poplars and drove clouds of tan-bark dust into the air. The river, immediately after the bridge, lowered its muddy loins. It was made of earth, ice-blocks, wrecked branches, and clots of black grass. From time to time its strength forced the great granite boulders rolling in the depths of its waters to leap up into the air.

One could hear all the mountain tributaries rumbling. Through a fleeting gap in the fog Antonio could see more than a hundred living waterfalls, hanging on the peaks.

The girl brought the brandy.

"What's your name?" Antonio asked.

"La Bioque."

"You alone?"

"My mother's out."

She had just trimmed her bodice with a paper rose.

Sailor slowly shoved his big wine-glass towards the bottle. "That sound is good," he said, looking through the panes.

Antonio stroked his blond moustache with the whole length of his fingers. The first glass of alcohol had provided work for his desire. He felt his warm and rested body.

"It's moving," Sailor said, pointing to the river. "Perhaps . . ."

"Perhaps what?" Antonio asked.

"Who do you take me for?" Sailor said. He had propped his elbows up on the table. He thrust forward his old face, furrowed all over with wrinkles under the stubble of beard.

"I take you for what you are, not for somebody else."

"Don't try, my boy," Sailor said. "I know my own reckoning. I'm not afraid of it. D'you think death frightens me?" His hand passed over the table. "Dust!

"One thing," he said, lifting his finger, "if I didn't say it, I would be a liar: to take them back, both of them, to Nibles—him and the girl—see Junie once more, and then say: I'm ready to go now! That's all. You're all swaggering about. You think I don't see you? There's the other shit up there with his herbs. Death, death, we know it's bound to come. No, all I ask is a little more time, almost nothing. Set them free to see them start life properly. That's all I ask. And then, Junie. Nothing more."

"For me, it's just the reverse," Antonio said. "I say: at once. And then damn everything."

"Fill it up," said Sailor.

"I said 'perhaps,'" Sailor went on. "I see the awakening, it wakens me."

"At once, you see," Antonio said, "at once. Peg out straight away here, on my chair. What's the good of living?"

"That's what I say."

"That's all right for you, but for me? And then," Antonio said, putting his fists on the table, "you say afterwards: 'I'm ready to go, I don't care, so you see!' You say: 'I'll get my twin out of here, I'll see Junie once more, and then I don't mind dying.' You see."

"I wouldn't mind staying, either," Sailor answered quietly. "Fill it up. Yours too."

"I'm not forgetting myself, you can be sure," Antonio said.

The vultures had flown down from the mountain. They were hovering over the eddies of the river.

"What the devil am I here for, in this world?" Antonio asked. He drank. "Look, this is what's worth while, but otherwise . . . Now look here."

He pushed his stool forward and rested his arms on the table. He licked his moustache.

"Many other things are still worth while," Sailor said;

"you've got to admit it. This, if you like, on a day like to-day."

He touched the bottle. The bridge had just spurted out all the accumulated ice-blocks, and the river was crying like a madman.

"Nothing," Antonio said. "That's nothing." He raised his glass. "It's still worth while because we're such shits. That's all. Such shits. All of us. What the devil are we doing, I ask you? Yes, some of 'em are lucky. Right enough. But me? Alone."

He paused a minute to listen to the tumult outside.

"Whether it wakes up or not, I don't care a damn. That's on one side, I'm on the other. It gets on with its business. I'm doing mine. Always the same. What are we waiting for? Since I've been looking, listening, hearing, I've seen everything, heard everything. The game's over."

Then he poured himself some alcohol, bending his head a little to see whether the glass was brimming.

"You're speaking of a reckoning," he said. "The reckoning's soon done." He opened his empty hands. "Nothing; that's my share. Well, then, what are you going to answer the man who tells you: 'I'm fed up'? Isn't that true? Who can force him?"

"That's funny," Sailor said, rubbing the stubble of his beard with his hand.

"What?"

"I thought you were . . ."

The little girl had stayed near the stove. Now and then she frizzled with her fingertip the paper rose in her bodice. She looked at the effect, creasing her chin, then pulled her skirt over her bare legs. She was squatting on her chair, with her feet on the rungs and her hands clasping her raised knees. She unclasped her hands and smoothed her thighs. Finally she jumped down and ran towards the kitchen.

"I thought you were self-possessed," Sailor said.

"I'm as self-possessed as anybody," António answered. "What d'you think you've been doing yourself?"

"Oh," Sailor said, lifting his hand, "not much! Pour out some more."

Antonio drew his face towards Sailor's.

"Come here and I'll tell you something."

Under his heavy eyelids, he had only a thin thread of an eye left. The weight of brandy pulled down the two corners of his mouth.

"Nothing," he said. "Shall I tell you? Woman! People think it'll do that"—he slowly made the gesture of catching a fly with his big awkward hand—"that's the result. More of a fool than before. And that's what I am. You can't make yourself understood by others. D'you get me? Never anything. Never a bit of what one's got inside; one's never properly understood. There are no words"— he sniffed with open nostrils, suddenly wrinkling his face all over—"it ought to be smelt, like a smell. It's all a damned lie! You may well have wife and child, you're always alone. The world's nothing, that's what I make of it."

He fell back against the back of his chair. His head was swimming with eyes closed.

"Good God," he said with clenched teeth, "I'd like to break somebody's jaw."

The sound of a guitar made him open his eyes. The little

[242]

girl had now come back and was sitting on her chair again. She held a full-sized man's guitar on her knees and in her arms. She was fondling it with her hand as a big sister would a child. She strummed the bass strings always in the same rhythm, and the rumble of the river, the noise of women running in the street, the neighing of horses set free, and of the wind echoed all round.

Gradually everything took shape and became music. Night had fallen. Children were running about the town flourishing torches of dry lavender. A pallid phosphorescence oiled the leaping river, and its bulging meanders lighted up the distant plain like moons. The whole warm sky beat against the window. One could hear the life in the earth of the hills, which was now freed from frost. Far away, up in the mountain, avalanches thundered down, cutting through the fog and bespattering the night with great round flashes, like wheels.

Sailor was looking straight in front of him. He was beating time, slapping the table with his flat hand.

"What are you playing?" Antonio asked.

"Sad things," she said.

"What's it?"

"Nothing," she said; "made up."

"Strike up a dance for me," Antonio said. "Come on."

He got up. He kicked his chair aside. He was fierce in heart and heavy with drink. He took two steps, spreading out the beam of his arms.

"Hoy!" Sailor cried. And he started to bang his hands on the table. "Put your heart into it."

Antonio looked round with a small grey smile. "Oh, the heart's there, sure enough," he said.

[243]

He stretched his arms wide open. He put his right foot forward, then his left, bending his knees, then his right, then again his left. He knelt gently on the air at each step, and leaned his head forward. He offered his open arms. His big shoes creaked. Step after step, with the "pluck-pluck" of the guitar and the hollow answering blows struck on the table, he drew near the little girl. He stayed there, stamping his feet, with scarcely any gestures: slightly bending his knees in quick cadence, his arms quivering, his hands hardly so, with a soft waving of his slender burning body, like a wrecked tree in the middle of an eddy.

Night had settled almost everywhere. The little girl played on, leaning on her guitar, moved to the quick by her music. All that could be seen was her long shiny hair, and her white hand dancing on the dark strings opposite the man.

Sailor opened the window. The rumble of the river blew mightily, carrying sprays and warm gusts.

Antonio spun round three times, then he was carried about the room in the circle of his spinning. The hob-nails of his shoes rang on the flagstones.

Down below in the river big trees drifted with their arms outstretched. The fire of the lavender torches set the streets ablaze. The little girl lifted up her head. Antonio was spinning round. She gazed at him with a broad smile, and nervously twanged the strings more vigorously. At each twang he suddenly bent his knees, flung his arms up in the air like a man sinking into water, then straightened himself up again with ease on his outstretched arms and swayed, inclining his head as if to dive into a new hole of the music; the depressing notes of the guitar came upon him, and he sank on his knees, with arms upturned, and a great exhausting sigh.

He was laughing too, with a laugh meant for nobody. He danced. He stooped his shoulders and raised his arms above his head. His hands drooped like weary leaves. Meanwhile his feet beat on the flagstones. He caught the rhythm again, raising his body with the supple undulation of a whip-thong, and then he threw his head backwards like a tuft of wool. Thus he went on, always bending his legs, as if trampling in a vat.

The door suddenly burst open. A woman ran in.

"Hide me," she said.

She crouched behind the stove. She was all quivering with joy, effort, cunning; she peeped at the street where the lads, carrying their lavender torches, were running after her. She glanced at Antonio, Sailor, and the little girl, all stock-still.

A sound died away in the guitar.

The lads passed down the street flourishing their torches; one could hear them going hither and thither about the square, searching behind the big elms. The woman got up again.

"Thanks," she said.

She flew away like a bird. Antonio sprang after her, in pursuit. The door remained open.

"And that's that," said the little girl after a pause.

Outside it was the first spring night. The whole town knew it, the whole of Rebeillard knew it, the whole earth seemed to know it.

"It's the time of the star."

"The sky."

"The moss."

"Wine," said a girl, dark as night.

"Why wine?"

"Yes, the flower of wine."

"Perhaps," said the boy.

"She's cheating," cried the girls, "and so are you, Gaubert, you cheat. The flower of wine is not a star."

"It is a star," said the boy. "Your turn, Dorothée."

"My turn?"

"Yes, yours. Quick, or you'll have to run."

"Water." She pointed at the river leaping under the last gleams of the day.

"It's not stars, it's moons."

"And those," Dorothée said, "aren't they stars?"

The spray sparkled over the river like St. Anthony's path.

"It's the time of the star. Now your turn, Marie."

"Eyes."

"Lamps."

Lamps were kindling behind the windows.

"Torches."

"Lanterns."

"Me, me," said a girl, stamping in her place and beating her fists, "I don't know, I don't know . . . I know, but I want to run."

"Catch the star!" cried the boy, and they all rushed after her.

The town was full of songs, games, torches, and lanterns. The lavender torches emitted a thick smoke which smelt of warm hills. Old women laughed noisily in the corridors.

The rumble of the river swayed to and fro among all the echoes in the mountains. Under the open sky, full of tumult, the Rebeillard country quivered like a mare's hide.

Antonio had run after the woman into a long lane ascending with stairs and vaults right the way up. He could see nothing. He heard footsteps in front of him. He leapt, she leapt. He climbed two stairs at a time, so did she, with a little laugh. For a time he heard nothing more. He called out: "Hey!"

She stopped a moment without answering, then burst out laughing near him. He rushed upon her with his arms open. She was already leaping up there from step to step.

> "Turtle-dove, turtle-dove,
> Turtle-dove has only one wing . . ."

She sang to indicate that she was a little tired. Up the lane there was a street-lamp, a small square, a fountain, and a tree. She hid behind the tree-trunk. Antonio heard the water. He had stopped to consider where the turtle-dove with one wing could have disappeared. He heard the water. The fountain had just been set free. The basin was filling with a broad song. Under the brass spout he saw the glistening jet of water.

Antonio felt within himself all his clear river, his summer river, rocking broad pebbles of light on its meagre waters. He thought of Clara.

The woman behind the tree whispered: "Turtle-dove." Then she ran forward, and he had just time to press her as she went. She slipped away from between his arms. Some warmth remained in his hand, and the shape of a breast.

She ran forward like a doe: her head high, her legs slen-

[247]

der, leaping over the earth, bound after bound. She looked round. He could see her face. Her eyes were like mint leaves. The green flash of her eyes thrilled him. He was almost out of breath, more from those looks than from the race. He ran heavily but with a good stock of strength and time, sure as he was of catching up with her when she floated some way in front of him, hesitating between two streets; he swung his body only slightly as he ran, ready to start the race again. Now and then, although his prey was far in front of him in the shadows which seemed bespattered with fire, he held out his arms ahead of him, to get used to the gesture of clasping her.

"Turtle-dove has both wings,
Turtle-dove, turtle-dove . . ."

The whole crowd playing the star game suddenly issued from the street. There were boys and girls, and they too were chasing a little woman who moved like a partridge. She did not run fast, but she fluttered from one wall of the street to the other, turning round the trees and lowering her loins to avoid the hands that were trying to catch her. She hid behind Antonio. She pulled him by his coat. She pushed him along. She used him as a shield against her pursuers. Antonio let her do so. There were five, ten Claras around him. Each of them had big mint-leaf eyes. They could see and laugh, like all other women. They smelt of healthy sweat and spring. Suddenly the partridge sprang away and they ran after her. The one-winged turtle-dove was waiting at some distance under the street-lamp.

"Wait," Antonio said. He rushed forward. She stumbled as she sprang forward again. He bounded upon her. He

[248]

caught her in both arms. The whole spring night flowed into him. But she was already off, running towards the streets along which streamed the blaze of the torches.

The sky was heavy, soft and starless, without light, and so low upon the earth that it was torn by the tree-tops. The night was already renewed. It smelt of warm rain. It had become human and sensitive.

Just after he had touched the woman with his arms and breast, Antonio stood motionless for a moment, filled with the deep knowledge of his own bitterness at being aimless while the world was being renewed. He started to run again.

The turtle-dove had just entered a bright street. She had looked round to see whether he was following her. He was. He cried: "Clara!"

He breathed deeply in that oozy night, thick with things to come like the seed of a beast. Here, he could see the woman better: her back, her hips, where, if he pressed with his hands and squeezed, he could stop her flight, and hold, and keep both the movement of the race, and the flight itself. When she turned round to look at him, he could also see that movement which was love! But here she was more difficult to catch, for the street was packed with people going down the square on the quay where the May bonfire was to be kindled. Running was out of the question. They walked along now at four or five yards' distance from each other, separated by groups of tanners, drovers, housewives, little girls. From time to time Antonio shouldered his way between two men and slid along to catch up a bit. In front of him he saw the undulating hips, the body shivering from the flight and constrained energy. He would have liked to catch her, to stop her and hug her, but she gained on him, slipping forward between one group and another. Now and then she looked round to see what distance there was between them. At the same time she glanced at Antonio, and smiled repeatedly, for she saw in the midst of the other men that he was tall and that he had a good-looking face which was still young, with a soft golden moustache. Thus, he saw her eyes. They seemed to be very dark blue or else violet. By the street-lights they seemed to be black, but they glowed and showed reflections. All that he was looking for on that woman were places to prey on, places on that body which he could seize and hold in his hands. Yet whenever she looked at him, he suddenly felt a deep tenderness in the midst of his strength and desire.

On the embankment square, the howling of the river struck the men full in the face. It was sufficient to make them grave and anxious. The waters had not stopped rising all day long. The ice-blocks crashed against the keystone of the bridge. At times the pale crest of a wave glistened like the back of a fish above the embankment. The women looked timidly at the gravity and anxiety on the men's faces. Great love was making ready.

Maudru's drovers had carried the mother of wheat into the middle of the square. It was a great sheaf of last year's wheat, with almost black straws, but still with golden hair. The old sheaf, made with the last stalks in the fields, had been dressed in three skirts and a big belt of twisted oats. There it stood, pregnant with man's toil, with its belly sagging under the weight of seeds, its straw breasts, and its old head of ears of wheat. The yoked oxen sniffed at it and stamped their hoofs in the mud. They shook their necks of bronze and the yokes creaked. They tried to turn round and flee, dragging the carts behind them. Antonio stopped.

A drover had taken a lavender torch. He tucked up the skirts of the mother of wheat. He began to make love to her underneath with his blazing torch, and suddenly she took fire. The roaring of the flames, the sputtering of the bursting ears, and the moaning of the straw, squeezed in between the skirts, drowned the howling of the river. The blaze broadened out under the low sky like a ripe harvest. The men shouted: "Wheat for the fire! Wheat for the fire!"

The woman of straw was writhing on her burning belly.

Antonio drew near the woman of flesh and bones, the one he could seize by the light nape of her neck, under her dark hair. She understood that he was coming. She took two steps sideways, as if for a dance. He took two steps sideways. She advanced. He advanced. The eddying crowd carried her towards the elms. He made his way towards the elms. She was out of the crowd, on the verge of the shadows. He walked towards her. She was waiting for him, and ran backwards.

"I'll catch you," Antonio said.

"Yes," she said.

And they sprang forward into the shadowy lanes.

Sailor was listening to the river and to the fullness of spring, running riot in the night sky. On top of his brandy he had just swallowed two measures of red wine, draught after draught, alone, face to face with the phantom of the sea.

The noise of waves and sails filled his head, and from time to time he expanded his shoulders, clenched his fists,

[251]

and with both arms tugged at a long rope full of splinters on board a phantom ship. A glow lit up the sky.

"What's that?" he asked.

"It's their May fire," said the little girl.

Sailor looked at the open door and the empty chair. "He's not come back, then?"

"He'll not come back," said the little girl.

When she spoke, her guitar trembled on her knees, and also spoke with its own voice. It faded away and was then mute.

"How much do I owe you?" Sailor asked.

"Ninety sous for your share."

"I'll pay for both."

"Then," she said, "seven francs."

He drew a handful of coins from his pocket. "Pick out the right amount," he said. And he spread the money out on his hand. He tied up what was left in his handkerchief.

"Order's necessary," he said.

He lifted up a finger in the air and tried to smile to make her understand the archness of it all. He felt under his tongue the salt tang of the sea.

"Could it be my hour?" he said.

"To go to bed," said the little girl.

"Yes," Sailor said. "Give me your hand, girlie."

She held out her hand and he weighed it in his.

"Not heavy," he said, "but a lot in it. . . . Well, then, farewell."

"Farewell," she said, "but aren't you coming back?"

"No," he said, "I sail tonight."

He walked out. People were coming back from the May

fire. The night smelt of burnt straw. Red reflections still lingered in the sky.

"It's queer," he said, "but it's things like that one regrets. Those hands are quite small. Made of nothing, yet strong as a buffalo. Pull straight, Sailor. Don't lean on the left like that . . . there."

Between his half-closed eyelids he saw the people around him, men and women tired at last of games, going home to bed. In groups of five or six, arm in arm, Maudru's drovers made their way towards "Diversion Inn."

"The fact is," Sailor said to himself, "it's just like setting out anywhere else. Always the same. If you've done it once, you've done it a hundred times. Always beginning again. On shore, it's all right. You start, you come back, you get a foothold, the shore carries it." He repeated slowly: "The shore carries it! Right enough, but then, without land, that's the question. Now, my man. Shut your trap," he said to himself.

He walked on, without thinking about anything, light and vacant.

Now and then he heard the wind whistle in the rigging and the great sails clack. Hulls were moaning. It smelt of fir timber. A great port was splashing around him.

"It seems as if there were a tide ebbing in the earth."

He felt drawn forwards, drawn towards the quays; already he felt the flexible sway of the gangway under his feet. "When you must go, you must go," he said. "Yes, home, it'll be all right at home. No good thinking too much. I shouldn't have touched that little girl's hand, I just couldn't help it. They have thin sort of skin between their fingers, as feeble as a duck's web. It's soft and yet as strong as a buffalo. Funny to be hooked to earth like that. . . . All right, I'm coming, Captain," he said after a while.

He had just entered a zone of shadows and silence. The noise of the river could no longer be heard, and the movements and smells of spring were absent, but close to the ground there was a soft rustle of sleeping waves. Sailor was singing:

> "There's never a hedge on the open sea,
> There's never a pot-house here,
> But old man death is everywhere.
>
> Of land and home there's never a shade,
> Only the shade where all's forgot,
> Only the trail, till you lose the lot.
>
> There's no comfort, and there's no rest,
> There's no pleasure, and there's no jest,
> Never a tree, or a hedgerow lane,
> Only the sea, and all the same."

Two drovers, a dark one and a hairy one, were standing on the doorstep of "Diversion Inn." "That's him from up there, isn't it?" they said.

They looked at Sailor climbing towards the upper town with difficulty. He was singing:

> "Ah, Captain,
> If you'd listen to me . . ."

"He is all alone," said the dark man.

Suddenly, at the corner of the road, Sailor found himself in front of the mountain. The night-wind had unveiled it completely. All the glaciers were quivering.

In spite of the great wind, the ship of death had all her sails out, up to the top of the sky, like a mountain.

"So you're here," Sailor cried out, lifting up his arms.

At that moment they stabbed him in the back with their knives.

"Where are you?" Antonio called out.

The woman had disappeared. Just as he was about to catch her she had slipped off behind a wall and had vanished. He looked all around him. He was on the church square.

Suddenly something told him: "Go. Go that way, go and see. Go." And he was all of a sudden sick with hope, as if a big bird had started to flap its wings in his breast, hitting at his heart and liver.

He went forward. There it was, right at the bottom of the lane ascending to Toussaint's house. It was an old winter sledge. It had been rigged with wheels. The horse was still panting. When it moved, one could feel the heat of its sweat. It had just arrived.

"The man from Nibles!"

He had thought about that sledge for such a long time that he would have recognized it out of a thousand, even if he had seen it glide across the sky with the speed of a star. And suddenly Clara began to hurt his whole body like a big wound.

"Clara!"

He heard Toussaint's door open and shut up there, then a man's step going down the alley steps.

He had no strength left. He could not move his little finger. He had all he could do to breathe.

"Hallo," said the man.

"It's me," Antonio said.

"I've been after you up there."

"Got any news?"

"Yes."

"Well . . . ?" Antonio said a good while after.

"The child's dead," said the man.

Antonio took a deep breath.

"And Clara?" he said.

"She's there."

"Where?"

"Up there. She came with me."

"Thank you," Antonio said.

He began to go slowly up the alley.

"It's a long way," said the man.

"I know, a long way," Antonio said. "Thank you."

He opened the door. The house was full of shadows and silence. He stood in the hall, listening. He felt dry and all ablaze. Only the clock beat time as usual. He did not dare to call or move. He looked for a presence with all his senses.

"I see you," said Clara, from the depths of the night.

He could not speak. He needed all his strength just to breathe, to remain standing and not to lie down on the flagstones and remain there, happy and peaceful, since all he had wished for had happened.

"I've been very lonely without you," she said. "I've come," she said at last, "because you cannot deceive me. I can see you."

[256]

"Where are you?" Antonio said.

"In front of you, come along."

He groped forward in the dark. And, all of a sudden, he came upon her.

CHAPTER VI

Toussaint awoke.

The wind stirred up the night with sweeping, velvety movements. Downstairs, only the tread of the clock.

He lit his candle and listened. All right, nothing. Yet he felt that something was wrong in the house. The shadows were quivering like sand worked by the water from underneath.

He went and listened at Sailor's door. He pushed it open. The room was empty, the bed cold. In Antonio's room, nobody. Then he went downstairs. He walked noiselessly, barefooted on the flagstones. He held his candle high above his head to see well in front of him.

He stopped. A woman was sitting at the foot of the stairs. She was gazing at him with large green eyes, full of colour to the brim like mint leaves. She held Antonio's sleeping head in her lap. She seemed to have reached the moment of happiness when one no longer sees anything around one, and her eyes were filled with an indefinite light.

"Woman," he said in a low voice.

She did not move, but only asked: "Who's there?"

"What shall I say," he answered with a bitter chuckle, "to let you know who's really there?"

"I feel you're not to be feared," she said. "This is a house of kind people, here. You're the second one I've heard here, and I cannot tell who's the kinder of the two, the man sleeping in my lap or you."

Thus he understood that she was blind.

"Why is he sleeping?"

"He was waiting for me," she said. "He's resting now. Leave him alone."

Toussaint went down the stairs slowly. She still looked upwards, at the place from which his voice had come.

"We'll have to wake him," he said. He touched the woman's shoulder to let her know that he was close to her. "I fear a misfortune has come upon us. Antonio!"

"What?"

"Wake up."

"Here I am."

"How about Sailor? Sailor," Toussaint repeated, "he's not gone to bed." The candle trembled in his hand.

"It's true," Antonio said. He got up. "I left him in a wine-shop, one in which the window faces the river, in the lower town. Hasn't he come back?"

"No."

"I'll go and get him."

"The town is packed with drovers."

"Give me my gun."

"I'm going with you," said Clara.

"I don't know," Antonio said. "You'd better stay here. Perhaps I'll have to fight."

"Good and bad luck for both of us now," she said. "You can't ask anything else from me."

Toussaint lit the lantern. "I'm going too," he said.

Antonio went down the street first, with his gun in front

[259]

of him. Clara followed, grasping his coat. Toussaint followed twenty paces behind, carrying the lantern.

"That laurel bush in front there's dangerous," said Antonio in a low voice. "Usually they lurk about there."

"Stop," Clara said.

He stopped with the butt on his hip, his finger on the trigger, and the gun levelled at the black tree.

"Go on," Clara said, "there's nobody."

They went on.

"Lend me your lantern," Antonio said.

He examined the tree. Somebody had lain there in ambush some time ago. Hob-nails had bruised the bark not long before.

"The guard has gone," Antonio said.

"Yes," said Toussaint. He had taken his lantern again, and he lit the shadowy places close to the ground. "What are you looking for?"

"Sailor."

"Let us go on," Clara said. After a time she asked: "Does the street open onto a square?"

"Yes."

"Be careful at the turning. You can go on now," she said after a pause. "There's nobody."

Toussaint caught up with them on the deserted square. The sky was terrible to look at. It was not in its usual place up there, but down on the earth, making wild gestures around the lantern.

"He must have stayed down there," Antonio said. "He must be sleeping on the table."

"Hardly likely," Toussaint answered. "Did you drink?"

"Yes."

"He must have gone straight off in the dark. Why did you leave him?"

"I don't know," Antonio said. "Let's go on. . . ."

"Stop here," Clara said, "and look about you."

Behind the elm they found Sailor lying with his face in the mud. A long flaying-knife was buried between his shoulders. It was no good trying anything. His mouth was choked with mud. His nose and ears had bled. His face was not calm; around his open eyes and his distorted mouth one could see the frightful wrinkles of the last despair.

"I left him," Antonio said, "I left him!"

"Carry him now," Toussaint said.

Now Antonio felt proud of his strength. He could lift up this body, carry it in his arms like a baby, do something for it. He heard Clara say: "Wait, I'll help you." And she laid her hand on his shoulder.

"I thought so," said Toussaint. "When I saw nobody in the laurel bush, I thought they had done it, right enough. Sailor! Rebeillard has been your meeting-place, too."

Antonio carried the body. "I left him, I left him," he said to himself.

There was nothing good left in the world except Clara's little hand resting on his shoulder.

Toussaint entered the house first and opened the kitchen door.

"Here," he said.

"We ought to lay him on the easy chair."

"No," Toussaint answered, "here on the floor, like a dead man, here in front of the fireplace and the kettles." He looked around him. The deep wrinkles of his face were full of shadows. "You see: the table, the pot, the hearth,

[261]

and Sailor dead, that's what I want." He turned his eyes towards Antonio, and Antonio saw in his glance a queer fury beyond man's scope. "Maybe we've no longer any twin; he's sleeping. You never know what a big-mouthed woman can eat up in a man. I want him to see Sailor there on the floor, among the everyday things of life. To make him understand, if he can still understand."

He went out. He walked along the passage, towards the twin's and Gina's room.

"Were you fond of him?" Clara said.

"An old pal."

"And is it your fault?"

"Yes."

"Come in," Toussaint said.

The twin came in.

"You too."

Gina came in.

"There," Toussaint said.

"Who's that?" the twin asked.

"Your father."

He leaned over the blood-smeared face.

"My father," he said, "why?"

He looked at Antonio, then at Toussaint, then at Clara, then about him: at the chairs, the hearth, and the cauldron. "And now . . . ?" he said.

Suddenly he broke away from Gina, who was clasping his arm. He touched Antonio's arm. "Come along," he said.

CHAPTER VII

THEY left the town by the north. The wind was blowing. Now and then the clouds uncovered the moon and they could see a hirsute stretch of land still bedrabbled with mud and melting snow.

"I haven't got my gun," Antonio said.

The twin walked in front with long strides. "No need for it," he said.

The noise of the river was a long way off. They could hear the voice of a great marsh full of young reeds.

They were still walking on firm ground, but close to them they could hear the rustle of water, big splashes, and at times the quiver of a rippling wave hissing among the reeds.

"How many hours before daybreak?" asked the twin.

"Five."

"We'd better run a bit," he said. "We're following the dike. The way's clear."

He started to trot stealthily, scarcely making any sound. After a while the clouds parted. In the distance ahead the moon lit up a wide stretch of flat water, strewn here and there with small islands and reeds, but where glistening ripples of wind glided unhindered.

At the end of the dike the twin peered down into the shadows.

"Wait for me."

He climbed down to the water. Antonio heard him paddling. "See if there's not a pole up there. On the ground." There was one, right enough. "Come on."

It was a queer sort of raft, with a low rim, half like a boat.

"Let's wait till the moon's hidden."

Great shadowy waves were still being carried along by the wind. The two men did not move. They were looking at the mountains. From time to time, far away in the distance, they could see gleaming rocks, snow-fields, and glaciers, but all along the mountain slopes, heavy black mists, thick as forests, were oozing out; they could be seen swelling their gigantic foliage. The two men had to wait for the wind to catch the mists and blow them down. Then the night would be pitch-black and moonless. It came at last. The wind, too heavily laden, floated about for a time, striking the water of the marshes with its smell of trees.

The whole marsh was lost in darkness. The twin pushed off with his pole and began to steer. A small circle of moon still remained on the water, but when it reached the hilly fir-groves it receded at full speed and vanished far away on the opposite side. All that remained was the splash of the pole in the water and the smooth swish of the flat boat. There was a good smell of mud and decay, and then the heavy breath of reeds full of green sap. There was an animal smell of water fowl, the downy hollow of the nest, the smell of the long-billed spawn-eaters, and the smell of black eels. The flight of a web-footed rat roused the smell of osier roots, then there was the smell of the small floating nest with the warm female lying in it.

The twin steered the raft in clear water. He seemed to know the way. He weighed regularly on his pole. He drew it out of the water, and at the place where it emerged a small glimmering circle widened out, like the flower of a water-lily. The pole glistened and dripped all over. He plunged it into the water. All was dark again. Some water animal passed them with a moan. It smelt of dead fish and wet fur. It disappeared into a clump of oat-reeds, scattering an odour of pollen and honey.

For some time Antonio had seen in the distance a small red speck glowing like an ember. The twin headed towards it. A smell of trampled earth and dung also came from that direction.

"It's a lamp," Antonio said to himself.

A fish leapt out of the water with a smell of aniseed and water-cress.

In front of them there was now a glow behind windows, probably the glow of a big fireplace, a kind of scarlet halo throbbing slightly. Inside there were brighter specks twinkling like stars or lamps. The smell of dung became heavier. A smell of walls too, of wet plaster, of torches, of thatch, and of slate. In the low sky, brushing against the water, there floated a smell of dry hay, straw, smoke, bulls' urine, pelts, sweat, and men.

The light seemed to sink into the earth, and then disappeared. They were landing at the bottom of a high bank of damp earth. From time to time clods crumbled down and fell into the water.

"Wait here a bit," said the twin. He jumped out and climbed along the slippery bank. Antonio heard the twin throw himself down on the ground above. Then there was a heavy sort of cry which was slowly snuffed; the twin's short breathing in gasps; bones crackling; a short groan; a deep breath; then silence.

Antonio jumped out. As he was rounding the top of the bank, the claw of a beast scratched his cheek. He ducked his head and struck into the darkness with his big hand. The claw was at the end of a long, stiff, motionless paw. He bounded up, rolled onto a body which was still warm and limp as otter skin. It was covered with fur. His hand slipped on a slobbering tongue, cold teeth, and a mouth which smelt of carrion.

"Shut up," said the twin. He was lying near him on the ground. "It's the dog," said the twin. "Wait a bit."

Now they could see at some distance before them the big body of a house. Its frame was blacker than the night, blacker than the hills behind it; the light burned in the main building, beneath an arch.

A great smell of bulls, as thick as mortar, lay sleeping on the surface of the pasture.

"At the end of the third pasture," said the twin. "That's where we are."

The huge bull farm loomed before them at the far end of the pastures. A number of stables with pale roofs spread out to the right and to the left.

They crossed a ditch, a barbed-wire fence, and an old pasture; here and there the grass was eaten down to the stones; another wire fence; a somewhat richer pasture; a wider ditch, deeper and half full of water and water-weeds, cress and hawk-weed. On the other side of the ditch a meadow. Judging by the smell, it seemed to be occupied. There were mangy bulls in it, alone in the night. The beasts

[266]

got up. They sniffed at the men and stamped on the heavy ground. They cricked their necks. The twin whistled. The bulls lay down again.

There was the wall. From the bank of the marsh, where the twin had strangled the dog, up to this first wall of the farm, one had to count more than a thousand steps. It was a wall slightly over a metre high, built of big granite blocks.

Antonio jumped over it. On the other side, he felt fresh dung under his feet.

The twin said: "I think it's on the right."

A great black barn loomed in front of them; it breathed out a smell of dry hay. A hollow shed buzzed with the noises of the night; it echoed their steps. The two men stopped; the shed smelt of iron and wood. It doubtless sheltered new carts. They stole like cats along a grassy path. It took them to the well. They stopped a moment to take their bearings.

They could no longer see the light. They had penetrated too deep into the body of the farm. From there they could see only the reflected light on the wall of another barn. There was no noise except the low murmur from the shed.

"I'll get at them," said the twin.

"Who?"

"All of them. All of them," he repeated.

He looked at the small reflection on the wall.

"One after the other, each in his turn, each as he deserves. All of them, up to the last man."

He struck in the grass with his fist. The dim light reflected from the wall was cast on him: he was squatting like a cat with his head forward and his chin protruding.

"It's time," he said.

He jumped forward. Antonio ran behind him. From the angle of the barn there was a path of light up to the porch of the farm. They went forward with measured strides.

They could see the big window. Inside it was light: fireplace and lamps. Six drovers were sitting with their elbows wide apart on the table. Maudru stood near the hearth, with the lower part of his face in his hand. His thumb and forefinger were on his cheeks and his mouth was in his palm. Gina, wearing the mourning dress of a woman of the mountain, walked up and down. Now and again she spoke. They could not hear what she said. Nobody could have heard, not even those inside. They remained motionless. At last a drover turned towards her and started to reply. He explained with gestures of his hand; he seemed to be speaking of open country, then he lifted his arm as much as to say: "Far as hell, down over there." Gina stopped in front of him. She remained motionless as she spoke to the man. Only her lips moved. She seemed to be talking of Maladrerie, for as she spoke the drover looked up in the direction of the mountains. Gina turned to Maudru. She seemed to say: "Well, then, and you, what do you think about it?" Maudru did not move. He remained as he was with his mouth in his hand.

The twin counted them: "Six, seven, eight."

"Nine," said Antonio.

"Nine? Where?"

"Look down there, near the door."

It was Delphine Melitta, neat and smart as usual, with her small knitted cap aslant on her fair hair. They saw her profile, with her low forehead and her big, stubborn chin.

"There remain two men in each stable," the twin said.

[268]

He drew near Antonio. "First, you'll follow me, then you'll do your own job, without troubling about me."

"I've got to trouble about you," Antonio said.

"I tell you . . ."

"I tell you I'm not likely to take orders," Antonio rejoined. He heard the twin grind his teeth like a bear. "Go on," Antonio said, "I'll follow you; afterwards we'll see."

The stables extended on either side of the main body of the farm: five to the right, seven to the left.

"Now for the first," the twin said. He peeped through the cat-hole. It was as he had thought: the lantern was there, the bulls were loose, and the two men asleep. Even better than he had thought: they had just strawed the stable and the straw of the litters was quite dry. He lifted the latch gently. He opened the door. It was a high ship of a house, with a ridge of beams like a bird's breast-bone. A lantern lay near the sleeping men; a sort of storm-lamp with a bulging gasolene tank.

The twin approached the men. He hit them under the chin with all his might. One of them without moving started bleeding from the nose. The other raised his arm and dropped it again.

"Let's drag them out. Far from the stables," said the twin in the dark.

They hid them in an angle of the wall near the well.

The twin touched Antonio's shoulder. "Those two'll be quiet for a good quarter of an hour."

"Perhaps longer," said Antonio. He had carried out the man with the bleeding nose. He had blood on his hands.

"Yes, perhaps longer," said the twin, "but in a quarter of an hour they may wake up and it won't matter."

[269]

They went back into the stable. The twin rummaged in the drovers' chest. He took out two leather coats marked with an M.

"We'll put these on," he said; "they'll hide us for a time all right." He pulled a cap over his red hair. "And now . . ." he said.

From time to time the twin had said: "And now . . ." He had started on leaving Villevieille. He said it to himself, as if he had come to the end of a movement that flung him into another movement, that flung him towards his vengeance, always further on in regular order, where everything had been foreseen and nothing could escape him.

"And now . . ."

He did not hurry. He simply trembled a little.

"And now . . ."

He walked forward among the slumbering bulls.

"Oh, ox-carrion," he said, "it's for you I'm doing this."

The beasts seemed to know him. He stroked the withers of a light-horned bull. He kicked a red bull gently in his side.

"Come on, bulls," he said, "up you get."

There was a soft, light noise made by the beasts as they rose. Then they stopped still, standing on all fours, still full of sleep. They looked at the twin. He went from one to the other. He spoke to them in a low voice.

"What's he going to do?" thought Antonio.

The twin seemed to him to have grown.

"What are you going to do?"

"Fire the place."

They looked at the beasts. They had all got up now and some of them were already shaking their heads.

[270]

"Open the door, just one wing," said the twin. Then he took the lamp and unscrewed the small cap of the gasolene tank. He heaped up some straw. He poured gasolene over it. As he emptied the lamp, the flame dropped and then went out altogether. Nothing remained but the red glow of the wick. The twin blew on it. He threw it onto the heap of straw.

There was a moment of darkness and silence, then all of a sudden a puff, and the flame burst in the straw like a red bubble.

They left the stable. They went to have a look at the two stunned drovers. They were still sleeping.

The fire had already filled the frame of the door with red, but there was no sound of burning. They could only hear the bulls beginning to prance.

"You," said the twin, "you go and set fire at the end, there"—he pointed to the dark stables on the right—"and I'll go down there. . . . The whole lot," he said.

Before the lighted window of the house, they saw old Gina's shadow going up and down. She was still speaking.

"The tongue sucks where the tooth aches," said the twin. He touched Antonio's arm. "My father . . ." he said.

That was what flung Antonio into the night. As he ran, he touched his pocket. He had his tinder. He looked behind him. The twin was running the other way. Smoke, flickering with red flares, came from the stables. A bull bellowed in dismay. They could hear the trampling of hoofs inside, the blows of the bulls' horns on wooden walls, and great bodies shoving against the wing of the door with its iron frame. A bull bounded out into the yard. He dragged a wisp of flaming straw between his legs. The window opened.

"What!" Maudru cried. Then: "Fire!"

He shouted another great cry in bull language, and the beasts jumping about in the fire answered him. The bull which had escaped galloped to the window.

The twin had disappeared the other side of the smoke. Antonio started running again. He threw himself flat on the ground behind the watering-trough. Two drovers came running out of the black stables. They went towards the fire. It was now full of terrible vigour. It leapt towards the sky, full of smoke and shadows, and with bulls scattering about in it, straining with their horns towards the cool of the night. Men's shadows were gesticulating before the blaze. The house creaked with all its beams. Antonio got up. He went to the big door of the last stable. He fumbled for the latch. Inside, the bulls realized that the guards had gone. They were breathing hard. They were questioning one another in low voices. They were walking gently on the straw towards one another.

Antonio stepped in. The lighted lantern had been left there. He poured the gasolene onto the straw. The flame shot up at once. These were younger bulls. They blew heavily and stamped on the ground. They shoved one another with their buttocks against the wall at the far end. Drooping wisps of dry hay fell from the traps of the barn. The flame climbed right up. It dug its way underneath for a time, then was suddenly heard gutting the fodder in the long, draughty barn.

Antonio saw a small door in the wall on the right. The flame made it sparkle, for it was studded all over with iron nails. He sprang towards it. He pushed it open. He found another quiet stable behind it, where the farm continued;

a stone stable, with a vaulted ceiling. Cows and calves. Bundles of straw, bound with cords. He drew his long knife. He cut a cord. He scattered the straw and looked around him. At the far end he saw a big gable window which was round, like those in churches, and wide open. It would make a good chimney. A little fire, and it would draw like the devil under those vaults. The uneasy cows got up. They made their tongues smack in their nostrils. The calves drew towards them. The first stable which Antonio had set on fire was now emptying its bellowing bulls into the night. He could not hear the other fire on the other side. The walls were too thick.

Antonio was about to strike a light. He lay down in the straw. A door had just been opened. Between the legs of the cows he saw the legs of a man. As they approached him, Antonio gripped them in his arms, and the man fell. Antonio hit him in the ribs. The man's fist missed him and struck the straw. He had got him. Antonio rose on his knees. He seized the man's hair and pulled his head backwards. He hit him twice very quickly on the point of the chin, then again in the ribs. He could see nothing, so he touched the man's face with the palm of his hand. The mouth was open, the lips curled up, the teeth cold, and the eyes closed. Antonio dragged him by the arm to the door through which he had just entered. It led into the house itself. He stretched him out on the flagstones. He went in again and struck a light. He set fire to the straw in five places. He returned to the house and closed the door.

The man had red skin with freckled cheeks. The blows had galled his chin. The cows in the shed tried hard to get out. They did not low. They rushed all together against the little door; at each attempt one or two got through, then they started battering the walls and the door again. The house trembled every time, as if a great ax had struck at its foundations. The fire in the barn burned merrily with a long, low roar. A calf lowed and beat its head against the house door. Thick smoke oozed slowly through the door.

Here was the room where a few moments ago Gina had been walking up and down and speaking. There was no longer anybody in it, only the deserted table, the over-turned wooden stools, the hearth with its homely fire, and the open window. The night-wind made the shutter bang. Outside, he could hear a tumult of bellowing and the crack-ling of the huge arms of the fire. Antonio licked his lips. It was the heart of the farm. A cupboard stood with its doors open, full of account-books. A large board with prints of all the bulls' marks hung on the wall. The orders were written in Gina's handwriting. Antonio licked his lips again, and went nearer to read:

"Servery, enclosure number 5.

"Ressachat, enclosure number 9, needs salt.

"Burle—the biggest of the old ones—take to the high pastures . . ."

The house trembled. The wind shut the door of the accounts cupboard. A huge mass of flames, crushed down by the wind, lighted up the outside, and he saw the frantic race of bulls showing up black in the night. Antonio passed his hand over his face. There was not much to set on fire here. Books burn badly. A staircase rose in the corner near the hearth. It probably led to the bedrooms. He went up.

Better go carefully. Of course, they must all be out, try-ing to . . . but . . .

At that moment he heard someone open the door downstairs, and a heavy step, stumbling among the stools.

"Tavelé! Tavelé!"

It was Maudru. He grunted a curse, then went out again running.

Outside, the noise swelled and fell again, like the language of a strong wind. At its highest pitch, it intermingled the roar of the flames, the cracking of walls, beams, and doors, the echoes from the sheds, the bellowing of the bulls, and the muffled cavalcade of beasts in the meadows near by. When all that had subsided a little, and the noise had flown away up into the night, a sputtering of fat could be heard in the fire near the ground. Above it there was the sound of the drovers' shouts and, in the midst of it, the louder shouts of Maudru himself, with his deep voice, ringing like a valley. It was hard to say whether he was speaking to the men or to the beasts. Men answered and beasts answered to that voice.

From the heights of the night the blue flail of the flame fell down roaring, and the whole farm crackled under it.

The house had only one story. Antonio pushed a door open. He struck a light. It must be Maudru's bedroom, he thought; a small, narrow iron bedstead on rollers, a grey sheet, still crumpled, a pillow which had become blackened with the grease of his head. In the middle of the bed a big hollow had been worn. Yes. The water-jug, the bearskin coat. That was Maudru's room.

Lowering his tinder, Antonio lighted up a leather trunk in the middle of the room, a suitcase for town use, with brass corners and leather, marked D. M. It must have been brought there, then opened and closed again in a hurry; a

[275]

strip of ribbon protruded under the lid. Antonio opened it. It was full of women's things. Silk. All sorts of things. D. M. Delphine Melitta.

Antonio thought of the big man, bitter and tender by turns, talking on the edge of the grave at Maladrerie. The night, the rustle of the cypresses, and that great voice ringing in the depths of the darkness, speaking of a woman's movements as she carried glasses and a decanter.

Without the fire, Maudru would doubtless have been cured this very night.

"Oh, to win . . ." said Antonio to himself. He was thinking of all he had heard about Maudru and Delphine Melitta since she had begun to dangle around the master of the oxen. "I wonder if it's she who's winning in all this business."

He was thinking of that big man, sick at heart and bitter.

He set fire to old Gina's room—in the straw bed, in the mattress which he had ripped open, among the skirts, the dresses, and the scarves. He broke the looking-glass and a bottle of scent. He opened the door and the window to make the fire draw well.

He thought of Tavelé lying on the floor downstairs, with his chin swollen from blows. He would have to drag him out of there. He went down. People were talking in the kitchen. He went barefooted to the turning of the stairs. He looked. Old Gina and a man.

"He must have bumped against something," she said.

"And those two, against the wall?" the man said. "And the fire which has started on all sides?" the man went on. "Take his feet, Mistress," he said.

[276]

They bent over Tavelé. The man took hold of the head and Gina the feet. They carried him outside. Gina walked backwards. "And all for that whore of a girl," Gina said.

Antonio stole out through the small window of the rinsing-room. It opened on the beech wood behind. On this side, all was ablaze. The wind lashed the flames along. They glided in the grass, then a little further on bent their knees, and with a great blue leap lost themselves among the trees and in the night.

Antonio ran to the wood. The big beech trunks crackled under the heat from over the way. A bull had stopped there. His eyes were lighted up by the bounding flames. From there one could see everything. There was nothing left of the farm except the frenzy of fire and smoke. It was now blazing from one end to the other. No solid part of the structure remained. It was all loose and eaten up by the flames. All the bulls had left it. They could be heard bellowing and galloping about in the fields. But the cows and calves must have remained. A smell of charred flesh and bones filled the smoke. A horn sounded far away in the mountains.

"And over the other side?" Antonio said to himself. He meant: And what's happening to the twin on his side? All the sheds on the right, seven of them in all, were on fire, but he heard the men shouting. He had seen nobody on his side except Tavelé, whom he had stunned with blows. They all seemed to be hunting over there. The wind and the eddies of the fire made their shouts whirl in the air like a flight of birds.

Antonio buttoned up his "Maudru" coat, pulled his

drover's cap down over his head, and went towards the shouts and the hunt in the smoke. He said to himself: "What about the twin?"

Maudru was standing on the biggest dung-heap. He was directing his bulls. He was trying to make them understand that they had to leave the yard and gallop away to the surrounding pastures, without minding about the fire any more. He was telling them that day was coming, that the fire was what it was, but was nothing much, after all. What mattered was that on the very next day they would leave for their summer pastures. It was a bit early, but they had sheds up there.

"Off with you!" Maudru shouted, and he pointed to the great nocturnal meadows.

But the bulls would keep on sniffing the stench of charred meat. From time to time, in the glowing cinders on the left, the belly of a cow burst: udder, stomach, and everything; then all of a sudden there was a smell of tripe, milk, and sour grass. The bulls rose on their hind legs like fighting he-goats, and tried to gore the flames with the tips of their white horns. They snorted heavily. They had big clots of slobber dripping from their chaps. When they fell back, they remained motionless for a long time, like bulls of stone, listening to nothing, only gazing at the dancing flames.

Antonio approached. Maudru called Aurora. A drover came running up.

"Have you got him?" Maudru asked.

"It's him who's got us."

"Still?"

"There are three of 'em knocked out over there." He

pointed to the corner of the shed across the smoke. "I be-lieve Carle's among 'em."

"He was here a minute ago," Maudru said.

"Well, he was . . ."

"Well, then, perhaps it is so . . ." said Maudru. "I don't know." He called Aurora again.

Antonio went into the smoke with the drover. He saw a familiar figure in front of him. But it was enlarged by the smoke and the bursting flames. The drover trembled like a man about to fall.

"Hey!" shouted Antonio.

"Is that you?" said the twin. He had clasped the drover by the collar and was holding him. The man's neck was already limp and his arms dangling. He stretched him out on the ground with another blow.

Antonio and the twin rushed into the thick of the smoke. Antonio too began to strike whenever he came across a drover alone. When they were two or three, he went by, shouting. Every time a man was alone in front of him, he struck with all his might. "But what's the matter?" the astonished man would say, and then fall.

Just when the main body of the house was blazing from top to bottom, sputtering like burning figs, with its pine beams and its greasy wainscoting, the twin caught hold of a big, bearded drover. He seemed old. His shoulders were stiff. He received the blow in his beard, but dodged a little and rushed forwards, wheeling his long arms in the air like hammers. His knuckles hit the twin's lip. Smoke whirled round them. The drover caught the twin by the waist and bent him backwards. The twin lost his foothold. He seized the man's neck between his hands. He drove his thumbs

[279]

into the groove of his throat. They both fell. The drover's mouth smelt of onions. The twin got up.

The enormous roof of the barns fell in. A wall collapsed and all its stones crashed into the meadow. For a time the great flames burned silently. Maudru was still speaking to the bulls. They were beginning to understand and were looking at the pastures. The green light of dawn began to shine on the grass.

The twin stuck his fingers into his mouth and started to whistle. The blood of his split lip spurted between his fingers.

"Who's whistling?" Maudru shouted.

The bulls listened to the whistle. They seemed more inclined to obey that whistle which drew them towards the fire. Maudru got down from the dung-heap and walked through the smoke towards the place from which came the other order to the beasts. Antonio saw him coming. He walked, dragging his leg, the way he did up at Maladrerie. The reflection of the flames lit up his dog-like nose. But he still had his tender eyes, and a grey, weary bitterness. Aurora followed him. The bull was suspicious; he looked to the right and to the left through the smoke. Maudru went straight up to the whistler, slowly and deliberately.

Antonio hid himself behind a bin of grain. It was dawn. The heavier air had brought the smoke down and the flames had become clearer in the sky, which now admitted some light. The farm was nothing but a huge charnel-house with its charred beams and rotten walls. From time to time a long, yellow flame sprang out of the heap of dead cows and, like a jet of gold, burst into the air, throwing out a heavy stench of burnt fat.

[280]

Maudru walked forward, dragging his leg. There was nothing more to be done for Puberclaire—walls and beams —but there was still something to be done for Puberclaire bulls. The beasts must be persuaded to leave for the distant pastures. At once. Give them grass and quiet. At once. Far from that red fire, far from that stench. They were already circling round in full gallop. All at once, or else the dance would begin. Aurora bellowed towards his brothers.

The twin was crouching in a ditch. The smoke twined itself round him like a ball of black wool. He whistled short calls, swinging his head, and his whistle seemed to come from all the corners of the wind.

Antonio started to crawl under the smoke. Maudru strode over the ditch. The twin turned round slowly in his hole. He held his knife open in his hand. He got up to pounce on Maudru, who was walking in front of him towards the beeches. A man fell with all his weight on the twin's shoulders. They both rolled in the ditch. The twin struck with his knife. The blade buried itself in the earth. An iron hand clasped his wrist. He bit the arm with all his teeth. The hand gripped firmly on the nerve of the thumb. He dropped the knife. He received a blow on the joint of his jaw, but he was on top. He raised his head. He held his assailant fast under his knees and the man writhed underneath.

"Let me go!" Antonio shouted.

The twin hit him on the forehead, near the temple.

"It's me!" cried Antonio.

Again the twin struck his temple. He tried to free himself to run after Maudru.

[281]

"Leave him," Antonio said. "Delphine Melitta, the suit-case, leave him."

He struck a number of blows at the twin's belly. He tried to turn round, to overthrow him, to lie on him and hold him down.

"It's light, it's light," cried Antonio. "Leave him. Come on, Twin, enough of this."

He bent his leg and kicked at the twin's head with all his strength. The twin belaboured his sides. He received two or three blows. He gasped. Antonio kicked him in the haunch. The thighs which squeezed him loosened a bit. He swelled up his loins. The twin wavered. He tossed him over into the ditch.

Beyond, near the beeches, Maudru was calling the bulls. The whistle was no longer calling. They began to respond to his voice. The frantic gallop stopped. Then the bulls started to run off towards the master.

"Enough of this," Antonio said. "Leave him that. We've more than squared accounts. Come along."

The twin hit him as hard as he could in the face, but the blow was limp. Antonio caught hold of his wrist and began to twist his arm.

"Day is on us," Antonio said. "Come along. Let's go, now we can. Gina . . . D'you hear me? Let's all go to-day, the river, now we've a chance. D'you hear me?"

With his free knee the twin pounded the soft of his belly. Antonio struck him in the nose with his elbow. He con-tinued to twist his arm.

"Listen," panted Antonio, "listen. We must go today with Gina. D'you hear me?"

He struck him under the chin.

"We must get away, back to your country. The forest. Don't you remember?"

Suddenly he howled like an animal; the twin had caught him with his leg right in the middle of his belly.

As they lay together in the ditch, covered with smoke, the flames flapped gently in the rising daylight like big sheets hanging from a line. The bulls could be heard starting off for safety on the foothills of the mountain.

The twin strode over Antonio. He lay outstretched on top of him. He was panting with long, slow breaths. He put his limp mouth close to Antonio's ear.

"My father," he said, "my father, my father!"

His cheek was all wet with tears.

PART THREE

I T W A S the great disorder of spring. The fir forests puffed up clouds from their trees. The clearings smoked like ash-heaps. The mist ascended across the fan-like branches; it emerged from the forest like smoke from a camp-fire. As it hovered aloft, thousands of similar curls of mist hovered beneath the forest like thousands of camp-fires, as if all the gipsies in the world were camping there. It was only spring rising out of the earth.

Little by little the cloud of mist took on a dark colour, as if reflecting the heavy branches. It also had the heaviness of that great mass of trees; it throbbed like them and carried the smell of their bark and of the ground. It weighed down on the hollow vales, resting on a rim of new grass.

The pastures, furrowed by new-born springs, sang a muffled, velvet song. The tall trees creaked as they swayed to and fro like masts of ships. A black wind arrived from the east. It brought with it one storm after another and extraordinary sunlight. The clouds in the vales throbbed under it, and then suddenly tore themselves away from their bed and bounded in the wind. Heavy grey rains drove across the sky. Everything was blurred over: mountains and forests. The rain hung from the north wind like long hairs from the belly of a he-goat. It sang in the trees and sailed noiselessly across the open pastures. Then came the sun, a thick, three-coloured sun, more russet than a fox's coat, and so heavy and hot that it quenched everything, noise and motion alike. The wind rose in the sky. Everything was steeped in silence. The branches, as yet without leaves, sparkled with a thousand tiny silver flames, and under each flame a new bud swelled in a glittering raindrop. At times, a heavy smell of sap and bark rose in the still air. Rain that had already fallen started pattering from the branches to the ground. The new rain drove through the firs. The wind came down again with all its weight, and black splashes of rain swept across the sun, over the whole countryside lying beneath far-flung rainbows.

Clouds began to thicken in the punchbowls with sudden spurts, like flour soup in a cauldron. From time to time gigantic bubbles burst, throwing out flashes of lightning. The thunder rolled its heavy wooden blocks through all the mountain valleys. Then the storm reared in its lair. It trampled the villages and fields underfoot and split trees asunder with its golden claws.

The streaming waters danced, and burrowed beneath the undergrowth. The swirling springs leapt from the sloping banks, spitting like cats. The snows had already completely melted. They had left uncovered a black earth with red veins, filled with water that oozed under the light tread of birds. Glaciers, worn by sun and rain, slid down in torrents, along narrow defiles encumbered with enormous boulders.

The wind dropped. The clouds, brought to a standstill, heaped on the horizon their thick dappled foliage, their caverns, their dark steps, and the blue abysses in which all the beaming lights of the sun lost themselves. It was warm. The very shade was warm. The last bounds of the wind jolted out a few showers of hailstones. Day by day the sun recovered its natural colour. It rose every morning through a flock of clouds, then started to roll gently over the fine sand of uncovered sky. Furred animals, feathered animals, sleek-skinned animals, cold-blooded animals, warm-blooded animals, burrowers, gnawers of wood and borers of rock, swimming kinds, running kinds, flying kinds—all began to swim, to run, and to fly, with memories of former movements. Then they all stopped, sniffed at the warmth, and, amidst the shivering flaxen netting of light, sought out with their muzzles the syrupy tracks of love. During the long twilights, the sun went down behind ringing vales, amidst the calls of animals and the manifold streaming of waters.

The glaciers were melting. They had only small, slender tongues between the grooves of rocks; the mountains, covered with waterfalls, rumbled like drums. There were no longer any tiny brooks, but muscular torrents with terrible loins, which carried away ice-blocks and rocks, bounded above the fir trees, shining and steaming all over with foam underneath their deep banks, and swept away tatters of forest. Waters, rocks, ice-blocks, and skeletons of trees, all twisted themselves into great steel-grey branches swirling across the whole countryside, and roared as they poured out into the giant river.

The river itself had spread out its waters so far from its usual bed that it had almost stopped moving. It was encumbered with deserted farm-houses, clusters of trees, earthy knolls, and rows of poplars. Lost in the folds of the hills, it swelled slowly outwards. From its distant banks, one could just perceive, far away in the middle, the fleecy foam of the main stream.

Long ago the "houldres" had left the Ark cliff to go and herald spring far and wide. But the common birds flew back every evening to the big rock, overgrown with ivy and clematis. There were warblers, all manner of tits, nightingales, greenfinches, redfinches, magpies, ravens, and all the denizens of bush and forest, but only flesh-eaters. No seed-eaters. They were so fat and heavy that they could no longer fly or walk. They hung, clutching at the slender netting of branches and leaves which mantled the rocks, and they remained there awhile to recover from their day-long flight over the great open country full of warmth and hope. They blinked, they looked around, they whetted their bills, they picked at their fleas, then began to tell of what they had seen, or overheard, up there in the sky.

"Ice-gone, ice-gone, ice-gone."

"Too-true, too-true, too-true."

" 'Tisn't-true, 'tisn't-true, 'tisn't-true."

"But-where, but-where, but-where?"

"High-up, high-up, on the mountain top, on the peak, the peak, the peak."

Then they all bustled against one another to listen, to have their say, and it always ended in the departure of the ravens, because they were not very clever in speech, and always said the same thing over and over again.

What interested them all particularly was the river.

They well knew that it was not going to remain as wide as that for the rest of its life. They were waiting for the waters to recede and allow them to go hunting in the slime for worms, grasshoppers, water-beetles, and for the corpses of fish and their brown, greasy spawn.

A big white hazel-grouse arrived from the south.

"Come along. Push along, push along," it said. "Push along, do you hear? Let me be a bit at ease."

" 'T ease, 't ease," that is the last word of the hazel-grouse. Immediately afterwards it will strike with its curious sort of big, pointed bill. Everyone knows it.

"There you are. There you are."

Three greenfinches flew off, whirled around for a while, then clung on again lower down. The hazel-grouse settled on the branch.

"Come, come, come," it said, and it preened its neck. "It's warm here."

"Co-o-old," croaked the raven.

"Oh, no," said the hazel-grouse, "it's warm here. Down there, it's already full of flowers and the willows are so strongly scented that it's enough to choke you."

"Is it as warm as all that?" said the warbler.

"Well, I really mean that we're at ease."

The warbler hopped off towards its hole.

"Warm," said the hazel-grouse. "Leaves are out every-where, and there's shade, and that damned flower-dust which chokes you."

"How about worms, how about worms?" said the tomtit. "How about them?"

"Yes, of course."

[291]

"Here as well, over there where they've taken away the big raft from the water's edge."

"The raft," said the hazel-grouse, "I've seen it."

"Where?"

"Down there, far away, near Clape-Mousse. It's drifting along."

"By itself?"

"With men; it's almost reached the willow country already."

"Quite, quite," croaked the raven.

"Well, I'd really like to be at ease," said the hazel-grouse, and it jumped near the raven.

"Oh, quite, quite, quite," said the raven, and took to its wings. It hovered awhile over the rock, then flew away towards the ruins of Puberclaire.

The raft was heavily built, but it could be handled all the same on high waters. It had a rough ashen rudder astern, and Antonio needed all his strength to steer it. He had to hold the course steadily, for the mass of the fifty fir trunks obeyed sluggishly. At the bow, the twin held the pole and struck away all the flotsam. They floated along on one side of the river, near enough the main stream to be borne along, but out of the reach of waves and eddies. They went round islets of trees, hills, and wide stretches of shallow water, rippled by the wind.

They had tried to stretch a canvas awning over the two women. It had not held fast. They had just gone through two days' wind and rain, and added to the wind from the sky, on a level with the river there was the wind of the river, the air carried away by the waters, a sudden eddying and abysmal strength whose weight on the awning thwarted the rudder. They had almost got stranded on the sand in the middle of the river.

Then they had made a kind of horse-shoe in the middle of the raft with their belongings: a big trunk given by Toussaint, the bags, the roll of canvas, and the ballast. The two women took shelter there in the daytime, and slept there at night. For, since setting out from Villevieille, they had not once landed. To begin with, they wanted to get away quickly, and anyhow nothing solid or regular had been left of the banks, which were steeped in spring and alive with waterfalls and rain. It was better to keep in the offing and float down towards the warm south from which were wafted the scents of the trees.

The twin was at the bows and Antonio astern. Gina and Clara were in the middle, in the nest of luggage. They were huddled together inside, both wearing their great mountain cloaks. Gina had put on her hood, but Clara remained bareheaded under the rain.

"Cover your head," Antonio had said.

She had answered: "If I cover up my ears, and if I put that wool on my nose, it's like death. Let me be free, I enjoy it, I am not cold."

From time to time Gina's small face could be seen under the hood. She looked anxiously to the right and to the left, with her head sinking a little into her shoulders. She was frightened of that expanse of water, of the twin rooted there, barefooted on the firs, fighting with his pole against flotsam ten times bigger than himself, by Antonio propped against the helm, by that wild rain, cutting short the words and sounds, and biting their cheeks. She nestled against

[293]

Clara. The blind woman touched her hands, and felt for her wrists under her sleeves.

"It's spring," said Clara. "It'll soon be the heart of spring."

"How do you know?" And Gina looked at the dead eyes, still like mint leaves.

"It smells," said Clara, "and it has its own language." With her finger, she pointed at the noise of the waters, the noise of the full waters in the river, the noise of the clear waters pouring out from the rocks and mountains, yonder on the banks. She pointed out layers of rain, flapping a darker hue in their wings. She even pointed to land-slips before Gina had heard the crumbling noise.

"How do you manage it?"

"The smell," said Clara. "The smell of the earth came all of a sudden. It's clay. It's the edge of a meadow which has crumbled down. It smells of roots."

Gina looked at her, there, folded in her cloak: that female body, that fine face closed like a stone, sharp as a stone, that face which did not move, that face without eyes. She felt on her wrist the somewhat bony grasp of that hand.

"How do you know the meadow?"

"I moved about in them on all fours, when I was a little girl," said Clara. "I heard people say: 'the meadow.' I said: 'What is a meadow?' My father stamped his foot in the grass. 'That's what it is,' he said. I heard him stamp his foot near me. Now I call that sort of smell of plants a meadow. You know, those crackling things that people crush between their fingers, those things that smell"—she drew near Gina's ear—"that smell like a baby, or like when a man is lying on you.

"I know daisies, buttercups, oats, and sainfoin," she continued. "They're perhaps not the same names as you give them, but that doesn't matter as they're just names. It's not names that count. Are you listening, Gina?"

"I'm listening."

"It's not names. I don't quite know how to explain. If you were to close your eyes for a long time and get accustomed to everything with your body, and then, if everything changed meanwhile, on the day you opened your eyes again, you'd know everything. That's how it is. All the things in the world come to me in various places in my body"—she touched her thighs, her breasts, her neck, her cheeks, her forehead, and her hair—"they're tied up with me by tiny quivering strings. I myself am spring, now. I am greedy like all this around us, I am full of great desires, like the world now."

There was a smell of slime, of grass, and of warm rain.

"You're not afraid any more, are you?"

"No," said Gina.

"Pull left," cried the twin.

Antonio pulled the big bar to the left with all his might. The roof of a farm-house emerged from the water. The bottom of the raft scraped a little upon something beneath, then cut adrift, swept round the roof, and then glided along freely again. They neared a big hill entirely hemmed in by the waters.

"We ought to head more into midstream," Antonio cried out.

The twin came near the helm.

"Find the main stream," said Antonio, "and then straight along down at full speed."

[295]

"No," said the twin, "I know this place all right. Let's drift along easy for another three hours, and then, at night-fall, we'll reach a netting of half-submerged spinneys and sandbanks. The best thing will be to take advantage of that." He pointed to the hill. "Let's land, light a fire, and sleep. All's clear." He pointed to the waters all around.

"Right," said Antonio.

The afternoon was nearly half spent. Ever since the morning, they had drifted out of the rain. The scattered clouds were swinging light and shade to and fro like the branches of an orchard. The sun was sinking in the west.

The hill was clad with tall, crisp, evergreen oaks of an iron colour. It smelt as if the earth were already dry. It was like a hub with all the beams of the sun radiating around it. The raft glided into its shade. The spate of the river had filled up a whole vale. It formed a harbour fringed with chestnut trees. The leafy boughs dipped in the water. At the bottom of the creek three young fir trees stood out against the border of a meadow. A brook flowed along silently like oil in black moss. On that bank the waters of the river were asleep. They splashed gently in the branches of the trees. The peaceful air was all alive with the chirping of mole-crickets, crickets, and grasshoppers.

The twin moored the raft to the young firs. The hawser scratched off the white bark. The resin oozed. Its smell excited the smells of all the other saps. A chestnut tree was beginning to blossom. It was loftier than the rest. From its head, crushed under the glow of the setting sun, flowed a flavour of yeast.

"The grass is dry," Gina said.

"I'd like to know," said the twin, "whether the water is

all around us. Yesterday I saw a whole cavalcade gallop away over there on our right, and the herd of bullocks looked like a forest as it walked along the crest of the mountains."

"I'll see," said Antonio.

CHAPTER II

HERE it was a landscape of the south, with its dust and round pebbles. The undergrowth of the evergreen oaks was free from moss and clear. Animals ran about, scattering the dry leaves like foam.

Antonio led Clara, holding her hand. She followed him, bending her head and hiding her forehead in her folded arm to protect herself from the branches.

At the top of the hill, they lay down in the frizzy grass. The flooded river surrounded them on all sides. It was indeed an island protected by the main stream and by the wide stretch of waters. Along the ridge of the mountains which stood out like blocks in the evening light, there were only motionless woods. The only thing that moved was a silhouette in the distance on Uble Peak. It looked like a horseman sitting erect on the summit with his black cloak bulging in the wind. Perhaps it was a tree.

The spring of the south rose from the forests and waters. It had already conquered evening and night. It was the master of the length of the hours. The high ice-clad mountains rent the northern sky; a light sheet of clouds flapped on their flanks. But one no longer felt the cold. Fish leapt in the river. A fox called out with a small plaintive yelp.

Grey turtle-doves flew against the sun and the tips of their wings lit up. Kingfishers skimmed the water. Cranes, heading northwards like arrows, would pass aloft, screaming. Clouds of ducks crushed the reeds. A sturgeon with a back like that of a pig swam along the surface of the water. The sun glittered on its scales. A cloud of mud followed the beating of its tail. An extensive grove, all in blossom with catkins, trees with tufts of flowers, and trees with little sharp flowers like ears of wheat, barred the river downstream. They were bathed in water, shoulder-deep. Eddies made the boughs sway. Pollen smoked in the dusk like sand under gambolling colts. Otters would dive into the deep waters and emerge shiny and sleek as rifle bullets. Weasels mewed. A marten shot off the outskirt like a darting flame. A wolf kept on howling over towards Uble. A swarm of bees puffed up and down, lost in the sky. Swifts skimmed the water with their white bellies. Fish-spawn, set in motion by deep current, opened and closed its large reddish-brown foliage on the surface of the river. Pike snapped their teeth. Eels slithered among foam bubbles. Sparrow-hawks slept in the sunshine. Locusts crackled. The evening breeze wafted along the soft neighing of the river.

The sun set.

"I'd like to make you see," said Antonio.

"You worry too much about me, all of you," said Clara; "and I can see much farther than you."

"Evening has come," said Antonio, "and everything is speaking to me of you. Your hair is like the mountain firs."

"I wonder," said Clara, "what it means when you say 'see,' since every time your eyes deceive you."

She was facing the sunset. Her delicate face was some-

[299]

what lean, almost angular, and shaded under her heavy, dark hair which hid her forehead and her temples. Her mouth was thin and deep-set, her skin tanned, and her eyes were overbrimming with green and oval-shaped, like soft mint leaves.

"I remember," said Antonio, "what seeing you for the first time meant for me. At that particular moment it wasn't much, but afterwards . . ."

She remained silent.

"You've walked by my side along all the roads," he said. "Asleep or awake, I saw you all the time."

"Seeing, all the time seeing," she said. She touched his eyes. "So, from the depths of that country into which you went, you could still see me with your eyes?"

"No," he said. "You were alive in my head, with your own freedom, and you sometimes did things which were good for you and bad for me. That's the awful part of it all."

"I can see much better than you," she said.

Night had come down.

"Listen . . . the big fish is down there on the bank. It's lying on the water's edge. What do you call the thing that smells both of water and earth, and must be a mixture of them?"

"Mud," he said.

"It's swaying its tail gently in the mud," she said. "It's under those trees which smell like man's love. What's their name?"

"I don't know," he said.

"I'll show them to you, and then you'll know, and then you'll tell me. All over the hill there are paws, claws,

[300]

muzzles, and bellies. Listen to them! Hard trees, tender trees, cold flowers, warm flowers. Over there behind us there's a long tree. You can tell from its noise that it's straight. It makes a noise like running water. It has long flowers like cats' tails and they smell of unbaked bread."

They heard a poplar rustling.

"Can you see it?"

"It's dark," he said.

"What does that matter? Your wife knows a great deal," she said. "I'm afraid you take me for a little girl. I've known you ever since the minute you touched me with your hand, even before. Since the time I felt you at the foot of my bed. You didn't speak. You were breathing. And I said: 'There are three of you, and not two. There's someone there who hasn't spoken.' And I said: 'I want him to go out.' I didn't want you to know me in that sick bed, with the smell of the confinement. I didn't mind about the others, but I wanted you to get to know me with my heavy silk skirt on, swaying around me like ripe corn, and with my hood on my head. I wanted to be sitting on the grass in the meadows, in May, in the warm sun, and you to come along through the flowers, like in songs."

Antonio remained a long time without speaking.

"I'll tell you what you are waiting for," she said.

"I'd lie . . ." he said.

She added quickly: "You mustn't lie. It's no use, for I hear words just before they are on your lips, and when you speak to yourself, I hear you. I arrived quickly at maturity," she said, after a pause. She listened to a sigh from the river and the trees. "At times, according to where I am, I hear people say around me: 'the girl' and I hear the little girl

[3 0 1]

speaking half-words, bits of nonsense, like a bird. I don't remember ever being a little girl like that.

"My father was a man who had two voices. An ordinary voice, and in that one he was his real self. Then another which contained everything, and made your head swim till you could no longer distinguish what was wickedness and what was pain. Then there would be a tiny thread of something in the depths of that voice, as if a dog were licking its wounds. He often spoke with that voice. It went together with his footsteps as he arrived home and threw his ax in a corner. One day, when I was alone with him, I went and touched the ax; the handle was warm, and the iron cold, with a sharp cruel blade. His voice fitted in with the weight of his tread on the floor and with the creaking of the bench when he sat down. I said to myself: 'Lord have mercy!' just as I had heard my mother say it, and he began to speak with his evil voice. How old could I have been then? Very young, perhaps five. My mother had no voice of her own. She kept on repeating: 'Lord have mercy!' Outside there were trees, two at first, without the smell of trees. They were too near the house. They still smelt of the house, of slate, of stumps of wood, and smoke. Then, there was grass, a small rise and dip in the ground—and then trees. First, a place where they grew far from each other like my two arms outstretched. When I once got there, I felt the cool over my head. The branches were above me. At that time of the year, they smelt of honey and were alive like bee-hives. At the end of the year, they produced apples. You find them in the grass. Further on, there were trees pressed up against one another. Big trunks and small trunks, smooth barks, like skin, or gritty ones with everything, thorns; and then, if you entered, it was cold. A lovely cold, all of a sudden. And a rumbling coming from the depths of the trees, like when you are on the edge of a hole and listen.

"Don't suppose I am trying to find something to say," she said. "I'm thinking of what you are expecting, and I'm going to tell you. But all that is of some use—I mean for my excuse. If there's anything to excuse."

"There's nothing to excuse," he said. "I should think that I know things in life as well as anybody. And then . . ."

"And then," she said, "it all happened like this."

"That's not what I mean," he said. "I mean, and then I love you."

Night had settled and was entirely black, with a wide, double sky, full of stars in the heavens and in the reflection of the waters.

"Then to begin with," said Clara, "it's all rather a long story. There was I all that while, with the double voice of my father, the trees, the grass, the warmth, the cold, and then a new pleasure which stole upon me slowly: smells. My father's voice became less and less double. I heard his real voice only on rare occasions. My mother no longer moaned; she died one day—about the time when I discovered smells, and just after she had time to reassure me, as I was developing, about a thing that happens to women. So, you see how I was, don't you?"

"Yes," he said.

"I use your own word on purpose," she said, "to let you understand how I myself can see. That little girl, that was me. Think it over. The wind, the river. The night call of beasts.

"Give me your hand," she said. She married her fingers to his fingers. "You want to know how I came to have my little baby, and I'll tell you."

"If you think I'm asking you about that, you're mistaken," said Antonio.

"Your mouth says that, because one always boasts of being strong, with one's mouth, but your body is asking me about it."

She pressed Antonio's hand.

"O my boy," she said, "O angler and hunter, O man who carved wild-boar's meat, O king of the mountains! Tell me, tell me: Isn't it you who catch fish with your hands? Isn't it you who swim? Isn't it you who walk among the reeds? It's you who have a trick for catching the conger, just as you told the ox-driver near the door of the hut, when the two of us were listening with gaping mouths: he, and I who was bed-ridden and feeble all over, and there was that voice of yours which played like the big water-snake in my ears. It's you, is it?"

"Yes," said Antonio.

"Then it'll be all right," she said, "because our two bodies must be perfectly in tune. As for the little child, it was bound to happen, you understand?"

"Yes," said Antonio.

"I should like it to be well understood," she said, "and for that I'll have to tell you a great deal, and then a great deal more, and I'll have to explain things you'll know by yourself afterwards in me."

"There's one thing," he said, "which you may be glad to know. It's this: when I left you in the house of the mother of the road, Sailor and I walked. It was night like it is now, and I said to myself over and over again: She can't see! She can't see all those stars, like now, if you could see. And I wanted to make you see, to give you—you understand . . . ?"

"Yes, I understand," she said. "But why do you say that, just when I'm speaking of that child, and when I'm going to tell you all that happened before, everything? There's always a lot before a child."

"Speak, my little girl," he said; "you'll learn afterwards why I said that now."

"I'm not sure about that," she said.

"But I am," he said. "You are like someone who has climbed up a mountain more slowly than I. Sight deceives me. But, given plenty of time, nothing deceives you. The truth is that everything must obey."

"Yes," she said, "now I also know just what to say. I've known the meadow, the apple orchard, the forest, my father's flock—everything. The truth is that whatever one is, one has got to live, and there's no way out of it, but I ought to have found you before."

"You found me when you were destined to find me," he said; "you'll see . . ."

He unclasped his hand, he touched that face which he could no longer see. He drew near her in the grass and embraced her.

"Since I always come back to the night," he said with a little laugh, "and it's the same with a child who has found the alphabet. You can't feel the stars, or touch them; I want to give you the stars. And now, come along, my little girl. The twin has lighted a fire down there."

CHAPTER III

T H E Y broke camp at dawn. The chestnut-tree harbour was still steeped in shadows.

The twin was unfastening the mooring-knot.

"Wait a bit, my friends," said Antonio. He waded into the water. It was lighted up by the reflected gleam of the daylight rising on the evergreen oaks. A blue trout flapped its gills slowly on the rocky bottom. It was asleep. He stroked its belly, then gripped it under its front fins and raised it in the air, as it beat about wildly.

"Feeding on oats is good," said the twin. "Here we have colts at play as early as dawn."

"It's true," thought Antonio, "I am playing in the world now."

The twin carefully untied the knot, coiled up the rope, arranged the baggage, and tested the poise of the raft.

Antonio looked at the captured trout. It was still whisking its tail, opening out its pink fins which were flapping noisily, and it gaped with blood in its teeth.

"It's for our meal," he said.

"The four of us?" asked the twin.

"I'll catch some more," said Antonio.

"I want to get home tomorrow morning," said the twin.

Shreds of mist were trailing on the river and in the

mountains, full of silver mystery. The world began to sing gently beneath the trees.

Antonio was looking at Uble Peak. It was quite clean, high up in the sky and clear, like a fingertip.

"Last night, there was somebody up there," he said.

The twin stopped shaking the raft.

"I think," he said, "the battle's over."

He had put his arms akimbo, and was turning his head to the right and to the left like a man estimating the day's work around him.

"I want to get home tomorrow morning," he said, "and go up to Nibles, and begin straight away. I need thirty-five pounds of nails, thirty hinges—three for each door and window—and two locks. In the meantime Gina will sleep at Charlotte's house."

The morning was blooming like an elder-bush. Antonio was fresh, and taller than usual. New youth grew over him like foliage.

"It's well past its prime," he said to himself, as he heard the trout dying in his hand. Without realizing it clearly, he saw himself in his own island, standing with uplifted arms and his fists all aglow with joys torn from the world, golden, like captured trout; Clara, sitting at his feet, was hugging his legs in her soft arms.

"Youth," he said.

"Everything has an end," said the twin.

"I was talking to myself," said Antonio.

The raft was punted out of the harbour. A flurry of the current carried it away as it emerged out of the shadows and floated into spring. Antonio returned to the helm.

The trees called. A poplar said: "Good-bye, good-bye,

good-bye," with its small new leaves rustling in the breeze.

A black fir, half sunk in the river, raised its dark mouth, dripping with water. "Where are you going, my big children, where are you going, my big children?"

At about midday they crossed the broad chestnut grove which barred the river. They neared it slowly, noiselessly. They bent their backs. The raft glided beneath the trees. A momentous thing was happening there. The foliage nearly touched the river. It was full of sunshine, but the greatest light came from the flowers. Stars. Like those of the sky, bigger than a hand, with a smell of leavening dough. A smell of kneaded dough, the salt smell of men and women making love. The calm waters were covered with yellow dust. The raft went forward through a haze of pollen.

Clara turned her face towards Antonio.

"Tonio!"

She had almost cried out with a cooing in her throat like that of a turtle-dove. She remained with her lips half open, biting back the name.

Antonio was steering. He gazed in front of him at the mystery of shadows and the brilliance of the flowers. He steered the raft into the shade, then into the light. He knew whether Clara wanted the shade. He knew by the movement of her mouth, by the wrinkling of a cheek, by a sigh. He pushed the raft into the shade. He knew whether Clara wanted the light. He pushed the raft into the light. He knew whether Clara wanted branches. He pushed the raft into the low foliage, and Clara's face brushed aside the fresh leaves. He felt that she wanted suddenly, wanted intensely and immediately, flowers and that smell of warm

[308]

animals. He pulled at the bar with all his might, and the raft bumped sideways against the tree-trunks, and the flower-dust showered on Clara. Then she heaved deep, dark sighs, and all her body eased as if all her nerves were relaxing.

He was in Clara. He knew what she wanted better than she. He wanted what she wanted. Her joy was his joy. She was all around him. Her blood touched his blood, her flesh against his flesh, mouth to mouth, like two bottles of wine that you empty one into the other, and then turn upside down again, and they both glow with the same wine.

The twin was sitting at the prow. Gina was looking at him. She had impulses towards him, then she bit her lips and wrung her hands. His arms were hanging at his sides and he was waiting till the raft crossed through the trees.

Antonio thought: "Yonder, in front of that shadowy place. She does not know that I'll rush her into that . . ."

He pulled at the bar. Clara was quivering.

"She's beginning to know," he thought. He spied on her face the coming of the coolness. Then, at one pull, he pushed the raft right into the shadowy gulf. The flower-dust made their eyelashes sticky, the leaves rubbed against their cheeks, the branches crackled.

Clara moaned: "Tonio!" in the crackling of the branches. She thanked him with her smile, her panting breath, her way of biting at his name, with the white of her teeth.

At last, in the depth of the trees, Antonio saw the broad daylight and the open water. He felt that Clara was hungering and thirsting for the end.

He rushed the raft out of the grove, into dazzling sunshine whose very weight made him shiver as if he were cold.

Clara went back and lay amongst the luggage.

[309]

"Come near me," said Gina. And she hugged her in her arms. She leaned her head against her breast. She remained there, breathing with long, even breaths. Clara caressed her cheeks.

"You're weeping?"

"Oh, no," said Gina, "it's the sun."

They both lay down on their bed of blankets and started to sleep gently. Now and then they sighed.

As evening approached, the man who had been watching reappeared on Uble Peak. He was now in full view. It was not a tree. It was a big man on horseback. He was alone. He watched the raft pass before him, at the bottom of the valley. He saw it disappearing towards the south, then fade away in the night.

The stream carried hard. Stumps and shallows were no longer to be feared. They were on the swell of the water. All that had to be done was from time to time to pull slightly at the rudder. In the depth of the night, they heard the gorges blowing.

"We'll reach the isle of jays at dawn."

The twin came and sat near Antonio. The women were sleeping.

"All right?" asked the twin.

"All right," said Antonio.

"Those nails," said the twin, "those building nails that my father bought. D'you think they came from the smith's at Perrey-le-Terroir?"

"No," said Antonio. He was thinking that now, Clara and he, all the time together . . . "I think it was near Vuitebœuf," he said, "from the man who found iron ore on the hill, and who's building that smelting-house."

"I wonder if he still makes them?" said the twin.

Antonio was thinking that he had many things to teach her, that she was quite new to everything, that she had so far felt nothing, really touched nothing . . .

"And whether he'll be willing to sell me some?" said the twin.

"Why not?"

"I'll go and see him," said the twin. "How does one get there?"

"Villars-le-Terroir," said Antonio, "Prévouloup, then lower Combeyres and Lavaux Hill, then straight ahead. Orges, they call it."

"Three days?"

"More like five," said Antonio.

"Short trip," said the twin.

Antonio was thinking that he would be free and that he would keep her close to him, on the island. Very gently. Step by step. "Maybe I'll fasten her to me with the strap when we go towards the marshes. So that she treads where I tread. It's safer."

"What I want to make," said the twin, "is a good strong house, with big nails. Solid. I'll leave Gina at Charlotte's. Then I'll go to Orges. I've been thinking of those nails all the time. What do you think about it?"

"Nothing," said Antonio. He remembered the time when he was alone.

"At the west a wall ten metres long," said the twin. "At the east, two windows and the door. At the north, the sink-

[311]

hole, the granary, and a good store-pit for turnips, and then a terrace in front with three pillars, and a pent-roof covering it.

"The day after tomorrow, I'll leave for Orges. What do you think about it?"

"Nothing," said Antonio.

He was thinking that he was going to take Clara in his arms and lie down with her on the earth.

Printed in the United States
84355LV00001B/88-96/A